How to DeFi: Advanced
1st Edition, May 2021

Lucius Fang, Benjamin Hor, Erina Azmi, Khor Win Win

Copyright © 2021 CoinGecko
1st edition, May 2021

Layout: Anna Tan
teaspoonpublishing.com.my

All rights reserved. No part of this publication may be reproduced, stored in a retrieval system or transmitted, in any form or by any means, electronic, mechanical, photocopying, recording or otherwise, except brief extracts for the purpose of review, without the prior permission in writing of the publisher and copyright owners. It is also advisable to consult the publisher if in any doubt as to the legality of any copying which is to be undertaken.

"Probably the most comprehensive DeFi manual out there, a must-read."
— Hugh Karp, Founder of Nexus Mutual

"Education is paramount in DeFi and resources such as How to DeFi are so important. Not only is this an excellent sequel, but once again, the team at CoinGecko have managed to provide a comprehensive and in-depth overview of an ever-changing space."
— Ganesh Swami, CEO of Covalent

"This is the most comprehensive guide on DeFi anywhere, bar none. You should read this cover to cover."
— Leo Cheng, Co-founder of CREAM Finance

"If you want to learn the latest trends in DeFi, this book is the best of the best on the market."
— Yenwen Feng, Co-founder of Perpetual Protocol

"This book comes as an excellent follow-up to their first book, and provides a deeper dive into DeFi and on how to navigate the nuances in the space."
— Jocelyn Chang, APAC Growth Lead of MakerDAO Growth Core Unit

"Reading *How To DeFi* in 2021 is like accidentally meeting Vitalik Buterin by chance in a café in Zug in 2015 and discovering Ethereum first-hand. *How To DeFi* will help you make life-changing decisions when building and using DeFi protocols and applications of this decade."
— Molly Wintermute, Founder of Hegic

"DeFi isn't easy for newcomers—yet. But with this top CoinGecko guide, readers will very quickly discover how DeFi is not just the future. DeFi is now, and soon it will become a regular part of everyday life for many people across the world. This is probably the best guide right now to light the way on anyone's DeFi journey at any stage."
— Azeem Ahmed, Co-Founder of Armor

"This book is a tour de force through all of the important concepts and platforms that you need to know to engage meaningfully with DeFi. I'll be using this as a reference for both myself and newcomers to the space for a good long while."

— Laurence E. Day, Core Team of Indexed Finance

"The most in-depth and relevant guide to understanding DeFi and all its possibilities"

— DeFi Ted, Advisor of COVER Protocol

CONTENTS

Introduction	1
Part One: State of DeFi	3
Chapter 1: Defi Snapshot	5
DeFi Summer 2020	5
DeFi Ecosystem	8
Rise of Gas Fees	9
DeFi is Going Mainstream	11
Recommended Readings	12
Chapter 2: DeFi Activities	13
Yield Farming	13
Liquidity Mining	14
Airdrops	16
Initial DEX Offerings (IDO)	17
Initial Bonding Curve Offering (IBCO)	17
Liquidity Bootstrapping Pool (LBP)	18
Initial Farm Offering (IFO)	18
Yield Farming: Step-by-Step Guide	19
Associated Risks	25
Conclusion	25
Recommended Readings	26
Part Two: Evaluating DeFi Sectors	27
Chapter 3: Decentralized Exchanges	29
Types of DEX	30
Automated Market Makers (AMMs)	31
What are the existing types of AMMs out there?	33
How are prices determined on a Constant Product AMM?	35
The Various Automated Market Makers (AMMs)	37
Uniswap	37
SushiSwap	39
Balancer	42
Curve Finance	43
Bancor	45
What are the differentiators between the AMMs?	46
I. Pool Fees	46
II. Liquidity Mining	47
III Pool Weightage	48

Associated Risks of using AMMs	49
I. Price Slippage	49
II. Front-running	51
III. Impermanent Loss	53
Notable Mentions	55
Conclusion	55
Recommended Readings	56
Chapter 4: DEX Aggregators	**57**
DEX Aggregator Protocols	58
1inch Network	58
Matcha	60
Paraswap	61
DEX Aggregator's Performance Factors	62
Which DEX Aggregator offers the most value?	63
Associated Risks	65
Notable Mentions	66
Conclusion	66
Recommended Readings	67
Chapter 5: Decentralized Lending & Borrowing	**69**
Overview of Lending & Borrowing Protocols	70
Compound	70
Maker	72
Aave	73
Cream Finance	74
Protocols Deep Dive	75
Assets Supported	75
Revenue	76
Total Value Locked (TVL)	77
Utilization ratio (Borrowing Volume/TVL)	78
Lending and Borrowing Rates	79
Lenders	79
Borrowers	80
Associated Risks	81
Notable Mentions	82
Conclusion	83
Recommended Readings	84
Chapter 6: Decentralized Stablecoins and Stableassets	**85**
Centralized Stablecoin	86
Tether (USDT)	86
Decentralized Stablecoin	87
DAI	87
How do we resolve the stablecoin issue?	88

What are Algorithmic Stablecoins and Stableassets?	89
Rebase Model	90
Ampleforth	91
Seigniorage Model	91
Empty Set Dollar	92
Basis Cash	93
Frax Finance	94
How has Algorithmic Stablecoins fared so far?	95
Why has FRAX succeeded?	96
The Next Generation of Algorithmic Stablecoins and Stableassets	97
Fei Protocol	98
Reflexer	99
Float Protocol	100
How will these new Algorithmic Stablecoins and Stableassets fare?	101
I. Collateralization	102
II. Trader Incentives/Disincentives	103
III. Emergency Powers	103
Associated Risks	104
Notable Mentions	104
Conclusion	105
Recommended Readings	106
Chapter 7: Decentralized Derivatives	**107**
Decentralized Perpetuals	107
Perpetual Protocol	108
dYdX	109
Comparison between Perpetual Protocol and dYdX (Layer 1)	111
Notable Mentions	112
Decentralized Options	112
Hegic	113
Opyn	114
Comparison between Hegic and Opyn	115
Notable Mentions	116
Synthetic Assets	117
Synthetix	117
UMA	119
Comparison between Synthetic and UMA	121
Notable Mentions	122
Associated Risks	122
Conclusion	123
Recommended Readings	123

Chapter 8: Decentralized Insurance — 125
- What is Insurance? — 125
- How does Insurance work? — 126
- Does Crypto need Insurance? — 127
- DeFi Insurance Protocols — 127
  - Nexus Mutual — 127
    - Type of Covers — 127
      - 1. Protocol Covers — 128
      - 2. Custody Covers — 128
    - Cover Purchase — 128
    - Claim Assessment — 129
    - Risk Assessment — 129
    - Token Economics — 131
    - Wrapped NXM (wNXM) — 131
    - Protocol Revenue — 132
  - Armor Protocol — 132
    - arNXM — 133
    - arNFT — 133
    - arCORE — 133
    - arSHIELD — 134
    - Claim — 134
    - Protocol Revenue — 134
  - Cover Protocol — 135
    - Type of Covers — 136
    - Cover Purchase — 136
    - Claim Assessment — 137
    - Risk Assessment — 137
    - Protocol Revenue — 138
  - Comparison between Nexus Mutual and Cover Protocol — 138
    - Capital Efficiency — 139
    - Covers Available — 139
    - Claim Payout Ratio — 140
- Associated Risks — 141
- Notable Mentions — 141
- Conclusion — 143
- Recommended Readings — 144

Part Three: Emerging DeFi Categories — 145

Chapter 9: Decentralized Indices — 147
- DeFi ETF Landscape — 148
  - Index Cooperative (INDEX) — 149
  - Indexed Finance (NDX) — 150
  - PowerPool Concentrated Voting Power (CVP) — 151

Comparing the Protocol Indices ... 151
    Protocol Fees ... 152
    Protocol Strategies ... 153
    Fund Weighting ... 154
Associated Risks ... 156
Notable Mentions ... 157
Conclusion ... 158
Recommended Readings ... 158

Chapter 10: Decentralized Prediction Markets ... 159
How do Prediction Protocols work? ... 160
Market-Making ... 160
Resolution ... 161
Prediction Market Protocols ... 162
    Augur ... 162
    Omen ... 164
What are the other key differences between Augur and Omen? ... 165
Associated Risks ... 167
Notable Mentions ... 167
Conclusion ... 168
Recommended Readings ... 169

Chapter 11: Decentralized Fixed-Interest Rate Protocols ... 171
Overview of Fixed Interest Rates Protocols ... 173
    Yield ... 173
    Saffron.Finance ... 175
    Horizon Finance ... 176
Which FIRP should I use? ... 178
Associated Risks ... 179
Notable Mentions ... 180
Conclusion ... 181
Recommended Readings ... 181

Chapter 12: Decentralized Yield Aggregators ... 183
Yield Aggregators Protocols ... 184
    Yearn Finance ... 184
        Vaults ... 185
        Strategies ... 185
    Yearn Finance Partnerships ... 186
    Alpha Finance ... 187
    Badger Finance ... 189
    Harvest Finance ... 190
Comparison of Yield Aggregators ... 191
Associated Risks ... 192
Notable Mentions ... 192

Conclusion	193
Recommended Readings	194

Part Four: Technology Underpinning DeFi — 195

Chapter 13: Oracles and Data Aggregators — 197

Oracle Protocols	198
Chainlink	198
Band Protocol	200
Data Aggregators	202
The Graph Protocol	202
Covalent	205
Notable mentions	206
Associated Risks	207
Conclusion	207
Recommended Readings	208

Chapter 14: Multi-Chain Protocols & Cross-Chain Bridges — 209

Protocols and Bridge Overview	210
Ren Project	210
Lock-and-mint	211
Burn-and-release	211
Burn-and-mint	211
ThorChain	212
Binance Bridge	215
Anyswap	216
Terra Bridge	217
Notable mentions	218
Associated Risks	218
Conclusion	219
Recommended Readings	220

Chapter 15: DeFi Exploits — 221

Causes of Exploits	222
1. Economic Exploits / Flash Loans	222
2. Code in Production Culture	222
3. Sloppy Coding and Insufficient Audits	223
4. Rug Pull (Inside Jobs)	223
5. Oracle Attacks	224
6. Metamask Attack	224
Flash Loans	225
What are Flash Loans?	225
Usage of Flash Loans	226
Flash Loan Protocol: Furucombo	227
Case Study: bZx Flash Loans Hack	228

Flash Loan Summary	230
Solutions	231
Internal Insurance Fund	231
Insurance	231
Bug Bounty	232
Other Possible Solutions	232
Tips for Individuals	232
Don't Give Smart Contracts Unlimited Approval	232
Don't Give Smart Contracts Unlimited Approval: Step-by-Step Guide	234
Revoking Unlimited Approvals from Smart Contracts	237
Use a Hardware Wallet	238
Use a Separate Browser Profile	238
Separate Browser Profile: Step-by-Step Guide	239
Conclusion	241
Recommended Readings	242

Chapter 16: The Future of Finance — 243

How Long Before Institutions Build on These Networks?	244
Where Does This Take Us in the Next 5 to 10 Years?	245

Closing Remarks — 247

Appendix — 249

CoinGecko's Recommended DeFi Resources	249
Analytics	249
News Sites	249
Newsletters	250
Podcast	250
Youtube	250
Bankless Level-Up Guide	251
Projects We Like Too	251
Dashboard Interfaces	251
Decentralized Exchanges	251
Exchange Aggregators	251
Lending and Borrowing	251
Oracle and Data Aggregator	252
Prediction Markets	252
Taxes	252
Wallet	252
Yield Optimizers	252
References	253
Chapter 1: DeFi Snapshot	253
Chapter 2: DeFi Activities	254
Chapter 3: Decentralized Exchanges	254

Chapter 4: DEX Aggregators	256
Chapter 5: Decentralized Lending & Borrowing	257
Chapter 6: Decentralized Stablecoins and Stableassets	258
Chapter 7: Decentralized Derivatives	259
Chapter 8: Decentralized Insurance	260
Chapter 9: Decentralized Indices	261
Chapter 10: Decentralized Prediction Markets	262
Chapter 11: Decentralized Fixed-Interest Rate Protocols	262
Chapter 12: Decentralized Yield Aggregators	263
Chapter 13: Oracles and Data Aggregators	264
Chapter 14: Multi-Chain Protocols & Cross-Chain Bridges	264
Chapter 15: DeFi Exploits	265
Chapter 16: DeFi will be the New Normal	265
Glossary	**267**

INTRODUCTION

When we first wrote the *How to DeFi: Beginner (First Edition)* book in March 2020, we intentionally omitted a lot of information to make it easy for beginners to get started in DeFi. We knew that the book was only scratching the surface of what DeFi has to offer. Of course, it would not appear that way to beginners - many are merely trying to understand a rapidly growing industry infamous for its steep learning curve.

As our readers became familiar with the basics of DeFi, demand for more in-depth knowledge soon followed. We knew that we needed to write a follow-up for readers interested in exploring DeFi further, so we wrote this advanced book to serve this purpose.

We cannot understate how easy it is to get lost in DeFi. Every week, new protocol innovations occur, making DeFi more efficient and extending the use-cases further. Fully addressing this knowledge gap is impossible. However, we hope to bridge the gap through our research and analysis of key DeFi segments in this book.

In this book, we will be providing a rundown on the most current state of DeFi and what we can expect in the coming years. We will compare existing protocols under their respective sectors and offer some comparative analysis.

Throughout the book, we will also have **Recommended Readings** at the end of each chapter. In these sections, we will share supplementary reading materials that we believe will be useful as you dive deeper into the DeFi ecosystem. All credits, of course, go to their respective authors. Kudos to them for making DeFi more accessible!

This book is best for readers who already possess some basic understanding of DeFi and intend to become active users of DeFi. Therefore, we recommend beginners to start with our *How to DeFi: Beginner* book before continuing with *How to DeFi: Advanced*.

We hope that by sharing our learnings, you will have a deeper understanding of DeFi and will be able to decide better which DeFi protocols suit your needs best.

CoinGecko Research Team
Lucius Fang, Benjamin Hor, Erina Azmi, Khor Win Win
1 May 2021

PART ONE: STATE OF DEFI

CHAPTER 1: DEFI SNAPSHOT

The rise of Decentralized Finance (DeFi) took the crypto world by surprise during the summer of 2020, so much that we refer to the period as DeFi Summer 2020. Total Value Locked (TVL), a measure of the amount of capital locked inside DeFi protocols, has been increasing at a breakneck speed, breaching the magic number of $1 billion in May 2020 and ending the year with $15.7 billion in TVL.

Since then, DeFi has been growing non-stop, expanding into other non-Ethereum chains. DeFi TVL has reached an astounding figure of $86.05 billion in April 2021, showcasing the exponential growth of the crypto industry.[1]

In this chapter, we will zoom into key events of DeFi Summer 2020, take a look at the current DeFi ecosystem, the rise of Ethereum gas fees, and share our thoughts on DeFi becoming mainstream.

DeFi Summer 2020

The crypto space witnessed the meteoric rise of the DeFi sector in 2020, particularly from June to August. The market capitalization of DeFi protocols multiplied 12 times to $19.6 billion during the peak of the summer, now dubbed as DeFi Summer 2020. DeFi dominance, calculated by dividing the

---

[1] (n.d.). DefiLlama - DeFi Dashboard. Retrieved May 4, 2021, from https://defillama.com/

DeFi projects' market capitalization over the total crypto market capitalization, rose rapidly from 0.9% to 4.6%.

Source: CoinGecko

For those of you who were not involved with DeFi in 2020, we have a prepared a short timeline of key DeFi events in 2020 on the next page.

2020 was characterized by the protocol and token launches of many key DeFi projects. Many of these DeFi protocols introduced liquidity mining programs with high yields to attract users to their protocols.

Liquidity mining, a reward program that gives out the protocol's native tokens to users who provide liquidity on the DeFi protocol, is not a foreign concept in DeFi. It was first introduced by Synthetix back in July 2019 and was later popularized by Compound in June 2020.[2]

The popularity of these liquidity mining programs saw many projects launched in the summer of 2020, with many incorporating food and vegetables token names such as Yam and Pickle. Users had a busy summer being "yield farmers", actively rotating their capital into the various DeFi protocols searching for the highest yields.

---

[2] (2019, July 12). Uniswap sETH Pool Liquidity Incentives - Synthetix Blog. Retrieved March 26, 2021, from https://blog.synthetix.io/uniswap-seth-pool-incentives/

DeFi Snapshot

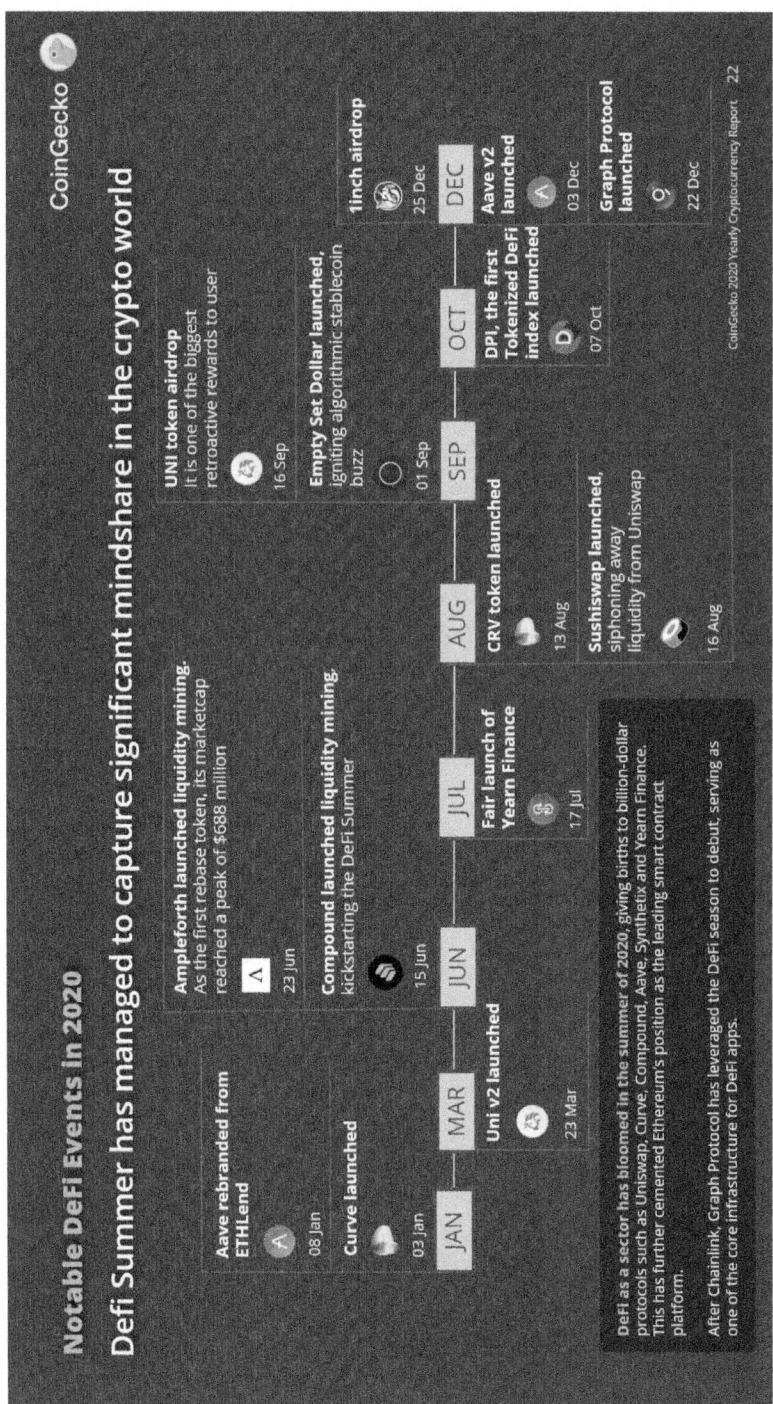

Source: *CoinGecko 2020 Yearly Report*

Yearn Finance, a yield aggregator, kicked off the "fair launch" hype in July 2020. YFI tokens were distributed fairly to anyone who wanted to participate without any private sales to earlier investors. The story continued with the "accidental" launch of the CRV token by Curve Finance in August 2020.

In the same month, SushiSwap, a fork of Uniswap, was launched. SushiSwap conducted a "vampire mining" attack to migrate liquidity away from Uniswap by introducing the SUSHI token to incentivize users.

Not to be outdone, Uniswap did a UNI token airdrop in September 2020, resulting in a windfall profit for all users who interacted with the Uniswap protocol. (Side note: if you had read our *How to DeFi: Beginner* book in 2020 and used Uniswap before the airdrop, you would have received the UNI token too!)

This kickstarted another wave of crypto frenzy, with many projects choosing to launch their tokens to attract more users and growth. Projects without tokens soon find themselves having to consider issuing tokens to compete effectively.

DeFi Ecosystem

DeFi's Total Value Locked (TVL) crossed an impressive $86.05 billion in April 2021. TVL is one of the most widely used metrics in DeFi because it represents the total amount of assets held by each protocol. As a rule of thumb, the more value locked in a protocol, the better it is for the protocol.

In most cases, the locked capital is used to offer services such as market making, lending, asset management, and arbitraging across the ecosystem, earning yields for the capital providers in the process.

However, TVL is not always a reliable metric because its levels can be volatile as capital can be mercenary with temporary incentives such as liquidity mining programs or external catalysts such as smart contract bugs. Hence, it is essential to look at TVL over time to measure the retention of capital and user stickiness.

DeFi Snapshot

With such a large amount of capital locked inside the space, various DeFi Dapps have emerged, challenging the norms of financial theories and boundaries. Novel financial experiments are happening daily, giving birth to new categories such as algorithmic stablecoins.

Below is an overview of the burgeoning DeFi ecosystem based on market capitalization. The Decentralized Exchange category is the highest valued category, followed by Oracles and Lending categories.

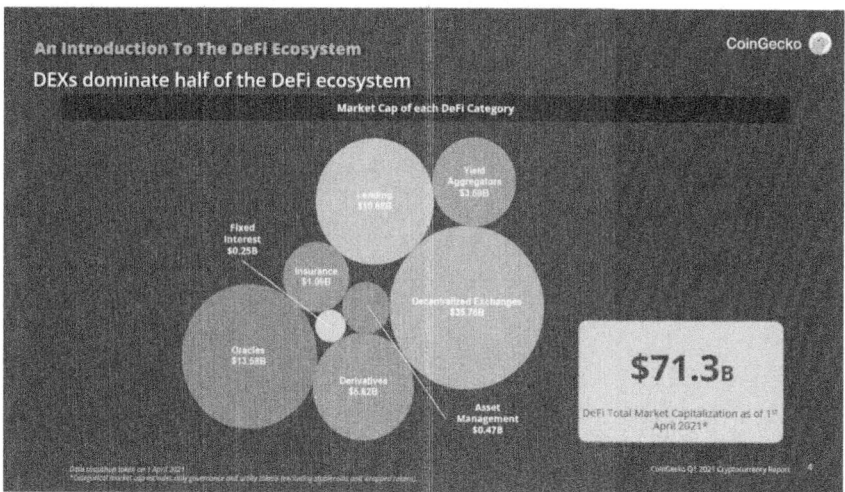

Source: CoinGecko Q1 2021 Report

Rise of Gas Fees

Since the start of 2020, the number of transactions on Ethereum has continuously risen and has exceeded one million transactions per day. The transaction-level seems to be on track to break 2018's peak transaction levels.

Source: Etherscan

The high number of transactions resulted in an uptrend of gas price, which hit a whopping 700 gwei per transaction by August 2020. Although gas price in 2021 is lower compared to DeFi Summer 2020, the price of ether in 2021 is much higher, resulting in the rise of overall transaction fees. Ethereum broke its previous All-Time High in January 2021 and recorded a new peak of $4,357 on 12 May 2021!

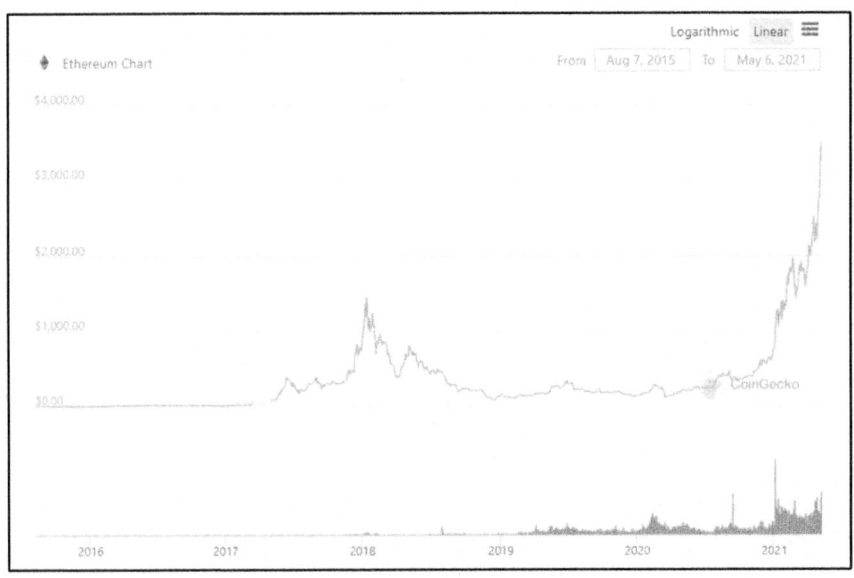

Source: CoinGecko

The high gas price and the increase in Ethereum price have made many DeFi Dapps on Ethereum no longer economically feasible for users to use without significant capital. Completing a simple swap on Uniswap in Q1 2021 can rack up fees of up to $100 per transaction, making it only feasible for large swaps. Transaction fees become even higher for more complex transactions such as yield farming transactions.

High transaction fees caused many Ethereum DeFi users to look for cheaper alternatives elsewhere. Some of the other options include moving to Layer-2 (e.g., Optimism, Arbitrum, and zkRollups), sidechains (e.g., xDAI and Polygon), or competing Layer-1 chains (e.g., Binance Smart Chain, Solana, and Terra). We will cover these in more detail in Chapter 14.

DeFi is Going Mainstream

The crypto industry captured a lot of attention in the first half of 2021. Significant events happening globally led to attention-grabbing headlines such as:

1. Tesla's $1.5 billion initial Bitcoin investment
2. Beeple's $69 million Non-Fungible Token art sale (Everydays: the First 5000 Days) on Christie's
3. Visa supporting USDC as a settlement option on Ethereum
4. Fidelity's plans for a Bitcoin Exchange-Traded Fund
5. Coinbase's listing on the NASDAQ
6. China's positive perception of Bitcoin and other cryptoassets as alternative investments

The increased media attention in the broader crypto market has also led to more eyes on DeFi. In particular, institutional investors started to take notice. For example, in Citibank's Global Perspective and Solutions (Citi GPS) report entitled "Future of Money: Crypto, CBDCs and 21st Century Cash," the 209-year-old lender espoused the benefits of DeFi, including the removal of third-party intermediaries and increased financial transparency.

Notably, the same report also explored various DeFi protocols such as Maker, Compound, Uniswap, and UMA. An in-depth report by the Federal

Reserve Bank of St Louis also highlights DeFi's potential to cause a "paradigm shift in the financial industry and potentially contribute toward a more robust, open, and transparent financial infrastructure".

We also see investment institutions entering the DeFi foray. Grayscale, one of the more famous digital investment funds, is actively offering exposure to DeFi assets (e.g. Chainlink) through share-based trusts. Bitwise Asset Management fund also has a DeFi Index Fund which offers exposure to over 10 DeFi assets such as Aave and Compound. When the fund opened in March 2021, it raised $32.5M in just two weeks.

DeFi is not stopping at the virtual line either. The envisioned "real world" use-cases of DeFi have already materialized where DeFi protocols are recognized as suitable alternatives from traditional banking instruments.

Centrifuge, one of the first "real world" companies to integrate with MakerDAO, is onboarding non-digital assets as collateral through their app, Tinlake. On 21 April 2021, the company successfully executed its first MakerDAO loan for $181k with a house as collateral, effectively creating one of the first blockchain-based mortgages.

Recommended Readings

1. Q1 2021 CoinGecko Report
   https://assets.coingecko.com/reports/2021-Q1-Report/CoinGecko-2021-Q1-Report.pdf
2. Understanding Eth2
   https://ethereum.org/en/eth2/
3. Beyond Ethereum: Ethereum Killers or Enhancers?
   https://peeman34.medium.com/ethereum-enhancers-or-ethereum-killers-a-new-ecosystem-dd7aeed3d440

CHAPTER 2: DEFI ACTIVITIES

In this chapter, we will look at the various ways you can participate in the DeFi ecosystem. DeFi protocols democratize access and allow unprecedented freedom for capital providers to offer financial services.

Activities such as market-making, insurance underwriting, and structured product creation were previously only accessible to institutions with a large capital base and specialized knowledge. DeFi has significantly reduced these barriers and availed these activities to the masses.

We will explain further some of the key areas and activities of DeFi, such as yield farming, liquidity mining, airdrops, and Initial DEX Offerings (IDO).

Yield Farming

Yield farming is perhaps one of the most innovative features of DeFi. It refers to the activity of allocating capital to DeFi protocols to earn returns.

Most DeFi protocols are peer-to-peer financial applications where capital allocated is used to provide services to end-users. The fees charged to users are then shared between the capital providers and the protocol. The fees that capital providers get are the intrinsic yield.

In crypto slang, we refer to these investors as "yield farmers" and the yield opportunities as "farms". Many yield farmers constantly rotate their farms in search of the highest-yielding opportunities.

Below are some examples of yield farming, where the capital provided will be used for a variety of purposes:

- **Exchanges** - Provide capital for market-making on decentralized exchanges, earning transaction fees in return.
- **Lending** - Provide loans to borrowers, earning an interest.
- **Insurance** - Underwrite insurance, earning premiums while undertaking the risk of paying out claims during disasters.
- **Options** - Underwrite options by selling call and put options to earn a yield.
- **Synthetic Assets** - Mint stablecoins or other synthetic assets, earning fees in return.

Liquidity Mining

Financial services is a capital-intensive industry and usually benefits from having economies of scale. This means the more capital that firms have, the better. DeFi protocols are no exception - obtaining sizable capital will be a substantial competitive advantage for DeFi protocols.

In crypto, DeFi protocols incentivize the provision of liquidity via liquidity mining programs. Liquidity mining refers to the reward program of giving out the protocol's native tokens in exchange for capital. These tokens usually come with governance rights and may have the possibility of accruing cash flows from the DeFi protocols.

When designed right, liquidity mining programs are a quick way to bootstrap large sums of liquidity in a short timeframe, albeit with a dilution of token ownership. These programs can also be used to incentivize new users to try out new DeFi protocols. You may think of these incentives similar to how Uber subsidizes rides in the early days using venture capital.

Liquidity mining programs are also a novel way to attract the right kind of community participation for DeFi protocols. As DeFi protocols are open-source in nature, it relies on voluntary contributions from the community. The token distribution encourages community participation in determining the future direction of the protocol.

While it may look like liquidity mining programs offer free rewards, by participating, you are locking up your capital for some time, and your capital has an opportunity cost of earning higher returns elsewhere. Additionally, in many instances, locking up your capital is not risk-free. Yield farming activities typically involve various risks that may lead to loss of money.

The most common form of liquidity mining program is the provision of native token liquidity on decentralized exchanges with base tokens such as ETH, WBTC, or USD stablecoins. Such programs incentivize the creation of liquidity surrounding the protocol's native tokens and enable users to trade these tokens on decentralized exchanges easily.

Example

In August 2020, SushiSwap, a decentralized exchange, launched its governance token named SUSHI and wanted to bootstrap the liquidity between SUSHI and ETH. The team offered to reward free SUSHI tokens to anyone that provides liquidity on the SUSHI/ETH trading pair on SushiSwap.

Users will have to provide both SUSHI and ETH in an equal ratio. Let's assume a user has $1,000 worth of ETH and would like to participate in this liquidity mining program to earn SUSHI tokens. The user first exchanges half of his ETH into SUSHI. Then he supplies $500 worth of SUSHI and $500 worth of ETH into the SUSHI-ETH liquidity pool. He will be given SUSHI-ETH Liquidity Provider (LP) tokens, representing his share in the liquidity pool that can then be staked in the SushiSwap platform to obtain the SUSHI token incentive.

Other types of liquidity mining programs have customizable names based on the intended use case of the capital locked. For example, Compound, a decentralized lending and borrowing protocol, gives out COMP tokens to lenders and borrowers to incentivize protocol activity. Nexus Mutual, a decentralized insurance protocol, has a Shield Mining program that gives out NXM tokens to NXM token holders who stake their capital on specific protocols to open up more insurance cover capacity. Hegic, a decentralized options protocol, gives rHEGIC tokens to option sellers and buyers to incentivize protocol activity.

There are several websites to monitor yield farming and liquidity mining opportunities:

- https://www.coingecko.com/en/yield-farming
- https://vfat.tools/
- https://zapper.fi/farm

Airdrops

Airdrops are essentially freely distributed tokens. Projects usually conduct airdrops as part of their marketing strategy to generate attention and hype around their token launch, albeit with the tradeoff of diluting token ownership.

Some projects also conduct airdrops to reward early users who have interacted with their protocols. Each protocol will have criteria for qualifying airdrop recipients, such as the timing of interaction and minimum amounts used.

Some notable airdrops are shown below:

Protocol	Token symbol	Date Airdrop	Initial Price	Price as of 1st April 2021	Return
Uniswap	UNI	16 September 2020	$3.44	$28.71	734.59%
1INCH	1INCH	25 December 2020	$2.36	$4.46	88.98%
PoolTogether	POOL	17 February 2021	$11.98	$23.11	92.90%

One of the most notable airdrops was the one conducted by Uniswap. Early users were awarded a minimum of 400 UNI.[3] As of 1 April 2021, the airdrop is worth as much as $11,484. (Side note: if you had read our How to DeFi: Beginner book in 2020 and used Uniswap before the airdrop, you would have received the UNI token airdrop too!)

Initial DEX Offerings (IDO)

Crypto projects have to be creative over their token launch and distribution strategies. With the growing popularity of Decentralized Exchanges (DEX), projects now have a viable option of going direct to users without paying sky-high fees to get listed on centralized exchanges. Crypto project teams can now list their tokens without the need for permission on these DEXs.

However, distributing tokens fairly and to a wide group of users at a fair price is still a difficult endeavor. There are various types of IDOs available, and we will be looking at a few popular types.

Initial Bonding Curve Offering (IBCO)

Initial Bonding Curve Offering, or IBCO, is a fairly new concept meant to prevent front-running practices. Essentially, as more investors provide capital into the bonding curve, the token price will increase from its initial value.

---

[3] (2020, September 16). Introducing UNI - Uniswap. Retrieved May 24, 2021, from https://uniswap.org/blog/uni/

However, it does not matter when you choose to contribute since all investors will pay based on the same final settlement price. Based on the price at the end of the IBCO, each investor will receive a portion of the tokens based on their share of the total capital invested. Projects such as Hegic and Aavegotchi have used this distribution method in their initial token launches with great success.

Liquidity Bootstrapping Pool (LBP)

Hosted using Balancer's Smart Pools, Liquidity Bootstrapping Pools (LBP) is a way for projects to sell tokens using a configurable Automated Market Maker. Usually, these pools would contain the project token and a collateral token, usually denominated in stablecoins. Controllers of the smart pool can change its parameters and introduce a variety of features to the sale, such as a declining price over time as well as pausing any further swaps due to high demand or external vulnerabilities.

Initial Farm Offering (IFO)

First introduced by PancakeSwap, an Initial Farm Offering (IFO) allows users to stake their Liquidity Provider (LP) tokens in exchange for a project's tokens. Using an overflow mechanism, users can stake as much or as little as they want. In the event of oversubscription, any excess tokens are returned to the bidder. IFOs on PancakeSwap use the CAKE-BNB LP tokens, where the project receives BNB tokens in exchange for their newly minted protocol's tokens, while the remaining CAKE tokens are burnt.

DeFi Activities

Yield Farming: Step-by-Step Guide

In this section, we will be going through a step-by-step guide on yield farming. Using the earlier SUSHI/ETH example in this chapter, we will show how to yield farm using Zapper.

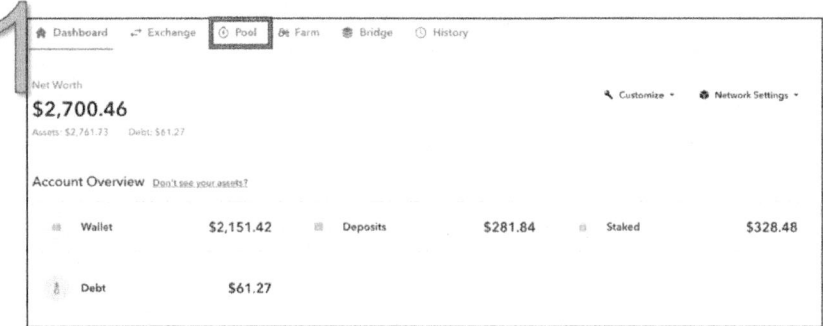

Step 1
- Connect Ethereum wallet at https://zapper.fi/dashboard
- Select the "Pool" tab

How to DeFi: Advanced

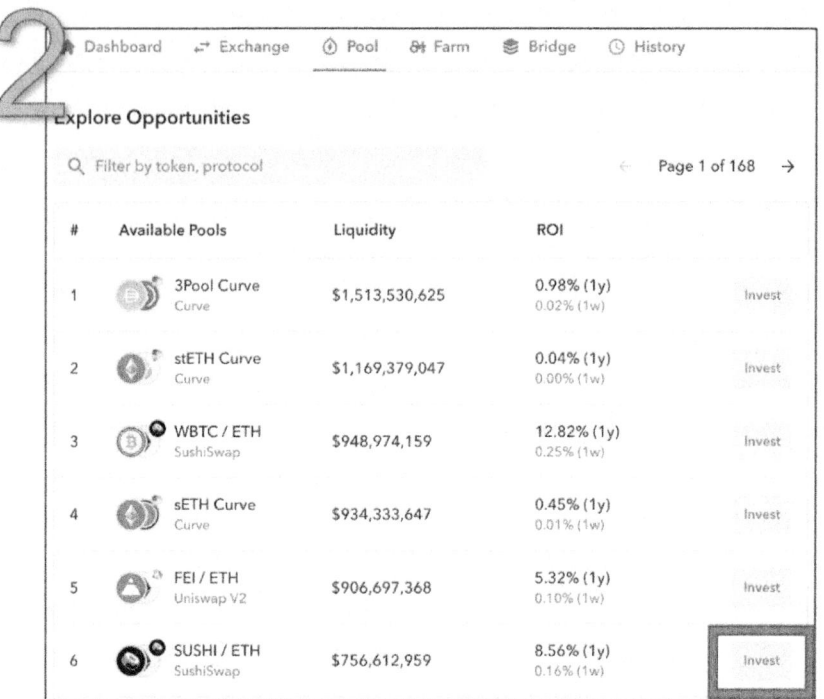

Step 2
- In this guide, we are going to yield farm SUSHI/ETH to get the SUSHI token.
- Click "Invest"

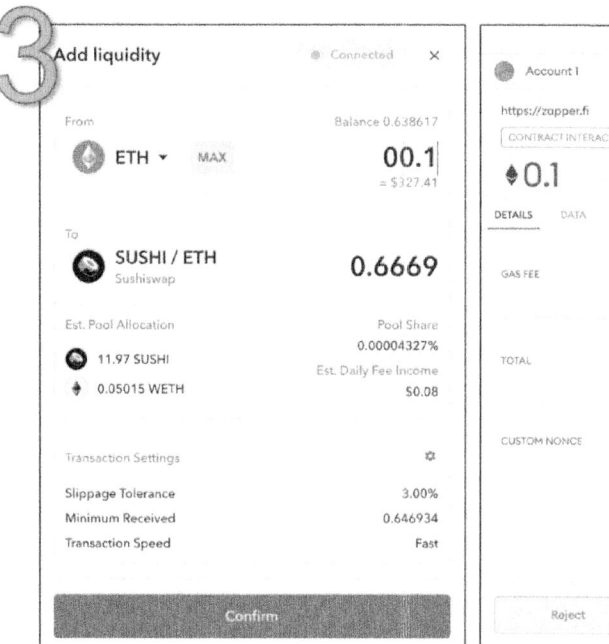
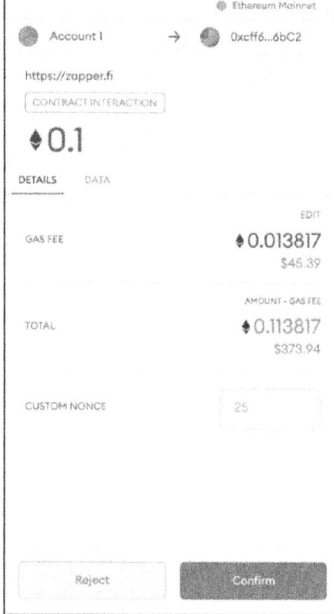

Step 3

- In Zapper, we can swap any single asset to any LP token. Here we will swap ETH to SUSHI/ETH.
- Confirm the transaction.

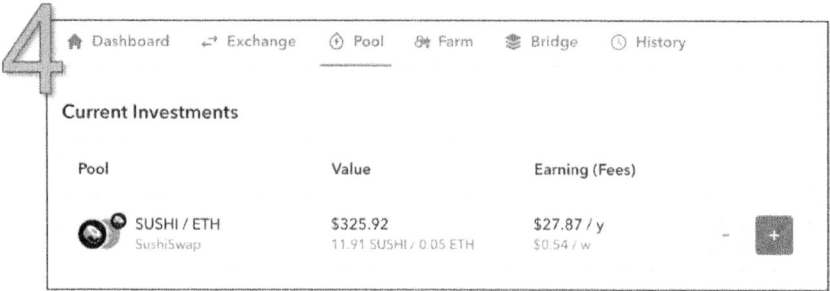

Step 4

- The SUSHI/ETH position will appear under the Current Investments section.

How to DeFi: Advanced

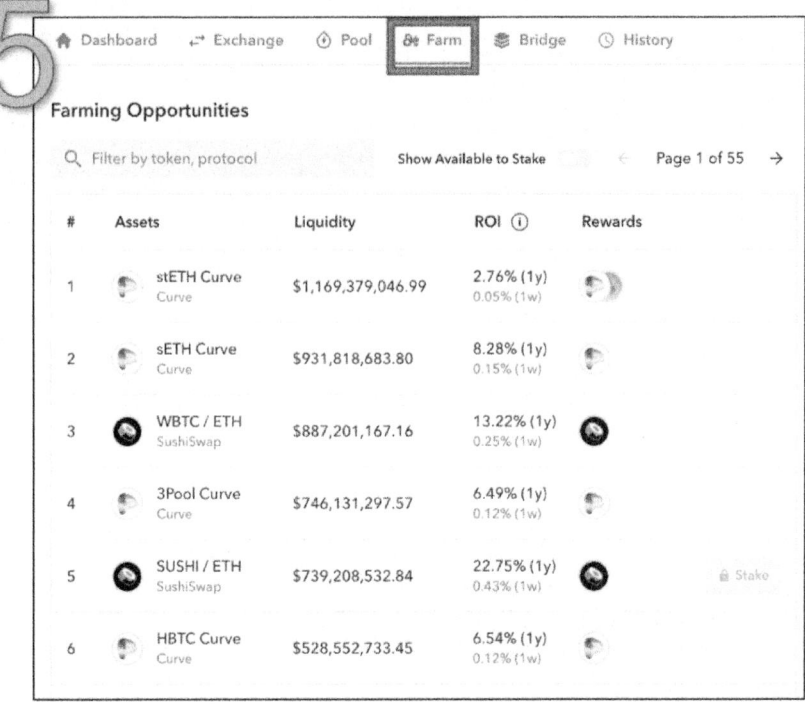

Step 5

- The "Farm" tab lists yield farming opportunities and their respective expected returns.
- A green "Stake" button will appear if we have the underlying asset for the yield farming opportunity.
- Click "Stake"

DeFi Activities

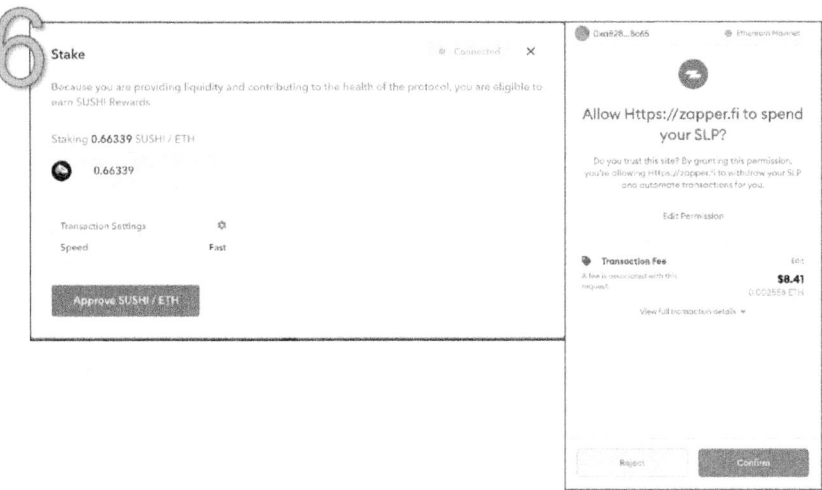

Step 6
- Approve the transaction. This allows Zapper access to our SUSHI/ETH LP token.

Step 7
- Confirm the transaction.

How to DeFi: Advanced

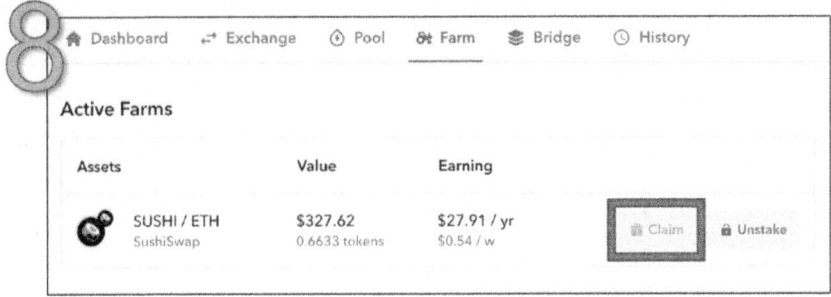

Step 8
- Now we will be able to earn the trading fees and the liquidity mining reward.
- Click "Claim" to see the rewards.

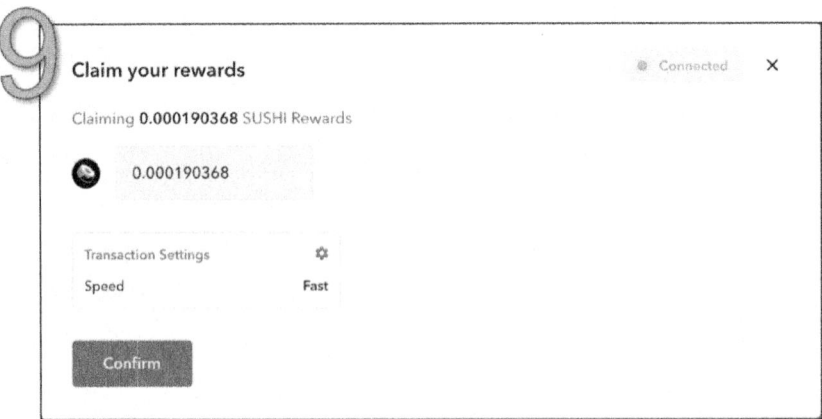

Step 9
- The rewards can be claimed by clicking "Confirm".
- We can exit the position by clicking "Unstake", as shown in the image at step 8.

Associated Risks

Once you are familiar with the DeFi ecosystem, you will inevitably see various protocols offering eye-popping yields, sometimes more than 1,000% Annual Percentage Yield (APY)! While it is tempting to plow your money in, such APYs are usually temporary and will eventually stabilize to lower numbers once other yield farmers start coming in.

Given the fast-paced world of DeFi, investors also have to make quick decisions on whether a project is worth investing in. Fear of Missing Out (FOMO) is real and should not be taken lightly.

Regardless of whether you are a trader, investor, or yield farmer, one should always be wary of the usual risks such as smart contract risk, impermanent loss risk, and relevant systemic risk. No matter how technically sound a project may be, liquidity exploits are always possible from malicious actors.

Users need to understand that the DeFi ecosystem is still nascent, and most DeFi activities are still experimental. We will be covering the different types of risks associated with each DeFi category throughout this book, and dedicate the whole of Chapter 15 to risks associated with smart contract exploits.

Conclusion

DeFi is groundbreaking. We are witnessing a financial revolution happening right in front of us, one which democratizes access to finance, promotes financial inclusion, and promises financial transparency. Although DeFi in its current iteration is not perfect, it does provide us with a glimpse of what the future may look like.

Anyone in the world with access to the Internet can now participate in this grand financial experiment. Crypto financial primitives such as being a liquidity provider and the tokenization of ownership allow new forms of organizations to be formed. It will not be long before we see DeFi protocols being more valuable than the largest companies in the world.

Recommended Readings

1. Governance Tokens: Investing in the Building Blocks of a New Economy
   https://thedefiant.io/governance-tokens-investing-in-the-building-blocks-of-a-new-economy/
2. New Models for Utility Tokens
   https://multicoin.capital/2018/02/13/new-models-utility-tokens/
3. Liquidity Bootstrapping FAQ
   https://docs.balancer.finance/smart-contracts/smart-pools/liquidity-bootstrapping-faq
4. What is Yield Farming
   https://learn.zapper.fi/articles/what-is-yield-farming

PART TWO: EVALUATING DEFI SECTORS

CHAPTER 3: DECENTRALIZED EXCHANGES

Whether you are trying to make a simple swap or actively trade, you will require the services of an exchange. Ideally, the exchange must have low latency and deep liquidity so that you have the best price execution and do not get impacted by price slippage.

Historically, Centralized Exchanges (CEXs) have provided better liquidity and have facilitated most large trades. However, they carry several weak points - the most notable being users of centralized entities do not hold custody of their assets. For example, in September 2020, KuCoin suffered a $281 million hack after a security breach.[4] CEXs could also halt trading and block users from withdrawing their funds at any time.

In 2020 and 2021, Decentralized Exchanges (DEXs) have grown rapidly and have started to rival their centralized counterparts. The Top-9 DEX-CEX ratio had improved from only 0.2% in January 2020 to 5.9% in December 2020. In 2020, top-9 DEXs recorded an exponential 17,989% growth to $30 billion in trading volume.[5]

---

[4] (2020, September 25). Over $280M Drained in KuCoin Crypto Exchange Hack - CoinDesk. Retrieved March 13, 2021, from https://www.coindesk.com/hackers-drain-kucoin-crypto-exchanges-funds

[5] "Q1 2021 Quarterly Cryptocurrency Report - CoinGecko." 15 Apr. 2021, https://www.coingecko.com/buzz/q1-2021-quarterly-cryptocurrency-report. Accessed 20 Apr. 2021.

Total Trading Volume ($ Billion)

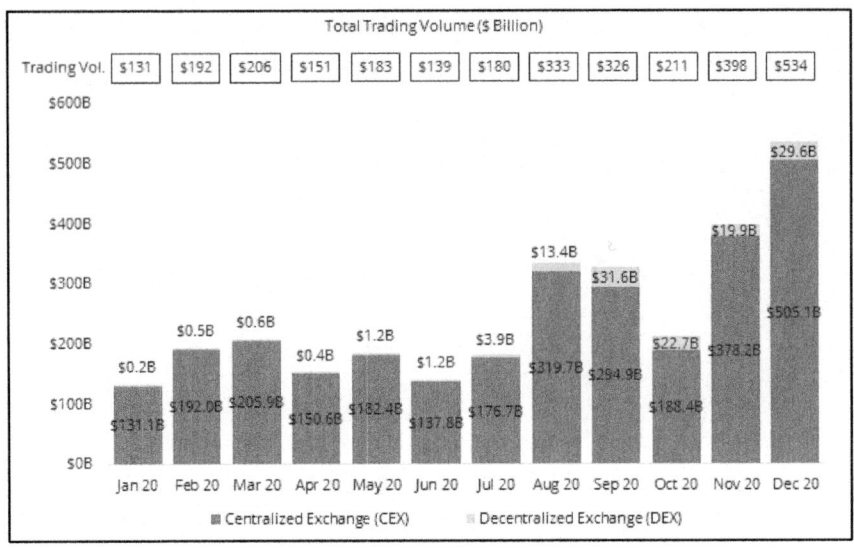

Month	Trading Vol.	CEX	DEX
Jan 20	$131	$131.1B	$0.2B
Feb 20	$192	$192.0B	$0.5B
Mar 20	$206	$205.9B	$0.6B
Apr 20	$151	$150.6B	$0.4B
May 20	$183	$182.4B	$1.2B
Jun 20	$139	$137.8B	$1.2B
Jul 20	$180	$176.7B	$3.9B
Aug 20	$333	$319.7B	$13.4B
Sep 20	$326	$294.9B	$31.6B
Oct 20	$211	$188.4B	$22.7B
Nov 20	$398	$378.2B	$19.9B
Dec 20	$534	$505.1B	$29.6B

Source: CoinGecko 2020 Yearly Report

But what exactly makes a DEX…a DEX?

A DEX is a platform that enables trading and direct swapping of tokens without the need for an intermediary (i.e., centralized exchange). You do not need to go through the hassles of Know Your Customer (KYC) processes nor are you subjected to jurisdictional limits.

Types of DEX

There are two types of DEXs:

1. **Order Book Based-DEXs**

    An order book is a list of buy and sell orders for a particular asset at various price levels.

    Order book-based DEXs like dYdX, Deversifi, and Loopring operate similarly to CEXs where users can set buy and sell orders at either their chosen limit prices or at market prices. The main difference is that in CEXs, assets for the trade are held on the exchanges' wallets, whereas for DEXs, assets for the trade are held on users' wallets.

Order books for DEXs can either be on-chain or off-chain. On-chain order book-based DEXs have all orders recorded on the blockchain. However, this is no longer feasible on Ethereum due to high gas prices. That said, this is still doable on Ethereum Layer 2 solutions like xDai or high-throughput Layer 1 blockchains like Solana.

Off-chain order book-based DEXs have trade orders recorded outside the blockchain. The trade orders remain off-chain until they are matched, at which point the trades are executed on-chain. Although this approach has lower latency, some may argue that DEXs that utilize this method are considered semi-decentralized.

2. **Liquidity Pool Based-DEXs**

    Liquidity pools are token reserves that sit on DEXs' smart contracts and are available for users to exchange tokens with. Most liquidity pool-based DEXs make use of Automated Market Makers (AMM), a mathematical function that predefines asset prices algorithmically.

AMM is one of the most innovative inventions from DeFi in recent years. It enables 24/7 market hours, higher capital accessibility, and efficiency. There are various types of AMMs, and different DEXs have implemented the various 'flavors'. The majority of DEXs that launched during the DeFi summer 2020 are AMM-based DEXs such as Uniswap, SushiSwap, Curve, Balancer, and Bancor.

Since many of the newer DEXs are AMM-based, we will focus the rest of this chapter going through a few examples of AMMs.

Automated Market Makers (AMMs)

In our *How to DeFi: Beginner* book, we have gone through Uniswap, the most popular AMM. Here is a recap of how liquidity pools in AMMs work.

Unlike centralized exchanges, which have bids and ask orders placed on order books, AMMs do not have any order books. Instead, it relies on liquidity pools. Liquidity pools are essentially reserves that hold two or more tokens that reside on a DEX's smart contract that are made readily available for users to trade against.

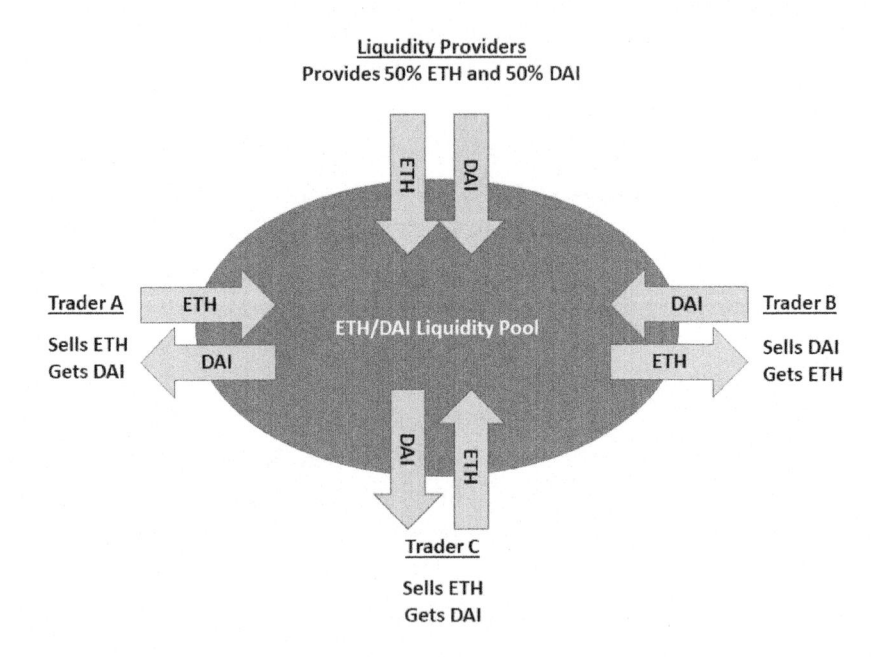

Liquidity Providers
Provides 50% ETH and 50% DAI

ETH/DAI Liquidity Pool

Trader A — Sells ETH, Gets DAI

Trader B — Sells DAI, Gets ETH

Trader C — Sells ETH, Gets DAI

You can think of liquidity pools as just pools of tokens that you can trade against. If you wish to swap ETH to DAI, you will trade on the ETH/DAI liquidity pool by adding ETH and removing an amount of DAI determined algorithmically from the liquidity pool.

Depositors, known as Liquidity Providers (LPs), seed these liquidity pools. LPs deposit their tokens into the liquidity pool based on the predefined token weights for each AMM (in Uniswap's case - 50% for each token).

LPs provide funds in liquidity pools because they can earn a yield on their funds, collected from trading fees charged to users trading on the DEX. Anyone can become an LP and automatically market-make a trading pair by depositing their funds into the smart contract.

With AMMs, traders can have their orders executed seamlessly without the need for a centralized market maker providing liquidity on a centralized exchange like Coinbase or Binance. Instead, orders are executed automatically via a smart contract that will calculate trade prices algorithmically, including any slippage from the trade execution. You may thus consider order book-based exchanges as following the peer-to-peer model while AMMs follow the peer-to-contract model.

What are the existing types of AMMs out there?

AMMs are a mathematical function to price assets algorithmically based on liquidity pools. Currently, several AMM formulas are utilized to cater to different asset pricing strategies.

Some of the more popular AMM formulas are as follow:

I. **Constant Product Market Makers**
$$x * y = k$$

The Constant Product Market Maker formula was first popularized by Uniswap and Bancor and the most popular AMM in the market. When plotted, it is a convex curve where x and y represent the quantity of two tokens in a liquidity pool, and k represents the product. The formula helps create a range of prices for the two tokens depending on each token's available quantities.

To maintain k as constant, when the supply of x increases, the supply of y must decrease, and vice-versa. Therefore, the resulting price is inherently unstable as the size of trades may affect the price in relation to pool size. Impermanent loss may occur by higher slippage caused by large trades.

II. **Constant Sum Market Maker**
$$x + y = k$$

The Constant Sum Market Maker formula creates a straight line when plotted. It is an ideal model for zero slippage trade but, unfortunately does not offer infinite liquidity. This model is flawed as it presents an arbitrage opportunity when the quoted price is different from the market price of the asset traded elsewhere. Arbitrageurs can drain the entire reserves in the liquidity pools, leaving no more available liquidity for other traders. This model is unfit for most AMM use cases.

III. **Constant Mean Market Maker**

$$v = \prod_t B_t^{w_t}$$

The Constant Mean Market Maker formula, or also known as Value Function, was made popular by Balancer. It allows for liquidity pools with more than two tokens and different token ratios beyond the standard 50/50 distribution. Rather than the product, the weighted geometric mean remains constant. This allows for variable exposure to different assets in the pool and enables swaps between any of the liquidity pool's assets.

IV. **Stableswap Invariant**

$$An^n \sum X_i + D = ADn^n + \frac{D^{n+1}}{n^n \prod x_i}$$

The StableSwap Invariant formula is a hybrid of the Constant Product and Constant Sum formula. It was made popular by Curve Finance.

Trading occurs on a Constant Sum curve when the portfolio is relatively balanced and switches to a Constant Product curve when imbalanced. This allows for lower slippage and Impermanent Loss but is only applicable to assets with a similar value as the price of the desired trading range is always close to 1. For example, this will be useful for trading between stablecoins (DAI and USDC) and wrapped assets (wBTC and sBTC).

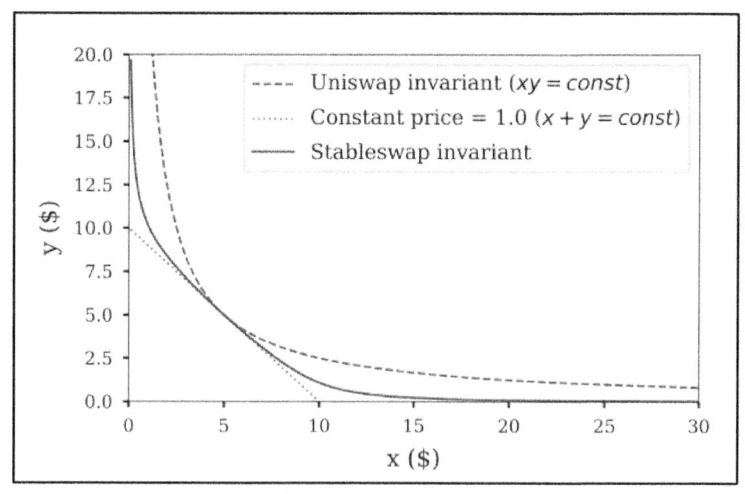

Source: https://curve.fi/files/stableswap-paper.pdf

This graph shows the Constant Product Market Maker (purple line) and Constant Sum (red line) curves with a Stableswap Invariant hybrid curve used by Curve Finance (blue line) in the middle. We can see that the Stableswap Invariant curve creates deeper liquidity near the Constant Sum curve. The result is a line that returns a linear exchange rate for most trades and exponential prices for larger trades.

How are prices determined on a Constant Product AMM?

Let's look at a simple example of a Constant Product Market Maker and see how asset prices are determined algorithmically. It works by maintaining a constant product formula based on the amount of liquidity available for each asset in the pool.

To see how it works via the popular AMM, we will look at constant product market makers that Uniswap popularized:

It is important to note that the market price on AMMs changes only when the reserve ratio in the pool changes. Thus, an asset price on AMM might differ from other exchanges.

> **Example**
>
> Based on the Constant Product Market Maker formula
>
> $$x * y = k$$
>
> x = the reserve token x
> y = the reserve token y
> k = the constant total liquidity that determines the price of tokens in the liquidity pool
>
> For example:
>
> There are 61,404,818 DAI and 26,832 ETH in Uniswap's DAI/ETH liquidity pool as of 21 April 2021. The reserve ratio implies that ETH's price at the time of writing is 61,404,818 DAI / 26,832 ETH = 2,289 DAI.

Assuming 1 ETH is now valued at 2,289 DAI on Uniswap. But when the price of ETH drops to 2,100 DAI elsewhere, such as on Balancer, an arbitrage opportunity presents itself. Arbitrageurs will take advantage of the price differences by buying cheap ETH on Balancer and selling it off on Uniswap for a quick profit (ignoring the trading fee for simplicity). Arbitrageurs will repeat this until the price reaches equilibrium between the two exchanges.

The Various Automated Market Makers (AMMs)

Uniswap

Uniswap is a decentralized exchange protocol on Ethereum that allows direct token swaps without giving up the custody of your funds. To use Uniswap, all you need to do is send your tokens from your wallet to Uniswap's smart contract, and you will receive your desired tokens in return in your wallet.

Uniswap's journey began in November 2018 when it launched its first iteration, Uniswap version 1. It is one of the first AMM-based DEX that popularized Constant Product Market Makers formula:

$$x * y = k$$

In May 2020, Uniswap upgraded its smart contract to Uniswap version 2 with added features. The new version expanded trading pairs to support any ERC-20 tokens.

On 5 May 2021, Uniswap released the latest iteration, Uniswap version 3. In the latest iteration, Uniswap introduced two main new features:

1. **Concentrated liquidity**
   With Uniswap version 3, LPs can control the price ranges where they would like to provide liquidity. For example, an LP for the ETH/DAI liquidity pool may choose to allocate 30% of his capital to the $2,000 - $3,000 price range and the remaining 70% to the $1,500 - $1,700 price range.

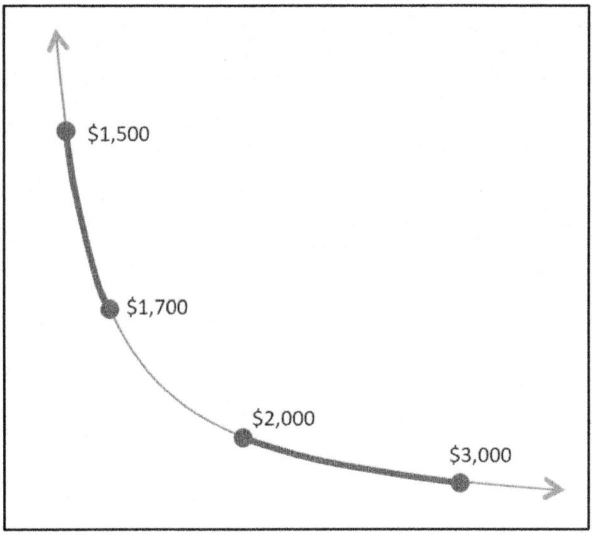
$1,500
$1,700
$2,000
$3,000

The new active management of liquidity on Uniswap version 3 now results in higher capital efficiency for LPs. A by-product of this is that LPs will receive Non-Fungible Tokens (NFTs) instead of fungible ERC-20 tokens representing their LP positions.

2. **Multiple pool fee tiers**
   Uniswap version 3 offers a three-tier pool fee that Liquidity Providers can choose accordingly:

   a. 0.05%
   b. 0.30%
   c. 1.00%

For example, the USDC/DAI trading pair has low price volatility and may warrant a lower 0.05% pool fee. The ETH/DAI trading pair has higher price volatility and would warrant a 0.30% pool fee. Meanwhile, the 1.00% pool fee may be more appropriate for more long-tail or exotic trading pairs.

SushiSwap

SushiSwap was launched on 28 August 2020 by a pseudonymous developer known as Chef Nomi. It was a fork of Uniswap's version 2 source code and utilized the same Constant Product Market Maker model. SushiSwap introduced a SUSHI token at a time when Uniswap did not yet have its UNI token. The attractive yield farming rewards offered by SushiSwap caught the attention of many people in the crypto community.

On 9 September 2020, SushiSwap launched a "vampire attack" on Uniswap's liquidity whereby anyone staking their Uniswap LP tokens on SushiSwap will have their underlying liquidity on Uniswap migrated over to SushiSwap. This attack drained over half of Uniswap's liquidity and saw its Total Value Locked (TVL) went from $1.55 billion to $470 million. Simultaneously, SushiSwap's TVL increased to $1.13 billion overnight.

Despite the "vampire attack", Uniswap has stayed resilient and recovered its TVL lead over SushiSwap very quickly. As of April 2021, SushiSwap now has $4.5 billion in TVL, slightly half of Uniswap's $10.3 billion in TVL.

SushiSwap has grown significantly and is now the second-largest DEX behind Uniswap. As of March 2021, Uniswap's trading volume is four times higher than SushiSwap's, signifying the substantial lead that Uniswap has in the DEX market. In the first two months of 2021, SushiSwap performed strongly and had 45% of Uniswap's trading volume.

Since its launch, SushiSwap has differentiated itself by offering a more comprehensive product range. It has also partnered (merged) with Yearn Finance, a yield farming aggregator protocol, and is now the AMM arm of

Yearn Finance.[6] The key difference between the two lies in the pool fees, available trading pairs, and supported blockchains.

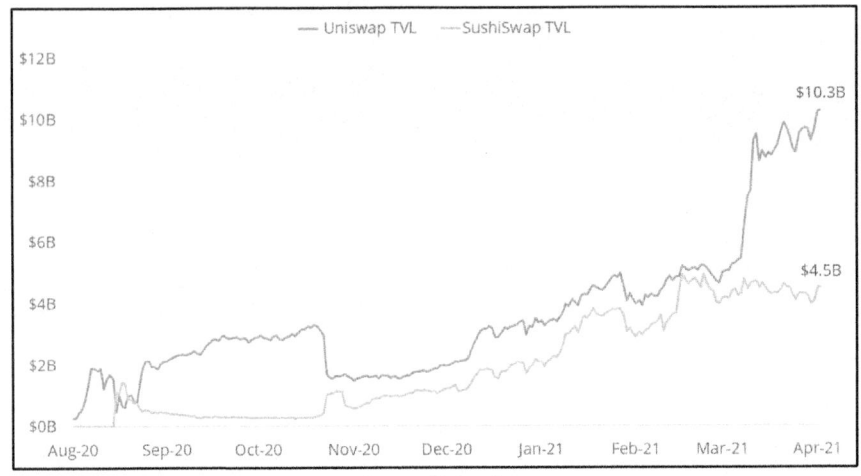

Source: DeBank

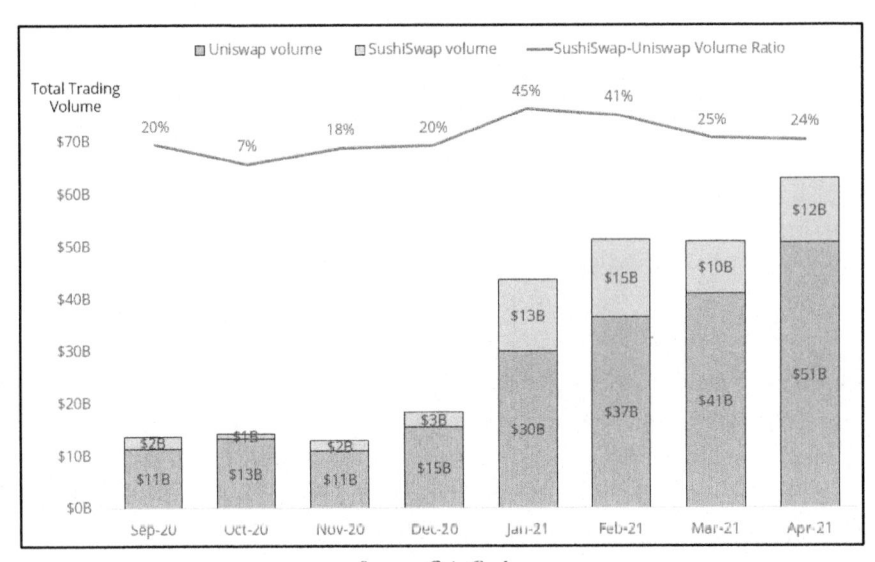

Source: CoinGecko

---

[6] "Yearn x Sushi 行ってきます. I had been outspoken in the ... - Medium." 30 Nov. 2020, https://medium.com/iearn/yearn-x-sushi-%E8%A1%8C%E3%81%A3%E3%81%A6%E3%81%8D%E3%81%BE%E3%81%99-41b2f78b62e9. Accessed 11 May. 2021.

Decentralized Exchanges

	Uniswap	SushiSwap
Type of fees	Fixed	Fixed
Pool fees	0.30%	0.30%
Protocol	0.00%	0.05%
Liquidity Providers	0.30%	0.25%

Pool fees as of 1st April 2021

From the table above, we can see that both Uniswap and SushiSwap have a trading fee of 0.3%. However, on SushiSwap, 0.05% of the trading fee goes to the protocol, which is then distributed to SUSHI token holders.

Uniswap does not currently distribute fees to UNI token holders, although this can be activated by UNI governance voting. As of April 2021, Uniswap's LPs receive a higher share of revenue (0.30%) compared to SushiSwap's LPs (0.25%).

We can see from the chart below that both Uniswap and Sushiswap's protocol revenues have grown significantly over the past year.

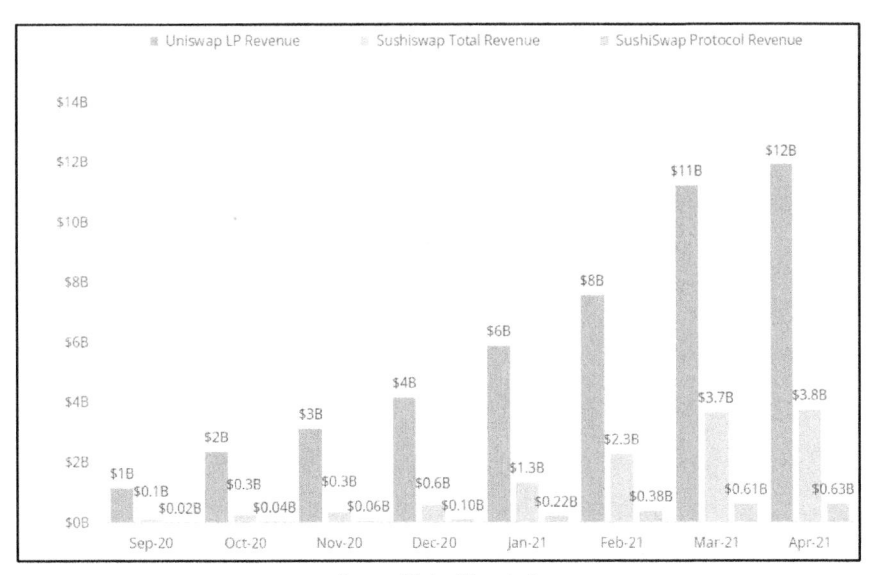

Source: TokenTerminal

Uniswap also has more than 2,000 supported trading pairs, which is approximately five times higher than SushiSwap - this suggests that there are more long-tail tokens supported and traded on Uniswap.

Uniswap currently only supports trading on Ethereum with plans to move to Layer 2 via Optimism. In contrast, SushiSwap operates on nine different blockchains, namely Ethereum, Binance Smart Chain, Polygon, Fantom, Huobi Ecosystem, xDAI, Harmony, Avalanche and OKExChain.

Balancer

Balancer positions itself as a portfolio manager in addition to its AMM-based DEX. Instead of paying fees to invest in a fund, Balancer pool holders collect fees from traders that arbitrage liquidity pools. This essentially creates an index fund that gets paid when the fund is rebalanced, adding another source of income for liquidity providers.

Unlike Uniswap that supports only two assets, Balancer supports multi-asset pools. Pool creators are also allowed to set customized fees ranging from 0.00001% to 10%. This flexibility opens up more possibilities to pool creations.

There are three types of liquidity pools:

1. **Public pool** - Anyone can add liquidity, but the pool parameters are permanently fixed. This is the most trustless pool.

2. **Private pool** - Flexible parameters. The owner is the only entity that can change the parameters and add liquidity. This makes the pool custodial and centralized.

3. **Smart pool** - Anyone can add liquidity. The pool supports fixed and dynamic parameters, which can be changed on an ongoing basis. This is the most flexible pool.

Balancer version 2 supports up to 16 different assets in a pool and allows for the creation of smart pools. Smart pools are especially useful for treasury management, where the pools can act as an automatic token buyback machine.[7] Plus, it also allows for idle assets in the pools to be lent out to lending protocols, improving the pools' yields.

Balancer has also introduced an innovative Initial DEX Offerings (IDO) method called Liquidity Bootstrapping Pools (LBPs). They are short-lived smart pools with dynamic weighting over time. Token price is set at a high price and is expected to fall throughout the sale. Whales and bots are disincentivized to buy the tokens all at the start, allowing for a more democratic way of fundraising.

Curve Finance

Curve Finance is an AMM-based DEX with the main focus of facilitating swaps between assets of similar value. This is useful in the DeFi ecosystem as there are plenty of wrapped and synthetic tokens that aim to mimic the price of the underlying asset. Curve Finance currently supports USD stablecoins, EUR stablecoins, wrapped/synthetic BTC, and wrapped/synthetic ETH assets.

---

[7] "Placeholder VC: Stop Burning Tokens – Buyback And Make Instead." 17 Sep. 2020, https://www.placeholder.vc/blog/2020/9/17/stop-burning-tokens-buyback-and-make-instead. Accessed 11 May. 2021.

For example, one of the biggest liquidity pools is 3CRV, a stablecoin pool consisting of DAI, USDT, and USDC. The ratio of the three stablecoins in the pool is based on the supply and demand of the market. Depositing a coin with a lesser ratio will yield the user a higher percentage of the pool. When the ratio is heavily tilted to one of the coins, it may serve as a good chance to arbitrage.

Curve Finance also supports yield-bearing tokens on Compound, Aave, and Yearn Finance. Curve collaborated with Yearn Finance to release the yUSD pool that consists of yield-bearing token yDAI, yUSDT, yUSDC, and yTUSD. Users who participated in this pool will have yield from the underlying yield-bearing tokens, swap fees generated by the Curve pool, and CRV liquidity mining rewards offered by Curve Finance. Liquidity providers of this pool are able to earn from three sources of yield.

To promote the liquidity of more long-tail tokens, Curve introduced the concept of base pools and metapools. A metapool is a single token pool with another base pool that allows users to trade the single token seamlessly. Currently, the most liquid base pool is the 3CRV pool.

For example, there is a metapool with UST (a USD stablecoin issued on the Terra blockchain) with the 3CRV base pool. Users can trade UST and the three USD stablecoins in the 3CRV pool. By separating the base pool and metapool, Curve is able to separate UST's systemic risks from 3CRV's liquidity pool.

The creation of metapools help Curve in the following ways:

- Prevents dilution of existing pools
- Allows Curve to list illiquid assets
- Higher volume and trading fees for CRV token holders

Bancor

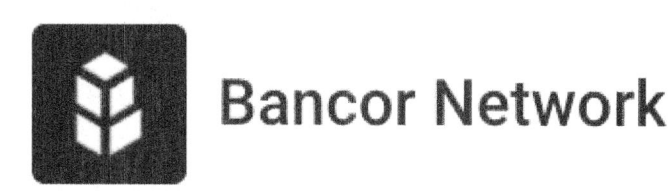

Bancor Network

Launched in 2017, Bancor was one of the first AMM-based DEX. Bancor utilizes a modified Constant Product Market Maker curve, similar to Uniswap. Bancor's approach to this model differs from the arbitrary two-asset curve formula used by Uniswap.

Instead of pairing a base token to any target ERC-20 token like Uniswap, Bancor uses its native token, Bancor Network Token (BNT), as the intermediate currency. There are separate pools for each token traded against BNT.

Bancor version 2 introduces several innovations such as single-sided staking and impermanent loss insurance.

Most AMMs require LPs to provide an equal ratio of each asset represented in the pool. This brings inconvenience to LPs who may only want exposure to a single asset. Bancor version 2 allows LPs to contribute a single asset and maintain 100% exposure on it. LPs can stay long on a single asset with single-sided liquidity while earning swap fees and liquidity mining rewards.

Impermanent loss is a risk that concerns most LPs on AMMs. Bancor incentivizes liquidity by offering compensation for any impermanent loss to LPs. Currently, the payout increases by 1% each day and reaches 100% after 100 days. This impermanent loss coverage encourages LPs to stay in the liquidity pool for at least 100 days. There is a 30-days cliff before impermanent loss protection kicks in.

Bancor also introduced vBNT and Vortex to improve the use cases of BNT tokens. Users receive vBNT when staking BNT in a whitelisted Bancor pool. The exchange rate of BNT to vBNT is 1:1. vBNT can be used for several functions:

- Vote in Bancor governance
- Stake in vBNT/BNT pool for swap fees
- Borrow other tokens on Bancor by using vBNT as collateral (Vortex)

Vortex allows BNT holders to borrow against their staked BNT. The proceeds can be used for leverage or any other purpose, increasing the capital efficiency of holding BNT.

What are the differentiators between the AMMs?

Now that you are familiar with the various AMMs in the market, let's look at three features that make each of them distinct. For simplicity's sake, we will focus on Uniswap v2, Curve, Balancer, and Bancor.

I. Pool Fees

To incentivize users to add liquidity, DEXs allow LPs to earn trading fees on their platform. The fees help LPs with price fluctuations and impermanent loss risks.

Below is a summary of pool fees for the four DEXs in April 2021:

	Uniswap	Curve	Balancer	Bancor
Type of fees	Fixed	Fixed	Variable	Variable
Pool Fees	0.30%	0.04%	Between 0.0001% and 10%	Up to 5.00%*
Protocols	0.00%	0.02%	Depending on each pool and it can be zero.	0.00%**
Liquidity providers	0.30%	0.02%	Between 0.0001% and 10%	Up to 5.00%*

Source: Uniswap, Curve, Balancer, and Bancor.

* The trading fee is controlled by the pool creator. The highest fee as of 26th April 2021 was 5%

** The accrued trading fee that goes to the protocol is used as impermanent loss insurance and not as revenue. It will be burnt once withdrawn from the pool.

Uniswap and Curve implemented a fixed trading fee for every swap made on their platforms. The main difference lies with the split -

Uniswap provides the entire trading fee to LPs while Curve splits the trading fee equally between the protocol and LPs.

For Balancer and Bancor, the trading fees are variable and controlled by the pool's creator.

II. Liquidity Mining

We have touched on this concept in Chapter 2. Briefly, liquidity mining refers to the process of providing liquidity to a protocol, and in return rewarded for the protocol's native tokens.

It is one of the most popular ways to bootstrap liquidity on a DEX and compensate liquidity providers for undertaking the impermanent loss risk.

Each of the four DEXs has its own native token:

Protocol	Coin name	Ticker
	Uniswap	UNI
	Curve Dao Token	CRV
	Balancer	BAL
	Bancor Network Token	BNT

As of 1st April 2021, Uniswap is the only DEX without an active liquidity mining program out of the four DEXs.

III. Pool Weightage

Most AMMs such as Uniswap and Bancor have a standard 50/50 pool weightage whereby liquidity providers must supply an equal value of the two tokens. However, Balancer has a variable pool supply criteria and Curve has a dynamic pool supply criteria.

On Balancer, users can set variable weights for each pool. Pools are constantly rebalanced to ensure they follow the variable weights set. For example, an 80/20 BAL/WETH pool on Balancer means that you will have to split your capital to 80% BAL tokens and 20% WETH tokens when supplying liquidity to the pool.

Pool address	Assets
0x1eff...a3d5	50% WETH • 50% WBTC
0x59a1...6fb4	• 80% BAL 20% WETH
0x5b2d...8801	• 86% wPE • 2% GIFT • 2% IMPACT • 2% YFU • 2% PIXEL • 2% NFTS • 2% LIFT • 2% STR

Source: https://pools.balancer.exchange/#/

On Curve, the pool weightage is dynamic and will change according to the reserve size. Unlike the other AMMs, Curve does not rebalance its pools or try to keep them in a balanced ratio.

Let's look at an example of the 3CRV pool consisting of DAI, USDC, and USDT. Ideally, this pool is equally weighted between the three stablecoins. However, the snapshot below had USDC with the highest weightage (41.98%) and DAI with the lowest weightage (24.80%). If you are interested in providing liquidity to this pool, you do not need all three tokens but simply contribute any of the three tokens to the pool. By doing so, you will alter the pool supply weight dynamically.

Decentralized Exchanges

```
Currency reserves

DAI:  357,291,966.27 (24.80%)
USDC: 604,680,912.75 (41.98%)
USDT: 478,432,441.58 (33.22%)
DAI+USDC+USDT: 1,440,405,320.61

Fee: 0.040%
Admin fee: 50.000% of 0.040%

Virtual price: 1.0161 [?]
A: 600
Ramping up A: [?] 200 -> 600
Ramp up A ends on: 25/02/2021 20:43:02

Liquidity utilization: 4.64% [?]
Daily USD volume: $66,842,947.61
```

Source: https://curve.fi/3poo as of 30th April 2021

Associated Risks of using AMMs

Using an AMM-based exchange does not come without risks. Below we outline three risks both from a Trader and Liquidity Provider perspectives.

I. Price Slippage

Based on the AMM formulas, the quoted price is dependent on the ratio of the token reserves.

In the Constant Product Market Maker formula ($x * y = k$), the larger the order, the larger the price slippage that a user will incur. This is subjected to the size of the liquidity pools - pools with lower liquidity will suffer higher price slippages on large orders.

Assuming current ETH/DAI price is $2,000 and the initial liquidity pair has 62,500,000 DAI and 25,000 ETH. This will give you a constant product of 1.56 billion. The table below illustrates the price slippage or premium that you will have to pay as your transaction sizes become bigger.

ETH Purchased	Cost per ETH in DAI	Total Cost in DAI	Premium	New DAI Reserve	New ETH Reserve	Product (k)
0	2,500			62,500,000	25,000	1,562,500,000,000
1	2,500.10	2,500	0.00%	62,502,500.10	24,999	1,562,500,000,000
10	2,501.00	25,010	0.04%	62,525,010.00	24,990	1,562,500,000,000
100	2,510.04	251,004	0.40%	62,751,004.02	24,900	1,562,500,000,000
1,000	2,604.17	2,604,167	4.17%	65,104,166.67	24,000	1,562,500,000,000
10,000	4,166.67	41,666,667	66.67%	104,166,666.67	15,000	1,562,500,000,000
20,000	12,500.00	250,000,000	400.00%	312,500,000.00	5,000	1,562,500,000,000
25,000	Infinity	Infinity	Infinity	Infinity	0	1,562,500,000,000

Here is another example of the price slippage example from Uniswap.

> **Example**
>
> Based on ETH/DAI pool on Uniswap, 1 ETH is now worth ~2,433 DAI
>
> You can set your slippage tolerance by going to the transaction setting. Uniswap sets 0.5% as default:

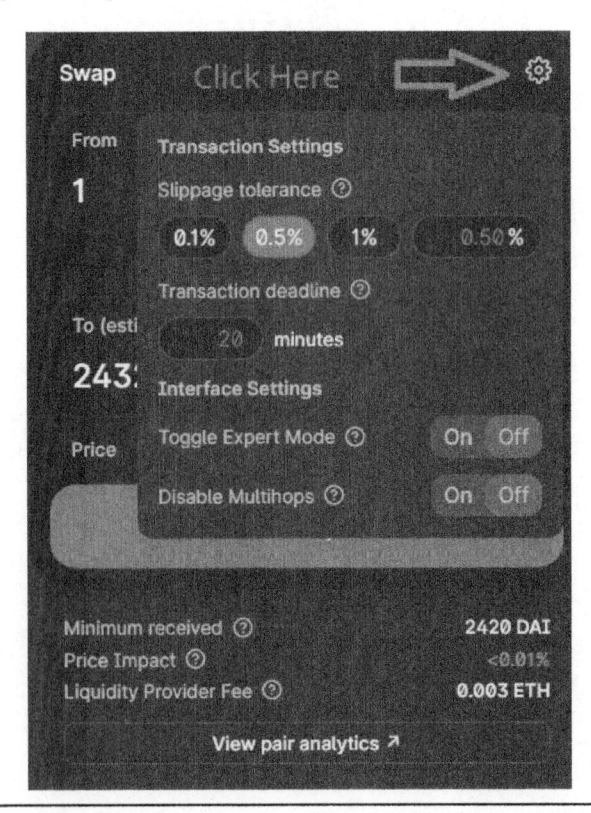

Decentralized Exchanges

> Focusing the indicators on the bottom of the image:
>
> 1. **Minimum Received** is the minimum amount of tokens you will receive based on your slippage tolerance. If your slippage tolerance is 0.5%, then the minimum you will receive is 2,433 DAI * 0.95% = 2,420 DAI
>
> 2. **Price impact** is the premium that you will have to pay, which will be reflected in the displayed price. The larger your order, the larger the price impact will be.

II. Front-running

As orders made on AMMs are broadcasted to the blockchain for all to see, anyone can monitor the blockchain to pick up suitable orders and front-run it by placing higher transaction fees to have their order mined faster than the target's order. The front-runner who makes this risk-free arbitrage has pulled an attack known as a "Sandwich Attack".

Below is an illustration of how this could happen:

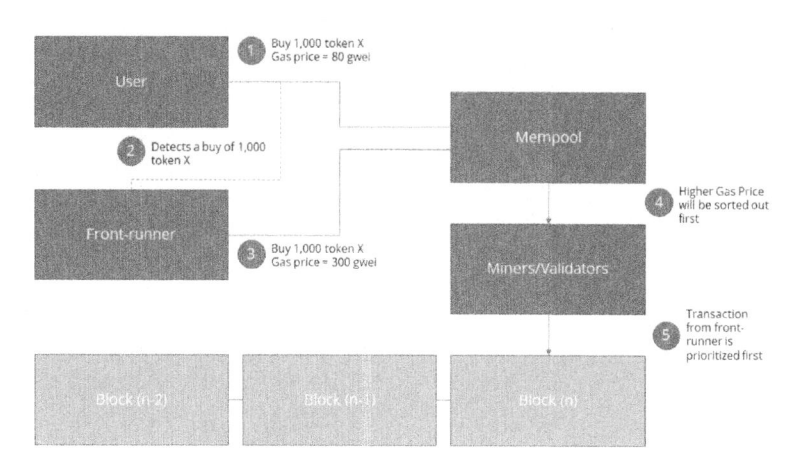

Below is a snapshot of a "Sandwich Attack" happening with Ampleforth's governance token (FORTH) on Uniswap.

How to DeFi: Advanced

FORTH Price = $41.81
Front runner = buy ~ 306 FORTH for ~ 12,796 USDT
Gas price = 126.2 Gwei ($35.45)

FORTH Price = $43.29
Victim buy = buy ~ 231 FORTH for ~10,000 USDT
Gas price = 126.0 Gwei ($31.84)

FORTH Price = $42.77
Front runner = sold ~ 306 FORTH for ~ 13,088 USDT
Gas price = 126.0 Gwei ($25.86)

Front-runner's cost = total gas = $61.31
Profit = $13,088 - $12,796 - $61.31 = $230.69

52

III. Impermanent Loss

Another downside of AMM is the impermanent loss that happens when you provide liquidity to the AMMs. Impermanent loss is similar to measuring your opportunity cost of holding the token within the pools versus holding them in your wallet. Note: the loss is not realized until you remove your tokens from the liquidity pool.

The higher the divergence between the value of holding your tokens in the pool and wallet, the higher is the impermanent loss.

Example

Assuming you created an ETH/DAI pool on Uniswap by providing 10,000 DAI and 5 ETH to the pool.

- Price of 1 ETH = 2,000 DAI
- The pool consists of 5 ETH and 10,000 DAI
- Pool liquidity uses the Constant Product Market Maker formula"
  $(x * y = k) \rightarrow 5 * 10,000 = 50,000$

Say the price of ETH doubles to 4,000 DAI.

- Arbitrageurs will arbitrage the difference in the ETH price quoted in Uniswap until it reaches 1 ETH = 4,000 DAI
- The pool will rebalance the reserve ratio until it matches the pool constant at 50,000
- The new pool ratio would become 3.536 ETH and 14,142 DAI

To calculate your impermanent loss, you can subtract your gains from holding outside the pool and within the pool.

At 1 ETH = 2,000 DAI, your original capital (5 ETH and 10,000 DAI) is valued at 20,000 DAI.

At 1 ETH = 4,000 DAI

- Your holding **within** the pool would be:

> - (3.536 ETH * 4,000 DAI) + 14,142 DAI = 28,286 DAI
> - Return on investment = +41% (ignoring earnings from trading fee)
>
> • Your holding **outside** the pool would be:
>
> - (5 ETH * 4,000 DAI) + 10,000 DAI = 30,000 DAI
> - Return on investment = +50%
>
> • Your impermanent loss is thus:
>
> - 30,000 DAI - 28,284 DAI = 1,716 DAI
>
> This loss is only realized if you withdraw your liquidity from Uniswap.

The graph below shows the opportunity cost you will get if you hold your tokens outside the pool and within the pool.

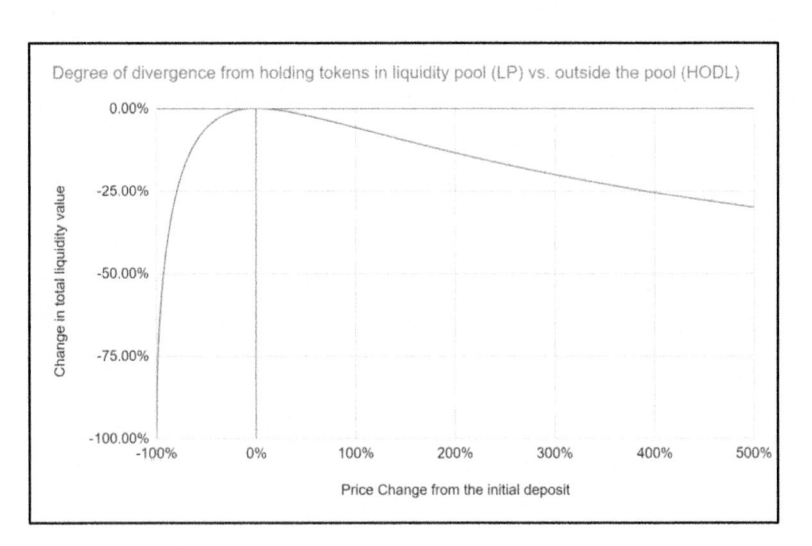

[Graph: Degree of divergence from holding tokens in liquidity pool (LP) vs. outside the pool (HODL). X-axis: Price Change from the initial deposit (-100% to 500%). Y-axis: Change in total liquidity value (0.00% to -100.00%).]

- 1.25x price change = 0.6% loss relative to HODL
- 1.50x price change = 2.0% loss relative to HODL
- 1.75x price change = 3.8% loss relative to HODL
- 2x price change = 5.7% loss relative to HODL

- 3x price change = 13.4% loss relative to HODL
- 4x price change = 20.0% loss relative to HODL
- 5x price change = 25.5% loss relative to HODL

Thus, trading pairs that trade within a small price range (e.g. stablecoins) are less exposed to impermanent loss.

Notable Mentions

- **PancakeSwap**

  PancakeSwap is a fork of Uniswap, but it is built on top of the Binance Smart Chain blockchain. It is the biggest AMM on Binace Smart Chain, and its volume is even higher than Uniswap as of April 2021.

- **TerraSwap**

  TerraSwap exists on Terra Chain, and it is the only DEX protocol on the Terra blockchain. You can choose your trading fees to be denominated in any Terra Chain assets.

- **0x Protocol**

  0x is a DEX infrastructure layer with two main offerings: a DEX aggregation API that allows projects to launch whitelabel DEX and a consumer-facing DEX aggregator called Matcha. Projects such as Tokenlon, Metamask, Zapper, and Zerion have integrated 0x to launch their exchange services.

Conclusion

DEXs play a vital role in powering the DeFi space as it depicts the current market behavior, especially the price and liquidity of cryptocurrencies. It determines the value of various cryptocurrencies relative to each other and illustrates the dynamic nature of trades and capital flow.

Recommended Readings

1. Understanding AMM Basics
   https://defiweekly.substack.com/p/understanding-amms-the-basics-f30
2. Types of AMMs
   https://blog.chain.link/challenges-in-defi-how-to-bring-more-capital-and-less-risk-to-automated-market-maker-dexs/
3. Understanding Price Impact on AMM
   https://research.paradigm.xyz/amm-price-impact
4. Front-running Issue on Ethereum
   https://www.coindesk.com/new-research-sheds-light-front-running-bots-ethereum-dark-forest
5. Uniswap V3
   https://uniswap.org/blog/uniswap-v3/

CHAPTER 4: DEX AGGREGATORS

Liquidity is essential to ensure trades can be executed without severely affecting the market price. The DEX market is extremely competitive, with multiple DEXs competing for users and liquidity. Liquidity is thus often disparate and leads to inefficient capital management.

While the impact on smaller transactions may be inconsequential, larger DEX transactions will be prone to higher price slippage. This is where DEX aggregators help traders with the best price execution across the various DEXs.

DEX aggregators look for the most cost-effective transactional routes by pooling liquidity from different DEXs. By routing a single transaction across multiple liquidity pools, traders making large trades can take advantage of gas savings and minimize the cost of price impacts due to low liquidity.

We covered DEX aggregators briefly in our *How to DeFi: Beginner* book using 1inch as an example. In the next section we will cover newer DEX aggregators such as Matcha and Paraswap, and offer some comparisons between each protocol.

DEX Aggregator Protocols

1inch Network

1inch Network is a DEX aggregator solution that searches for cheaper rates across multiple liquidity sources. The initial protocol incorporates the Pathfinder algorithm which looks for optimal paths among different markets. Since its inception on the Ethereum network, 1inch has expanded to support the Binance Smart Chain and Polygon networks. The 1inch Aggregation Protocol has also undergone two significant updates, and has been on version 3 since March 2021.[8]

As of 31 May 2021, there are 50+ liquidity sources on Ethereum, 20+ liquidity sources on Binance Smart Chain, and 10+ liquidity sources on Polygon. Notably, in just two years, the 1inch DEX aggregator has surpassed $40B in overall volume on the Ethereum network alone.

Unlike other DEX aggregators, 1inch has two native tokens. One is a gas token (CHI), and the other is a governance token (1INCH).

CHI is a gas token that takes advantage of the Ethereum storage refund. Gas tokens help smart contracts erase unnecessary storage during the transaction process and reduce gas fees. You can think of CHI as a discount coupon that can be redeemed for cheaper transactions, allowing users to save up to 42% of their gas fees.

---

[8] 1inch Network, (2021, March 16). *Introducing the 1inch Aggregation Protocol v3*. Medium. https://blog.1inch.io/introducing-the-1inch-aggregation-protocol-v3-b02890986547.

The 1INCH token, released in December 2020, propelled the protocol into becoming a more decentralized entity. Holders of 1INCH allow the community to vote for specific protocol settings under the Decentralized Autonomous Organization (DAO) model. The governance model enables stakers to control two main aspects:[9]

1) **Pool governance** - governs specific parameters for each pool, such as the swap fee, the price impact fee, and the decay period.

2) **Factory governance** - governs general parameters for all pools, such as the default swap fee, the default price impact fee, the default decay period, the referral reward, and the governance reward.

Also, through staking of the 1INCH token, users earn the Spread Surplus (positive slippage), which is the net positive difference between swap transactions when the executed price is slightly better than the price quoted. Notably, the 1inch Network also has many partnerships with other protocols where liquidity mining incentives are commonplace for 1INCH trading pairs.

Other notable features include limit orders and the option to select Pathfinder's routing process and choose between receiving maximum returns or minimizing gas costs.

The 1inch Network also incorporates its own Liquidity Protocol. The automated market maker protects users from front-running attacks and offers more opportunities for liquidity providers.

---

[9] 1inch Network. (2020, December 25). *1INCH token is released*. Medium. https://medium.com/1inch-network/1inch-token-is-released-e69ad69cf3ee.

Matcha

Matcha is a decentralized exchange (DEX) aggregator built by 0x Labs. Matcha is powered by 0x protocol, a protocol with various products, including a peer-to-peer network for sharing orders (0x Native Liquidity) and their proprietary API.[10] Matcha pulls data from the 0x API and efficiently routes orders across all the available liquidity sources (20+ as of 31 May 2021).

Unlike other DEX aggregators, Matcha utilizes a combination of on-chain and off-chain components throughout the trading experience. Quotes are generated off-chain via the 0x API to minimize gas costs before being utilized on-chain to execute orders.[11] The 0x API finds the most cost-effective trading path (including gas costs) and can even split individual orders across multiple liquidity sources automatically if it's better for the trader to do so.

To date, there have been four major updates to 0x's API (which powers Matcha), with the latest being 0x version 4 released in March 2021. Through this version 4 update, Matcha users should expect more gas-efficient orders (up to 70% gas saved for quote orders and 10% for limit orders) and better overall prices.[12]

Since 0x version 3, Matcha users are charged a small protocol fee (paid in ETH) on 0x open order book liquidity. The fee is proportional to the gas cost of filling orders and scales linearly with gas price. What is important to note here is that Matcha technically does not charge transactions other than

---

[10] Kalani, C. (2020, June 30). *Say hello to Matcha!* Matcha. https://matcha.xyz/blog/say-hello-to-matcha.

[11] Brent. (n.d.). *Does Matcha have a trading API?* Matcha. http://help.matcha.xyz/en/articles/3956594-does-matcha-have-a-trading-api.

[12] Gonella, T. (2021, January 27). *Say hello to 0x v4.* Medium. https://blog.0xproject.com/say-hello-to-0x-v4-ce87ca38e3ac.

the requisite network fees required by either the native chain or liquidity source.

Unlike 1inch, Matcha shares all positive slippage back to the user. Other notable features include limit orders and Matcha's recent support of the Binance Smart Chain network and Polygon network.

Paraswap

ParaSwap was first developed in September 2019 and uses its own routing algorithm, Hopper. ParaSwap examines the rate for the given pair on all supported exchanges and displays the effective rate (accounting for slippage) for each pair.

ParaSwap implements several solutions to reduce gas usage across the platform, such as implementing the REDUX gas token.[13] Gas costs are taken into account when analyzing swapping paths.

ParaSwap's most recent update, version 3, was introduced in January 2021. It included a significant UI upgrade and improved swapping contracts.[14] Emphasis was placed on reducing overall gas costs by 30%, especially for trades settled using only one DEX.

Protocol revenue is generated through two main avenues.[15] The first is through third-party integrators, where if they charge a fee on facilitated swaps, ParaSwap takes a 15% portion of the fee. The second is through

---

[13] Paraswap. (2021, April 11). *What is REDUX gas token?* Medium. https://paraswap.medium.com/what-is-redux-gas-token-cc20cc55fbd7.
[14] Paraswap. (2021, January 28). *Introducing ParaSwap's new UI & a significant upgrade for our contracts*. Medium. https://medium.com/paraswap/introducing-paraswaps-new-ui-a-significant-upgrade-for-our-contracts-ed15d632e1d0.
[15] *Fee Structure*. Learn2Swap. (n.d.). https://doc.paraswap.network/understanding-paraswap/fees.

positive slippage, where 50% is directed to the protocol and the other 50% is shared back with the user.

ParaSwap currently has 48 sources of liquidity. This is supplemented by native pools (ParaSwapPools), which are supplied by private market makers. ParaSwap also recently integrated with the Binance Smart Chain network and Polygon network.

DEX Aggregator's Performance Factors

There are many intricacies involved under the hood of DEX aggregators, making it difficult to compare them fairly. While users might focus on the quoted price, they are not necessarily reliable. Here's why:

> **Example**
>
> Let's say a user wants to swap 1,000 USDC for 1,000 USDT.
>
> Aggregator X quotes 1,000 USDT and has an estimated transaction cost of 5 USDT, giving a realized exchange rate of 1 USDC = 0.995 USDT. After swapping 1,000 USDC, the user will receive 995 USDT.
>
> Aggregator Y quotes 1,005 USDT and has an estimated transaction cost of 15 USDT, giving a realized exchange rate of 1 USDC = 0.990 USDT. After swapping 1,000 USDC, the user will receive 990 USDT.
>
> In this example, Aggregator X is more cost-efficient after taking into consideration the transaction fee. You have to remember that this example uses estimated figures that the DEX aggregator provides before swapping.

In reality, when a person performs a swap, the time difference between approving the exchange and the successful execution of the swap on-chain will affect the final price. During that period, external market forces such as network congestion and the size of selected liquidity pools may change. The protocol's routing algorithm will also affect the outcome as more efficient transactions reduce network usage and minimizes failed transactions.

Another point is the size of the transaction. The cost savings incurred from DEX aggregators are proportionally higher for larger transactions because they are more prone to higher price slippage. Smaller transactions may not need to rely on different liquidity pools because a single liquidity pool is the most optimal route.

If we categorize all these metrics, we get four primary factors that determine a DEX aggregator's performance:

1. Routing Algorithm
2. Sources of Liquidity
3. Current Market State
4. Size of Transaction

Which DEX Aggregator offers the most value?

DEX aggregators have become an essential part of the DEX economy. While it is difficult to ascertain which DEX aggregator offers the most value, the following table does offer some clarity:

As of 31 May 2021	1inch	Matcha	ParaSwap
Sources of Liquidity	80+	20+	48
Token	1INCH + CHI	None	None
Routing Algorithm	Pathfinder	0x API	Hopper
Limit Orders	Yes	Yes	No
Staking Features	Yes	No	No

As of 31 May 2021	1inch	Matcha	ParaSwap
Protocol Fees	Variable. At time of writing is 0.25% fixed fee on all trades.	70,000 gwei * Gas price of the transaction (where applicable)	None for users but third-party integrators are charged a 15% fee on facilitated swaps
Blockchains Supported	Ethereum and Binance Smart Chain, and Polygon	Ethereum, Binance Smart Chain, and Polygon	Ethereum, Binance Smart Chain, and Polygon
Transfer of Positive Slippage to User	Variable - At time of writing (May 2021), about 20% of positive slippage is given to referrers and 80% for 1INCH stakers.	100%	50%

1inch has a lot of first-mover advantages. As of 31 May 2021, the protocol has the most sources of liquidity, with over 80+ sources. 1inch is also the only DEX aggregator with its own native tokens, giving it a distinct advantage over other protocols and allowing users to stake 1INCH tokens and earn protocol fees. 1inch is also more decentralized than other protocols which lack a DAO. All these advantageous are reflected in trading volume, the most basic metric:

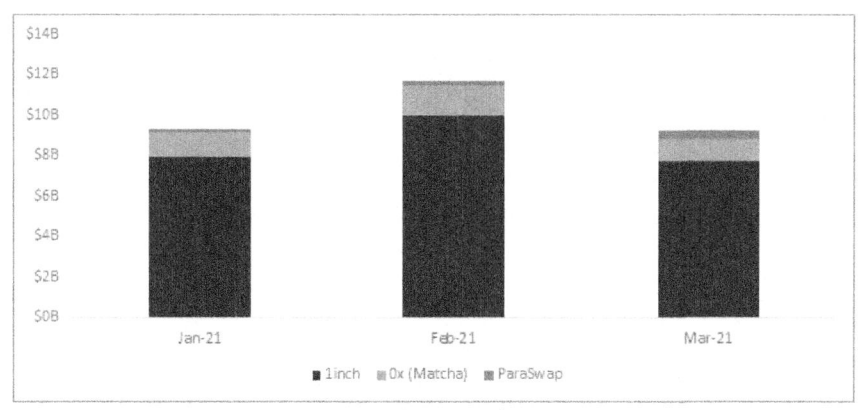

Source: Dune Analytics

The total trading volume for Q1 2021 is dominated by 1inch. In March 2021, 1inch had 84.2% of the total market share and $7.76 billion worth of trading volume. Of course, this could also be caused by a variety of reasons, including user loyalty and information asymmetry. However, when taken a whole, high-user retention rates suggest that the market recognizes 1inch's benefits.

Associated Risks

It is good practice to not treat quoted prices on DEX aggregators as gospel. While DEX aggregators aim to ensure that the executed transaction conforms to the quoted price, this does not always occur.

Another point is the size of the transaction. Although DEX aggregators offer better cost savings for larger transactions, it may sometimes be better for smaller traders to interact directly with a DEX.

DEX aggregators are usually reliable, but there have been instances where transactions are routed through small and illiquid pools. As a user, you should always check that your slippage is not too high before approving a transaction.

Notable Mentions

- **DEX.AG (rebranded to Slingshot)**
  DEX.AG is one of the smaller DEX aggregators which uses its own proprietary routing algorithm, X Blaster. The project rebranded itself to Slingshot in November 2020. At the time of writing (1 April 2021), the protocol is integrated with 18 liquidity sources, does not take any trading fees and has yet to release a live version of their update.

- **Totle**
  Totle is another small DEX aggregator which relies on their native API (Totle API). At the time of writing (1 April 2021), there are 15 liquidity sources.

Conclusion

DEXs are the lifeblood of DeFi. However, for many power users (whales especially), DEX aggregators are even more important as DEX aggregators can offer better cost efficiency for large transactions. DEX aggregators have even evolved to a point where they have their own liquidity pools, further blurring the line between DEX aggregators and DEXs.

The DEX sector is a prime example of DeFi composability. DEX aggregators are built on top of DEXs, to serve different user profiles. Thus, we benefit from a more comprehensive suite of innovative products borne out of increased competition and mutualistic integration.

Recommended Readings

1. Overview of DEX Aggregators
   https://www.delphidigital.io/reports/defi-aggregators/
2. Comparing Different DEX Aggregators
   https://medium.com/2key/defi-dexes-dex-aggregators-amms-and-built-in-dex-marketplaces-which-is-which-and-which-is-best-fba04ca48534
3. 0x's October 2020 Study on Dex Aggregators
   https://blog.0xproject.com/a-comprehensive-analysis-on-dex-liquidity-aggregators-performance-dfb9654b0723
4. 1inch's v3 Upgrade and Comparison with Other Dex Aggregators
   https://blog.1inch.io/introducing-the-1inch-aggregation-protocol-v3-b02890986547

CHAPTER 5: DECENTRALIZED LENDING & BORROWING

The capital market in the traditional financial system is not accessible by many - only the rich have the VIP card to access it.

Imagine you are a venture capitalist looking to finance your next business venture. You can take a loan and offer your assets as collateral. The collateralized capital will remain untouched and continue to grow over time, and can be redeemed at a later date. Of course, this is not a risk-free strategy. If you are not careful, you may default on your loan payment and lose your collateral.

Lending protocols in DeFi have now democratized access to debt for everyone. Using your cryptocurrencies as collateral, you can borrow from these protocols and leverage upon it. As one of the largest DeFi categories, decentralized lending and borrowing has grown exponentially, with borrowing volume reaching $9.7 billion in April 2021. That is an increase of 102 times compared to the year before!

The leading DeFi lending protocols are Compound, Maker, Aave, and Cream.

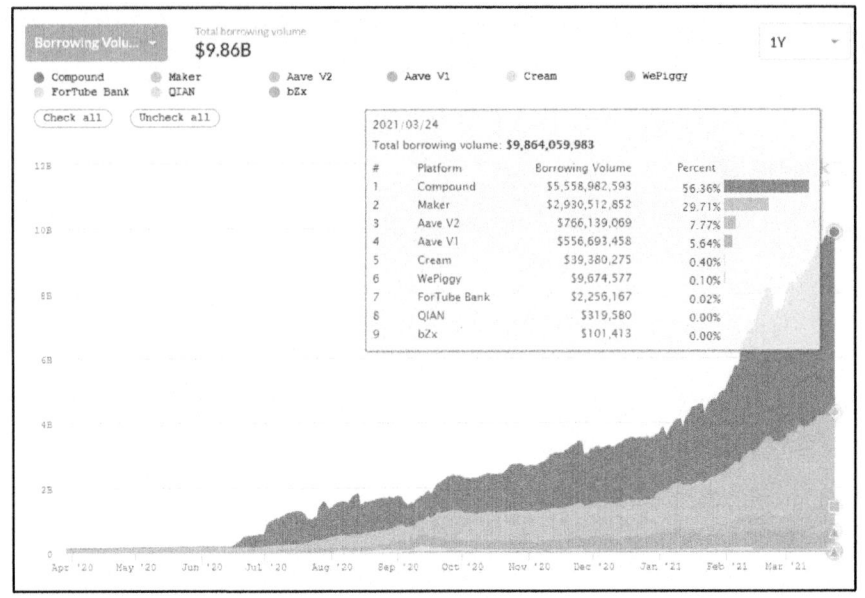

Source: DeBank

Overview of Lending & Borrowing Protocols

Compound

Compound Finance is a money market protocol built by Compound Labs. It is an Ethereum-based, open-source money market protocol where anyone can lend or borrow cryptocurrencies frictionlessly. As of 1 April 2021, there are nine different tokens available on the Compound Platform.

1. 0x (ZRX)
2. Basic Attention Token (BAT)
3. Compound (COMP)
4. Dai (DAI)

5. Ether (ETH)
6. USD Coin (USDC)
7. Tether (USDT)
8. Uniswap (UNI)
9. Wrapped Bitcoin (WBTC)

Compound operates as a liquidity pool built on the Ethereum blockchain. Suppliers supply assets to the liquidity pool to earn interest, while borrowers take a loan from the liquidity pool and pay interest on their debt. In essence, Compound bridges the gaps between lenders who wish to accrue interest from idle funds and borrowers who want to borrow funds for productive or investment use.

In Compound, interest rates are denoted in Annual Percentage Yield (APY), and the interest rates differ between assets. Compound derives the interest rates via algorithms that take into account the supply and demand of the assets.

Essentially, Compound lowers the friction for lending/borrowing by allowing suppliers/borrowers to interact directly with the protocol for interest rates without needing to negotiate loan terms (e.g., maturity, interest rate, counterparty, collaterals), thereby creating a more efficient money market.

Compound is the largest DeFi lending platform by borrowing volume, with a 56% market share (Debank, 1 April 2021). In June 2020, Compound introduced its governance token, Compound (COMP).

Maker

Maker is the oldest DeFi borrowing protocol. It enables over-collateralized loans by locking more than 30 tokens supported in a smart contract to mint DAI, a decentralized stablecoin pegged to the USD.[16] Besides being a borrowing protocol, Maker also acts as a stablecoin issuer (DAI).

On 19 December 2017, Maker originally started with the Single Collateral DAI (SAI). It was minted using Ether (ETH) as the sole collateral. On 18 November 2019, Maker upgraded SAI to Multi-Collateral DAI (DAI), which can be minted with 29 different tokens as collateral.

Maker now even accepts USDC, a centralized stablecoin to help manage DAI price instability. Maker has made huge progress in bridging the gap with traditional finance by onboarding the first real-world asset as collateral through Centrifuge. On 21 April 2021, the company successfully executed its first MakerDAO loan for $181k with a house as collateral, effectively creating one of the first blockchain-based mortgages.

Unlike other lending protocols, users cannot lend assets to Maker. They can only borrow DAI by depositing collateral. DAI is the biggest decentralized stablecoin and has seen growing adoption in the DeFi ecosystem. We will look deeper into DAI in Chapter 6.

---

[16] (2021, May 10). Introducing The Redesigned Oasis Borrow - Oasis Blog - Oasis.app. Retrieved May 27, 2021, from https://blog.oasis.app/introducing-the-redesigned-oasis-borrow/

Aave

Aave is another prominent decentralized money market protocol similar to Compound. As of April 2021, users can lend and borrow 24 different assets on Aave, significantly more compared to Compound.

Both Compound and Aave operate similarly where lenders can provide liquidity by depositing cryptocurrencies into the available lending pools and earn interest. Borrowers can take loans by tapping into these liquidity pools and pay interest.

Aave distinguished itself from Compound by pioneering new lending primitives like rate switching, collateral swap, and flash loans.

Rate switching: Borrowers on Aave can switch between variable and stable interest rates.

Collateral Swap: Borrowers can swap their collateral for another asset. This helps to prevent loans from going below the minimum collateral ratio and face liquidation.

Flash loans: Borrowers can take up loans with zero collateral if the borrower repays the loan and any additional interest and fees within the same transaction. Flash loans are useful for arbitrage traders as they are capital-efficient in making arbitrage trades across the various DeFi Dapps.

Cream Finance

Cream Finance (C.R.E.A.M) was founded in July 2020 by Jeffrey Huang and Leo Cheng. Cream is a Compound fork that also services long-tail, exotic DeFi assets. Cream partnered (merged) into the Yearn Finance ecosystem in November 2020.[17] It is deployed across Ethereum, Binance Smart Chain, and Fantom.

Cream has a more lenient asset onboarding strategy as compared to Compound and Aave. Employing the fast-mover strategy, it has listed more assets than any other lending protocol at a faster speed. It has chosen to focus on long-tail assets - assets with lower liquidity or belong in niche categories. It was one of the first lending protocols to accept yield-bearing tokens and LP tokens as collateral.

Cream has also launched the Iron Bank, an uncollateralized lending service offered to whitelisted partners. As one of its partners, Yearn Finance can utilize the borrowed funds from Cream to further increase the yield obtained from its yield farming activities.

In anticipation of the upcoming launch of ETH 2.0, Cream also offers ETH 2.0 staking service where users can stake ETH for CRETH2, which can be supplied and borrowed against as collateral. All the ETH 2.0 staking work will be done by Cream, and the yield is shared with CRETH2 holders. Essentially, CRETH2 is a custodial staking service, with a fee of 8% on the validator reward. In addition to ETH 2.0, Cream also offers staking services for Binance Smart Chain and Fantom.

---

[17] (2020, November 25). Yearn & Cream v2 merger. Yearn and Cream developers ... - Medium. Retrieved May 28, 2021, from https://medium.com/iearn/yearn-cream-v2-merger-e9fa6c6989b4

Cream positions itself as a more risky lender against Compound and Aave, facilitating and enabling the market demand for leveraging and shorting niche assets.

Protocols Deep Dive

(US$ in millions) As of 24th March 2021	Compound	Maker	Aave	Cream
Number of Assets Supported				
Collateral Type	8	29	21	47
Borrowing Type	9	1	25	65
Borrowing Volume	$ 5,559	$ 2,931	$ 1,324	$ 39
Total Value Locked (TVL)	$ 6,910	$ 6,090	$ 5,010	$ 202
Utilization Ratio (Borrowing Vol/TVL)	0.80	0.48	0.26	0.19

Source: Compound, Maker, Aave, Cream, DeBank, Token Terminal

The table above gives information about the 4 largest lending protocols: Compound, Maker, Aave, and Cream.

We will go through each metric in sequence to assess the protocol's capital efficiency in terms of borrowing volume and total value locked (TVL). Subsequently, we will look at the associated risks for each of them.

Assets Supported

To ensure trustless loans can happen, borrowers will need to deposit assets (collateral) with greater value than the amount borrowed. This is known as over-collateralization and underpins the solvency of DeFi lending protocols. How much borrowers can borrow depends on the collateral ratio of each asset on the various DeFi lending protocols.

Amongst the DeFi lending protocols, Cream has the most supported assets - 45 assets can be used as collateral, and 65 assets available for borrowing.

In contrast, Compound has the least number of supported assets - only eight assets can be used as collateral and nine assets available for borrowing. Compound is more conservative with its asset onboarding strategy.

Revenue

One of the vital metrics for lending platforms is their borrowing volume. This metric is important because borrowers pay fees for their loans and thereby produce revenue for these protocols. Here is the breakdown of how each protocol earns revenues:

- **Compound**: A portion of the interest paid by the borrower will go to its reserve, which acts as insurance and is controlled by COMP token holders. Each supported asset has a reserve factor that will determine how much goes into the reserve.[18] You can check each of the reserve factors by clicking on the respective asset pages.

- **Maker**: When borrowers repay their loans, they will pay the principal along with the interest fee that is determined by the stability fee. Each supported collateral has its stability fee.[19]

- **Aave**: The platform has 2 types of fees:[20]
    - 0.00001% of the loan amount is collected on loan origination in Aave V1.
    - 0.09% is collected from the flash loan amount—more about flash loans in Chapter 14.

- **Cream:** A portion of the interest paid from the borrowers to suppliers goes to Cream's Reserve Protocol and is distributed to CREAM token holders as rewards.[21]

As of April 2021, Compound generates the highest revenue among the lending protocols. See below:

---

[18] (2018, December 5). Compound FAQ - Medium. Retrieved March 25, 2021, from https://medium.com/compound-finance/faq-1a2636713b69
[19] (n.d.). Oasis Borrow - Oasis.app. Retrieved May 22, 2021, from https://oasis.app/borrow/markets
[20] (n.d.). Introduction to Aave - FAQ - Aave Document Portal. Retrieved March 25, 2021, from https://docs.aave.com/faq/
[21] (2020, September 3). CREAM Reserve Protocol. The Reserve Protocol is the fee ... - Medium. Retrieved March 25, 2021, from https://medium.com/cream-finance/c-r-e-a-m-reserve-protocol-99f811e693e4

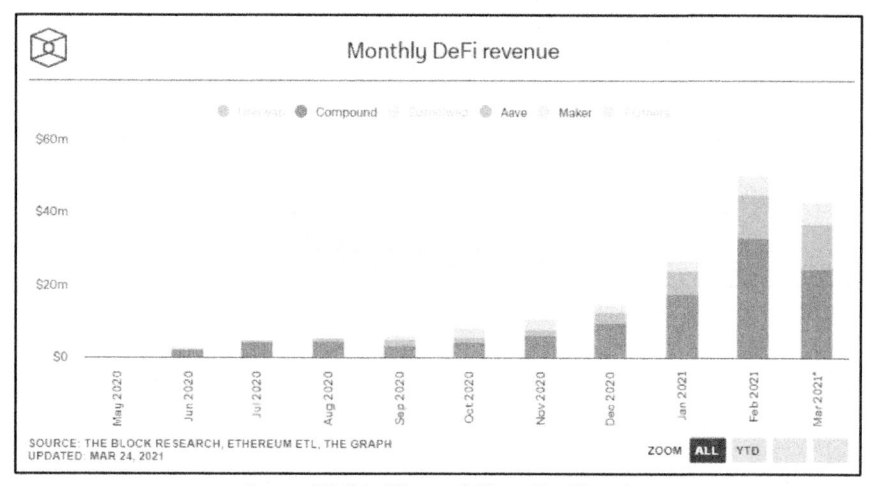

Source: TheBlockResearch Data Dashboard

Total Value Locked (TVL)

While all of the lending protocols have seen their TVL grow since October 2020, it is worth noting that the TVL for both Aave and Maker are more organic than Compound. This is because Compound has ongoing incentives for borrowers and lenders in their liquidity mining program.

Note: Aave recently launched a liquidity mining program at the end of April 2021.

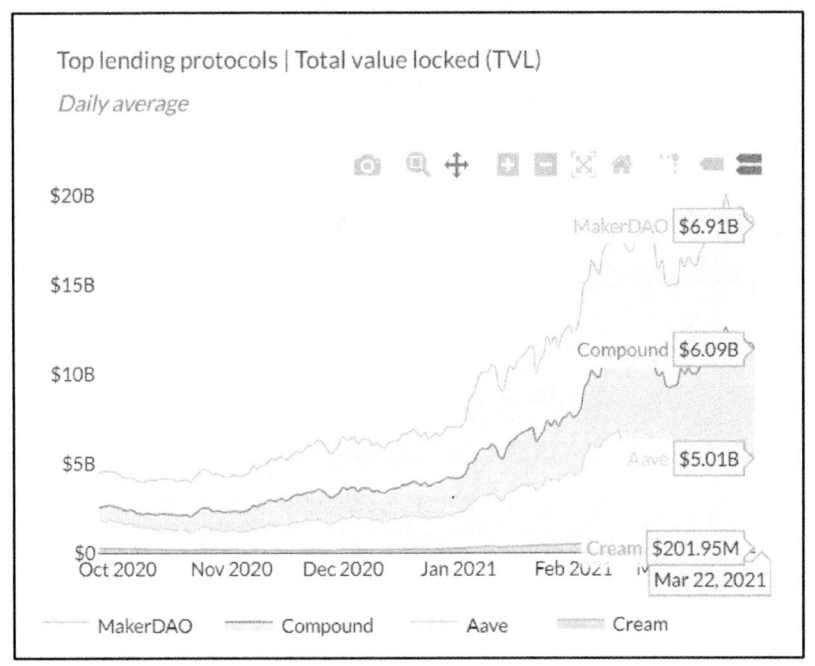

[Figure: Top lending protocols | Total value locked (TVL), Daily average — MakerDAO $6.91B, Compound $6.09B, Aave $5.01B, Cream $201.95M as of Mar 22, 2021. Source: TokenTerminal]

Utilization ratio (Borrowing Volume/TVL)

DeFi lending and borrowing protocols derive protocol revenue from their borrowings. Meanwhile, TVL in lending platforms is driven by users depositing their assets to earn a yield or to be used as borrowing collateral.

By dividing the above two figures, we can derive the utilization ratio of each protocol - the higher the utilization ratio, the more efficient the TVL is being put to work.

(US$ in millions) As of 24th March 2021	Compound	Aave	Cream
Number of Assets Supported			
Collateral Type	8	21	47
Borrowing Type	9	25	65
Borrowing Volume	$ 5,559	$ 1,324	$ 39
Total Value Locked (TVL)	$ 6,910	$ 5,010	$ 202
Utilization Ratio (Borrowing Vol/TVL)	0.80	0.26	0.19

*Maker is not included in this table because unlike its peers, the collateral cannot be borrowed.

At a glance, Compound seems like it has the highest utilization ratio at 0.80, and Cream the lowest at 0.19. However, Compound's high utilization rate may be due to its liquidity mining program that rewards borrowers with COMP tokens, while Cream's low ratio may be because it has suffered a couple of exploits in the past.[22,23] Given security concerns, Cream has stepped up their security coverage with a $1.5 million bug bounty with Immunefi, insurance coverage with Armor.fi/Nexus Mutual, and transparency report with Defi Safety.[24]

Lending and Borrowing Rates

Now, let us discuss the two primary users of lending protocols: the lenders and the borrowers.

Lenders

Supply Market (Snapshot on 24th March 2021)

	Compound	Aave	Cream
USDC	5.51%	7.50%	16.13%
ETH	0.16%	0.33%	1.60%
DAI	7.75%	8.71%	13.50%
WBTC	0.45%	0.18%	2.22%
USDT	2.43%	7.13%	26.11%

Source: Compound, Aave, Cream

Based on the table above, Cream provides the highest APY and Compound provides the lowest APY for most assets. As a lender, although it may seem like it is most desirable to earn the highest APY on Cream, the caveat with high APYs often means higher underlying risks of depositing your capital in these lending protocols relative to its peers.

---

[22] (2021, March 15). Another DeFi Hack: PancakeSwap, Cream Finance ... - Crypto News. Retrieved April 28, 2021, from https://cryptonews.com/news/another-defi-hack-PancakeSwap-cream-finance-websites-comprom-9548.htm

[23] (2021, February 13). DeFi Protocols Cream Finance, Alpha Exploited in Flash ... - CoinDesk. Retrieved April 28, 2021, from https://www.coindesk.com/defi-protocols-cream-finance-alpha-lose-37-5m-in-exploit-prime-suspect-idd

[24] (2021, April 20). CREAM Finance Is Working With Immunefi, Armor.fi, and ... - Medium. Retrieved May 28, 2021, from https://medium.com/cream-finance/security-immunefi-armorfi-defisafety-aa6e9e7c50e8

Cream has to offer high APYs to attract capital to its protocol as it has been hacked several times previously. Overall, Compound provides the lowest APY for all supported assets relative to its peers as its brand entity focuses on the platform's security.

Borrowers

Borrow Market (Snapshot on 24th March 2021)

	Compound	Aave (Variable rate)	Aave (Stable rate)	Cream	Maker
USDC	7.25%	8.23%	15.23%	23.20%	-
ETH	2.76%	2.06%	5.57%	8.02%	-
DAI	10.78%	14.71%	22.71%	21.26%	0% - 9% *
WBTC	4.82%	1.61%	5.01%	9.80%	-
USDT	3.67%	6.80%	14.80%	42.04%	-

* The interest depends on the collateral assets deposited on Maker

Source: Compound, Aave, Cream, Maker

As for borrowers, you would generally look at lending platforms that offer the lowest interest rate because that means cheaper borrowing costs. Compound offers the most competitive borrowing rates relative to its peers. However, Compound has a limited list of assets that users can borrow.

As for Aave, it provides two rate options for borrowers: variable rate and stable rate. Users can switch their rates at any point of time, whichever is cheaper.

Cream charges the highest borrowing rates - primarily because it has the most diverse list of assets for users to borrow. The higher borrowing rates on Cream are needed to compensate lenders' high APY requirement for taking the additional risk of supplying their capital.

Interestingly enough, some of Cream's borrowers are institutions using Cream's Iron Bank, such as Alpha Finance and Yearn Finance. Iron Bank provides a novel uncollateralized lending service where other protocols do not have to provide collateral to borrow from Cream.

Now, let's focus specifically on DAI's borrowers. Maker is the sole issuer of DAI, and it provides the cheapest interest rate to any of its lending peers using any of the supported assets. Maker's borrowing volumes are the second-largest behind Compound, and are locked mainly to mint DAI, which as of 1 April 2021 is the fourth-largest stablecoin in the world. This makes Maker an incredibly important player in the DeFi ecosystem.

Associated Risks

When using decentralized lending and borrowing protocols, you have to be aware of technical risks such as smart contract bugs. Hackers may exploit and drain the collateral held on these protocols if the developers are not careful with their code deployment.

Additionally, many lending protocols rely on price oracles (more on this in Chapter 12) to provide on-chain price data. Price oracles may fail or can be exploited. In November 2020, Compound's price oracle was exploited by driving up the price of DAI by 30% on Coinbase Pro, resulting in $89 million worth of loans being liquidated.[25]

However, as borrowers, the main risks involve losing your collateral through mismanagement of your collateral ratio. Cryptocurrency is known for its extreme price volatility, and you are at risk of having your loan go below its minimum collateral ratio and having your collateral liquidated. This is not an ideal outcome as you will take a considerable loss and pay a liquidation fee. It is thus vital to constantly monitor and maintain a healthy collateral ratio for your loans.

---

[25] (2020, November 26). Oracle Exploit Sees $89 Million Liquidated on Compound - Decrypt. Retrieved May 14, 2021, from https://decrypt.co/49657/oracle-exploit-sees-100-million-liquidated-on-compound

Notable Mentions

- **Venus**

  Venus Protocol is a money market and stablecoin protocol that operates on Binance Smart Chain. The protocol, initially incubated by Binance, is a fork of Compound and MarkerDAO. Swipe took over the work of developing the Venus Protocol since acquired by Binance.

- **Anchor**

  Anchor Protocol is a lending protocol operating on the Terra blockchain. The lending mechanics on the platform work similarly to Compound and Aave. Anchor Protocol has a 20% yield target for UST, a USD stablecoin native on the Terra blockchain.

- **Alchemix**

  Alchemix differentiates itself from other lending players by introducing self-payable loans without the risk of getting liquidated. Simply put, your collateral will be used to earn interest, and the interest earned will be used to repay the loan you made on Alchemix.

- **Liquity**

  Liquity is a DeFi borrowing protocol that lets you draw its stablecoin, Liquity USD (LUSD), without an interest fee. You will have to use Ethereum as collateral and maintain a minimum collateral ratio of only 110%. The repayment made will be in LUSD. The loans are secured by a Stability Pool containing LUSD and by fellow borrowers collectively acting as guarantors of last resort.

Conclusion

DeFi lending and borrowing protocols have seen incredible adoption - they have been dominating DeFi TVL ranking charts. However, the majority of DeFi lendings are currently still overcollateralized, signifying poor capital efficiency.

Traditional lenders utilize credit scores derived from personal information such as job, salary, and borrowing history before deciding to grant a loan. In DeFi, it is tough to develop a credit history with pseudonymous identities.

Several protocols aim to make progress on undercollateralized loans such as TrueFi, Cream, and Aave. In these protocols, selected whitelisted entities can obtain a loan without posting any collateral.

Undercollateralized loans will be the next stage of development for DeFi lending and borrowing protocols. Undercollateralized loans will be needed so that DeFi lending and borrowing protocols can be more capital efficient and compete effectively against traditional lenders.

While DeFi lending is currently still mainly constrained within the digital asset universe, with few links to real-life assets, Maker has made huge progress in April 2021 by accepting real-world assets such as real estate as collateral.[26] Thus, one may presume better integration between Traditional Finance and DeFi in the future.

---

[26] "DeFi 2.0 — First Real World Loan is Financed on Maker ... - Medium." 21 Apr. 2021, https://medium.com/centrifuge/defi-2-0-first-real-world-loan-is-financed-on-maker-fbe24675428f. Accessed 10 May. 2021.

Recommended Readings

1. Evaluating DeFi Lending Protocols
   https://messari.io/article/a-closer-look-at-defi-lending-valuations
2. How to Assess the Risk of Lending
   https://newsletter.banklesshq.com/p/how-to-assess-the-risk-of-lending
3. Dashboard on Lending Protocols
   https://terminal.tokenterminal.com/dashboard/Lending

CHAPTER 6: DECENTRALIZED STABLECOINS AND STABLEASSETS

In our *How to DeFi: Beginner* book, we established that stablecoins are an essential part of the crypto ecosystem. As of 1 April 2021, the total market capitalization for stablecoins is $64.5 billion - a whopping 12 times increase since the previous year.

As both institutional and retail investors flock to the crypto markets, the demand for stablecoins will continue to flourish. This is unsurprising as stablecoins are non-volatile assets that enable the global transfer of value.

Our beginner's book covered some of the key differences between a centralized stablecoin, Tether (USDT), and Maker's decentralized stablecoin, Dai (DAI). In this chapter, we will be looking at some of the shortcomings of Tether and Dai, before introducing other forms of decentralized stablecoins.

Centralized Stablecoin

Tether (USDT)

USDT (previously known as RealCoin) is a centralized stablecoin that first began trading on the Bitfinex exchange in 2015. Being the first stablecoin in the market, it has a strong first-mover advantage and has consistently maintained its position as the market leader for stablecoins. As of April 2021, Tether has a market capitalization of $40 billion, representing over 66% of the total stablecoin market share.

Tether maintains its $1 peg through a 1:1 collateral system. By holding cash as reserve collateral, an equal amount of USDT is then issued. In theory, this is a reliable and straightforward method to ensure USDT maintains its peg. After all, it is a reiteration of the Gold Standard, where the US Dollar used to be backed by Gold in the previous century.

However, the problem lies with Tether's non-transparent issuance process. Because of the centralized nature of its issuance, many people in the crypto community are skeptical that Tether has the reserves it claims to have. In March 2019, skeptics were partially vindicated when Tether modified its policy statement to include loans to affiliate companies as part of its collateral reserves.[27]

Over the years, multiple government agencies have opened up investigations into Tether's practices. In February 2021, the New York Attorney General's investigation into Bitfinex and Tether's internal finances concluded with no formal charges. However, the New York Attorney General did impose a

---

[27] Coppola, F. (2019, March 14). *Tether's U.S. Dollar Peg Is No Longer Credible*. Forbes. https://www.forbes.com/sites/francescoppola/2019/03/14/tethers-u-s-dollar-peg-is-no-longer-credible/?sh=43c247aa451b.

collective fine of $18.5 million to settle charges where Bitfinex commingled client and corporate funds.[28]

The Tether saga is a continuing one and unlikely to settle anytime soon. More recent events have lent further credence to its legitimacy, such as Coinbase's listing of Tether. Bitfinex's CTO, Paolo Ardoino has also reiterated that Tether is registered and regulated by FinCEN.[29]

Decentralized Stablecoin

DAI

Maker is one of DeFi's first attempts at a Decentralized "Central Bank". As a lending protocol, DAI is issued as a byproduct of borrowing demand when collateral (usually ETH) is deposited into Maker vaults.

These vaults are overcollateralized (generally 150% and above except stablecoins), which helps guard against black swan events where the value of the collateral assets drops significantly. Maker helps regulate the supply of DAI by controlling interest loan rates to influence buyers' and borrowers' behavior.

---

[28] Browne, R. (2021, February 23). *Cryptocurrency firms Tether and Bitfinex agree to pay $18.5 million fine to end New York probe.* CNBC. https://www.cnbc.com/2021/02/23/tether-bitfinex-reach-settlement-with-new-york-attorney-general.html.

[29] Mike Novogratz Doubts Dogecoin's Future — 'No Institution Is Buying DOGE, & Russian Lawmakers Move to Allow Crypto Payments Under Contracts. (2020, December 31). *Bitfinex CTO: Tether Is Registered and Regulated Under FinCEN- USDT Not Next Target of the US SEC – Altcoins Bitcoin News.* Bitcoin News. https://news.bitcoin.com/bitfinex-cto-tether-is-registered-and-regulated-under-fincen-usdt-not-next-target-of-the-us-sec/.

The problem with this setup is that over-collateralization limits capital efficiency, making it difficult for DAI to scale with demand. The arbitrage mechanics used to reduce the price of DAI require higher capital to redeem more DAI.

For example, ETH Vault-A, which has a collateralization ratio of 150%, would require a borrower to fork up another $1.50 to mint 1 DAI. This has led to scenarios where DAI's price increased above the $1 peg as it could not keep up with demand, such as the notorious Black Thursday run and Compound's liquidity mining launch.[30]

Maker has attempted to address these issues through multiple methods, such as its Peg Stability Module solution. However, it is clear that demand for DAI still scales with demand for leverage, rather than demand for a more decentralized medium of transaction.

How do we resolve the stablecoin issue?

Each stablecoin has its own set of issues and is not strictly limited to Tether or DAI. At the heart of the problem is balancing DeFi's ethos of decentralization against creating a currency that can reliably maintain its peg.

Although centralized stablecoins are effective, relying on them requires trust in an incorruptible central entity and offers exposure to the same systemic risks that plague traditional finance. On the other hand, although DAI may be somewhat decentralized, it is still capital-inefficient and cannot meet current market demand.

Several decentralized stablecoin protocols have since emerged, looking to improve decentralization, price stability, and capital efficiency. We call these protocols algorithmic stablecoins.

---

[30] Avan-Nomayo, O. (2020, May 4). *MakerDAO Takes New Measures to Prevent Another 'Black Swan' Collapse*. Cointelegraph. https://cointelegraph.com/news/makerdao-takes-new-measures-to-prevent-another-black-swan-collapse.

What are Algorithmic Stablecoins and Stableassets?

As its name suggests, algorithmic stablecoins utilize algorithms to control the stablecoin's market structure and the underlying economics. You may think of algorithmic stablecoins as an automated Federal Reserve, where instead of human-made decisions, pre-programmed code executes specific actions to control and influence the price.

While most algorithmic stablecoins are pegged to the US Dollar, some are not, and some even have a floating peg, thereby creating a new type of asset that we would classify as algorithmic stableassets. Unlike algorithmic stablecoins, algorithmic stableassets could be seen as another form of collateral rather than units of accounts.

If we were to categorize the stablecoins or stableassets market in its current state, the following illustration provides a concise overview:

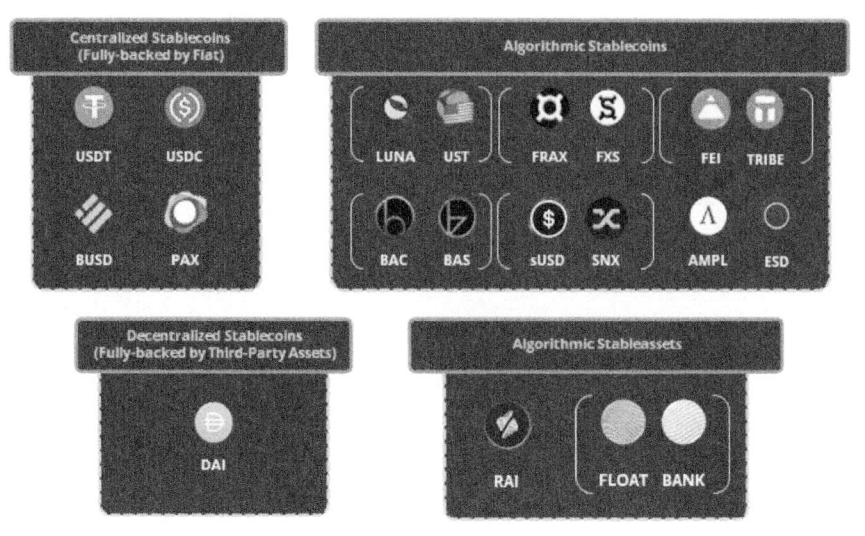

Source: CoinGecko Q1 2021 Report
*List is non-exhaustive

There are two ways of categorizing the various decentralized algorithmic stablecoins:

a) Has no collateral (ESD, AMPL, and BAC)
b) Is partially/fully collateralized by their own native token (FRAX, sUSD, and UST)

For the sake of categorizing stablecoins, we have bucketed UST and sUSD as algorithmic stablecoins because it is backed by its native token, unlike DAI, which is backed by third-party assets such as ETH and USDC. This is a key criterion because reliance on natively issued assets as collateral creates recursive value, requiring algorithmic functions to regulate the price.

Algorithmic stablecoins can be further broken down into different categories - the main sub-categories are rebase and seigniorage models.

Rebase Model

A rebase model controls the price by changing the entire supply of the stablecoin. Depending on whether the price of the stablecoin is above or below the intended peg, the protocol will automatically increase or decrease the supply in every holder's wallet over a fixed period.

The reasoning for this is that by forcefully controlling the supply, the price of the stablecoin can be influenced based on a simple inflationary/deflationary economic theory.

The pioneering protocol for this model is Ampleforth (AMPL), dating as far back as 2019.

Ampleforth

Every 24 hours, the entire circulating supply of Ampleforth (AMPL) is either proportionally increased or decreased to ensure the price remains at $1.[31] If the price of AMPL is trading 5% or more above the target of $1, the rebase will expand supply to wallets holding AMPL. If the price of AMPL is trading 5% or more below the target of $1, the rebase will decrease units in wallets holding AMPL.

Every wallet holder will be affected, but they will retain the same market share as before. The rebases, both positive and negative, are non-dilutive because they affect all AMPL balances pro-rata.

Since rebasing occurs at fixed intervals, users can time their trades to purchase or sell AMPL right before rebasing to increase the value of their holdings.

Seigniorage Model

A seigniorage model controls the price by introducing a reward system that influences market dynamics. If the price is above the peg, new tokens are minted and given to participants who provide liquidity or have tokens staked.

If the price is below the peg, tokens stop being minted, and mechanics are introduced to reduce the supply. Users may purchase coupons that burn the underlying tokens to remove them from the supply. These coupons may be redeemed for more tokens in the future, but only when the price returns or exceeds the intended peg.

---

[31] Ampleforth. (n.d.). https://www.ampleforth.org/basics/.

There are three basic iterations of this model:

Empty Set Dollar

empty set dollar

Empty Set Dollar (ESD) is a single-token seigniorage model. As the term implies, there is only a single token in this model. Users provide liquidity or stake in the Decentralized Autonomous Organization (DAO) through the protocol's native token - the ESD token effectively acts as both a stablecoin and governance token.[32]

At the start of every epoch, the system will measure the Time-Weighted Average Price (TWAP). If the TWAP is above $1, the protocol will enter an inflationary phase and mint tokens as rewards for DAO stakers and liquidity providers. Conversely, if the price falls below $1, the protocol enters a contractionary phase where users will stop receiving any rewards.

During the contractionary phase, users may purchase coupons by burning ESD to earn a premium of up to 45% if the protocol enters an expansion phase again. However, coupons only last for 30 days, meaning coupon buyers risk getting nothing if the system stays in a contractionary phase for over 30 days. Epochs in ESD lasts for 8 hours.

---

[32] *Empty Set Dollar Basics.* Empty Set Dollar Basics – Empty Set Dollar. (n.d.). https://docs.emptyset.finance/faqs/basics.

Basis Cash

ⓑ basis.cash

Basis Cash is a dual-token seigniorage model. As the term implies, there is an additional token known as the share token. Basis Cash's stablecoin is Basis Cash (BAC), while its share token is Basis Share (BAS).[33]

Like ESD, Basis Cash relies on a TWAP mechanism that will mint or stop minting BAC, depending on whether BAC's price is above or below $1. When BAC is above $1, the protocol enters an expansionary phase where users may receive newly minted BAC from the Boardroom DAO by staking BAS.

When BAC is below $1, the protocol enters a contractionary phase where no new BAC will be minted to BAS stakers in the Boardroom. Basis Bonds (similar to ESD coupons) become available for purchase and are priced at $(BAC)^2$. Purchasers of Basis Bonds will get to redeem BAC when the protocol enters an expansion phase again.

Basis Cash epochs last for 24 hours, and unlike ESD coupons, Basis Bonds do not have an expiry date.

---

[33] Dale, B. (2020, November 30). *'Basis Cash' Launch Brings Defunct Stablecoin Into the DeFi Era.* CoinDesk. https://www.coindesk.com/basis-cash-algorithmic-stablecoin-launch-defi-rick-morty.

Frax Finance

Frax ¤ Finance

Frax borrows principles from the seigniorage model to create its own unique model whose stablecoin (FRAX) is backed by two types of collateral - fiat-backed centralized stablecoin (USDC) and its native share token, Frax Share (FXS).[34] Although Frax currently employs fiat stablecoins as collateral, the protocol does intend to eventually fully diversify into decentralized collateral.

Unlike Basis or ESD, Frax takes a fractional collateralization approach. Frax has an adjustable collateral ratio controlled by a Proportional Integral Derivative (PID) controller. The collateral ratio is adjusted according to a growth ratio that measures how much FXS liquidity there is against the overall supply of FRAX.

Frax stablecoins (FRAX) can be minted and redeemed from the protocol for $1 worth of value. This incentivizes arbitrageurs to purchase or mint FRAX, bringing the price back to its peg. On the other hand, FXS accrues fees, seigniorage revenue, and excess collateral value. Notably, Frax launched veFXS which gives a portion of the Algorithmic Market Operations Controller (AMO) profits to FXS stakers, similar to how veCRV receives a portion of transaction fees on Curve Finance.

When FRAX is above $1, the PID lowers the collateral ratio by one step, and when FRAX is below $1, the PID increases the collateral ratio by one step. Both the refresh rate and step parameters can be adjusted through the FXS governance.

As of 8 May 2021, FRAX is 85.25% backed by USDC and 14.75% backed by FXS.

---

[34] Introduction. Frax Finance. (n.d.). https://docs.frax.finance/overview.

How has Algorithmic Stablecoins fared so far?

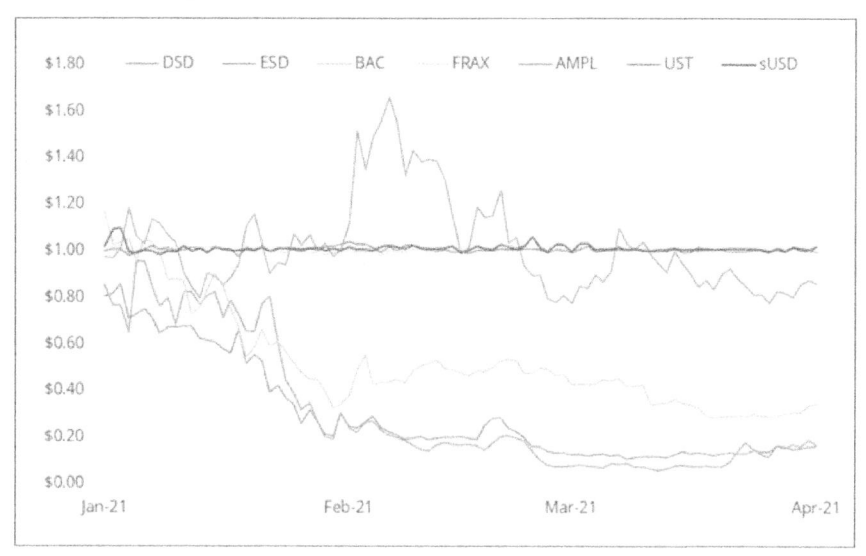

Source: CoinGecko Q1 2021 Report

Throughout the last quarter of 2020, we have seen many algorithmic stablecoins launched in the market. Many of these stablecoins use the seigniorage model.

Despite the crypto community's excitement, most of these protocols have failed. If we look at the historical price of the top-7 algorithmic stablecoins by market capitalization, only UST, sUSD, and FRAX have managed to maintain their peg to the US Dollar.

Although each protocol has its own design mechanics and unique reasons for failure, we are able to make some general observations on the issues with seigniorage-type stablecoins.

Historically, the fiat currency system was easier to implement because nations have centralized powers. For example, monarchies and governments have the monopoly to mint coins and guarantee their value. Contrast this with the stablecoin market where new protocols have to do the same overnight based on an experimental product, in a decentralized environment heavily saturated with competition and established incumbents.

To overcome this, algorithmic stablecoins offered eye-watering incentives in the form of extremely high liquidity mining rewards. The problem with this approach is that it primarily attracted speculators looking to make a quick flip, birthing a new species of yield farmers known as Algo-Farmers.

Algo-Farmers had one objective - look for new algorithmic stablecoin protocols before anyone else, farm the native stablecoin by providing liquidity, and exit the system once other Algo-Farmers start pouring in. Therefore, distribution was centralized within the first group of Algo-Farmers, and dumped onto latecomers. Algorithmic stablecoin launches effectively became a game of musical chairs as profiteers had little incentive to commit and proactively contribute to a single community, quickly moving on to other algorithmic stablecoins clones.

Unsurprisingly, the supply shocks led to massive price swings. Most algorithmic stablecoins were designed with a somewhat cooperative community in mind, but that failed to incentivize users to support the system during contractions or even counteract price manipulations by bigger players.

On top of that, algorithmic stablecoins are mostly traded on Automated Market Makers like Uniswap, which amplified volatility due to its constant product market characteristics. During the deflationary stage, liquidity providers are also disincentivized from supplying liquidity because of impermanent loss risk, leading to further volatility.

Why has FRAX succeeded?

While sUSD, UST, and FRAX have their own reasons for their successes, we will focus on FRAX because it has the best peg retention to date, with an average price of $1.001 throughout Q1 2021. Here are some of the reasons why we think they have been successful so far:

1. Frax is partially collateralized by USDC, which instills community confidence in the system to maintain its peg. As of 8 May 2021, 85.25% of FRAX is backed by USDC.

2. Frax keeps the collateralization ratio flexible, addressing market demands for pricing FRAX at $1.

3. Collateral is redeployed elsewhere to earn interest. This helps to bring in external revenue and keeps the protocol afloat, which is then used to buyback and burn FXS.

4. Price volatility of FRAX is shifted to FXS because of its buyback and burn mechanic.

While these are just simplified reasons, they will still need to be continuously reconsidered, especially in times of crisis when the price of FXS significantly drops and when liquidity mining rewards eventually stop.

The Next Generation of Algorithmic Stablecoins and Stableassets

While FRAX has largely been successful, one could argue that it is not truly decentralized. This is because it is still partially collateralized by USDC, which is backed by cash reserves held by a centralized entity (CENTRE Consortium - with Coinbase and Circle as co-founding members).

New entrants are trying to avoid this dilemma. They are still gravitating towards the collateralized system but have their distinctive takes, making it difficult to categorize under the existing umbrella of algorithmic stablecoins. We will cover three examples.

Fei Protocol

Fei launched at the end of Q1 2021. Much like Frax, Fei uses a partially collateralized system but is instead backed purely by ETH. Fei's stablecoin (FEI) is pegged to $1, which is underpinned by innovative concepts to maintain their peg and ensure the overall financial stability of the protocol.[35]

Rather than borrow collateral, Fei introduces a mechanism known as the Protocol Controlled Value (PCV). Essentially, Fei purchases ETH from users through newly minted FEI. Fei will then use the ETH to support their collateral-backed liquidity pools. Other common use cases include governance treasuries and insurance funds. During the initial launch, Fei allocated 100% of the PCV funded by the ETH bonding curve to a Uniswap pool using an ETH trading pair.

When the price of FEI is above $1, the protocol allows users to mint new FEI directly from the system at a discounted price (similar to FRAX) using ETH as payment. Traders may then arbitrage the price down until the price reaches its $1 peg. When the price of FEI is below $1, the protocol taxes FEI sellers (whose tax is then burned and removed from the supply), and awards extra FEI to buyers (on top of their initial purchase). The trading algorithm ensures that the tax amount exceeds the amount that buyers would receive.

In emergencies where the price of FEI is below the peg for an extended period, FEI may withdraw their PCV-backed liquidity from Uniswap and buy

---

[35] Fei Protocol. (2021, January 11). *Introducing Fei Protocol*. Medium. https://medium.com/fei-protocol/introducing-fei-protocol-2db79bd7a82b.

FEI from the market. At the same time, FEI is also burned. Once the peg is restored, Fei will resupply the remaining liquidity back into Uniswap.

Fei also has a native governance token (TRIBE) which will eventually become the foundation for a DAO. In the future, TRIBE holders will be able to decide on adjusting the PCV allocation and adding/adjusting bonding curves.

Reflexer

Unlike other algorithmic stablecoins, Reflexer's native token (RAI) is not meant to be a fixed-peg stablecoin. Launched in Q1 2021, RAI's intended purpose is to become stable collateral and replace existing collateral assets such as ETH or BTC, which are naturally volatile. RAI uses an ETH-based overcollateralized model and has a floating peg that was initially set to $3.14.

Reflexer uses managed-float regime principles, similar to how central banks operate.[36] Since prices constantly fluctuate, Reflexer designed a system where market interactions between RAI minters and traders (RAI holders) are incentivized to chase RAI's redemption price (floating peg) in order to keep the price of RAI relatively stable.

To mint RAI, users need to deposit ETH as collateral with a minimum of 145% collateralization ratio. Users are then charged a stability fee (borrowing interest rate). At the time of writing (May 2021), the stability fee is 2% per annum. However, it is variable and may be amended through a governance vote.

---

[36] Ionescu, S. (2020, October 29). *Introducing Proto RAI*. Medium. https://medium.com/reflexer-labs/introducing-proto-rai-c4cf1f013ef.

When the price of RAI is above the floating peg, the system lowers the peg. This allows users to mint more RAI and sell it back for ETH for a higher return. When the price of RAI is below the floating peg, the system raises the peg. This makes borrowing more expensive and incentivizes RAI minters to repay their RAI loans, thereby removing RAI from circulation and driving the price up.

In emergency situations (Settlement), the protocol shuts down and only allows both RAI minters and RAI holders to redeem ETH collateral from the system at the current redemption price.

Reflexer also has another native token (FLX) which acts as the lender of last resort, governs certain functions, and allows users to stake it in a pool that protects the system. There are also debt auctions, which are created to repay FLX in exchange for RAI - the RAI that is received by an auction will be used to eliminate bad debt from the system. On a longer time horizon, FLX is intended to be an "ungovernance" token, progressively automating the system over time and minimizing governance.

Float Protocol

Float is quite similar to FRAX, where it uses a two token seigniorage model and is partially collateralized by ETH. However, unlike FRAX, Float's native asset (FLOAT) has a floating rate but has an initial peg price of $1.61. Float's share token (BANK) also acts as both a governance token and regulating mechanism to support FLOAT's price.[37]

---

[37] Float Protocol. (2021, March 22). *Announcing Float Protocol and its democratic launch*. Medium. https://medium.com/float-protocol/announcing-float-protocol-and-its-democratic-launch-d1c27bc21230.

Float uses a similar mechanism as Fei's PCV where users may only acquire newly-minted FLOAT from the protocol. However, Float sells FLOAT through a Dutch auction where prices are listed at the highest possible price and descend downwards towards the minimum (reserve) price. To acquire FLOAT, users must pay with a combination of BANK and ETH. The asset payment ratio depends on the overall demand for FLOAT and the value of ETH in the basket.

If the basket is in excess, ETH is used to purchase FLOAT at the target price, and BANK is used to mint FLOAT. ETH (or any other future trading assets) earned from the Dutch auction is then stored as collateral in the protocol's collateral vault (Basket). BANK is burned whenever a user mints FLOAT.

When the price of FLOAT is above the floating peg, any user can start an auction. Initially it can only be started if a minimum of 24 hours has passed but this will be removed in the future once the team is satisfied that users are accustomed to the auction feature. Once an auction starts, the system mints and sells new FLOAT, starting at market price plus an added premium. Price will lower over time until it reaches the target price.

When the price of FLOAT is below the floating peg, the protocol offers to buy FLOAT from the market in the form of a reverse Dutch auction. This is where Float offers buyers what bids it would accept at incremental prices. FLOAT is bought with both ETH and freshly minted BANK.

Float's initial collateral ratio (Basket Factor) was set at 100% at launch but may be amended through governance voting. During emergencies, assets stored in the basket can be used to support the price of FLOAT if it is below its peg.

How will these new Algorithmic Stablecoins and Stableassets fare?

Older algorithmic stablecoins prioritized capital efficiency over everything else. Pegs were fixed and purely reliant on individualistic game theory mechanics, while untested bootstrapping methods were also prevalent.

Stablecoins were known for their peg to the US Dollar, but newer developments in the space have changed that very definition. We now have a new class of assets known as algorithmic stableassets.

We consider FLOAT and RAI as algorithmic stableassets primarily because they have a floating peg. Regardless, the focus should be on whether these assets can maintain a stable price or not. To answer this question, we considered three main factors.

I. Collateralization

Newer algorithmic stables are adopting a more conservative approach where collateralization takes precedence over capital efficiency.

Fei's PCV approach utilizes "liquidity collateralization" where collateral is automatically diverted to Fei's Uniswap liquidity pools. Governance voting (through the TRIBE native token) will allow users to control the PCV ratio, which is effectively the collateral ratio.

This is similar to Float's Basket Factor. However, Float has the added advantage of a floating peg and a share token (BANK) which is necessary for acquiring FLOAT. This increases its value and helps 'store' extra volatility into BANK as opposed to FLOAT. BANK can be used as collateral, though it would also be possible for Fei to collateralize TRIBE, albeit with less inert value since it possesses less utility. In other words, both Float and Fei let market forces decide on the ideal collateral ratio (similar to FRAX).

Contrast this with Reflexer's RAI, which is overcollateralized and is less prone to black-swan events. There is a minimum collateralization requirement but no maximum. Indeed, one could argue that Reflexer has a strong likelihood for success since it is a fork of Maker's Multi-Collateral Dai and managed to retain its peg after Black Thursday (despite the length of time it took). Furthermore, RAI does not confine itself to a fixed peg, thus giving it greater flexibility.

II. Trader Incentives/Disincentives

Algorithmic stablecoins and stableassets are designed to influence market behavior to help maintain its peg price. Older generations focused on rewarding "correct" user behavior (i.e., arbitrageurs). This still carries on for newer algorithmic stablecoins and stableassets where all three possess similar minting reward mechanics when the price is above the peg. There is, however, a noticeable difference in approach during the deflationary phase.

Newer protocols are incorporating "negative reinforcement" tactics. Fei penalizes sellers with a trading tax whenever FEI is sold below the peg. Reflexer indirectly raises the borrowing rate through the peg raise, which encourages borrowers to repay their loans (similar to Maker). Float is slightly different as it lets users' battle' it out in their reverse Dutch Auction. Rather than penalizing or rewarding users, Float lets market forces decide.

III. Emergency Powers

Perhaps the most interesting development is the push for stronger protocol powers. Each protocol's system design has built-in functions to protect its market when its native asset significantly devalues. One could draw parallels to traditional finance where regulators or centralized financial authorities step in during financial crises.

Fei essentially cuts off access to liquidity by removing their PCV-backed liquidity from Uniswap pools - similar to how a country might impose limits on bank withdrawals. Fei will then sell off its assets and offer to buy back excess FEI from the market. Float executes a similar tactic, except purchases are financed from the Basket. Reflexer halts all borrowings and only allows repayment of loans.

Associated Risks

We cannot emphasize enough that algorithmic stablecoins are still very much in the experimental phase. Protocols are still trying to figure out how to launch successfully without massive price swings.

Many algorithmic stablecoins protocols are also heavily reliant on competent arbitrageurs to maintain the price peg. If you are unsure how the protocol works, you would be at a severe disadvantage if you try to compete with savvy arbitrageurs (or even bots).

Algorithmic stablecoins require a strong community that believes in the project's fundamentals. More often than not, short-term profiteers will leverage their capital reserves to control and manipulate the price. In a decentralized market, only a cooperative community with strong underlying mechanisms can overcome this dilemma.

In other words, you would need to commit significant time and resources to understand each project. Only then can you decide whether it can compete with the many alternative stablecoins/stableassets that already have an established market presence.

Notable Mentions

- **Empty Set Dollar v2 (ESD)**
  ESD is migrating towards a dual-token stablecoin model by introducing a new token, ESDS. ESD v2 (also known as Continuous ESD) will be quite similar to Frax in having a partially collateralized stablecoin by incorporating a bank reserve backed by USDC. Together with ESDS, these two new features will hopefully help mitigate the volatility of ESD tokens.

- **Dynamic Set Dollar v2 (DSD)**
  While most stablecoin protocols are focussed on a partial or fully collateralized model, DSD (a fork of ESD) believes that this detracts from the ethos of decentralization. Despite its initial failure, DSD

has updated its model by introducing a new token, CDSD, which is partially redeemable 1:1 for DSD tokens. The idea is to transfer the volatility of DSD tokens onto CDSD - similar to Frax's model, but without any collateral.

- **Gyroscope (GYR)**
Gyroscope's mechanics is an amalgamation of multiple algorithmic stablecoin protocols with its own twist. GYR is over-collateralized and backed by multiple assets split into individual vaults (similar to Maker). Like most algorithmic stablecoins, there are arbitrage mechanics but with the addition of a complementary leveraged loan mechanism. During times of crisis, users will get a more favorable redemption rate the longer they wait to pay back their loans.

- **TerraUSD (UST)**
Similar to DSD v2, UST is an uncollateralized dual token model (along with LUNA) and fully relies on arbitrage to maintain its $1 peg. At the time of writing, UST is one of the only successful algorithmic stablecoins to maintain a stable price peg - likely due to strong demand and a flourishing ecosystem (Terra) that incorporates the mining network into its price stability mechanisms.

Conclusion

Algorithmic stablecoins are effectively DeFi's take on replacing a central bank, while algorithmic stableassets are DeFi's way to emulate the Gold Standard and create reliable digital collateral. In traditional finance, a successful monetary system requires a competent and independent financial authority. In DeFi, competency is sourced from pseudo-anonymous individuals who are incentivized to collaborate and act rationally.

Successful algorithmic stablecoins and stableassets require longer time-frames to prove themselves, especially during times of crisis. Neither short-term incentives nor short-term speculation is sustainable in and of itself - they need to become more than just a thought experiment and offer economic utility through widespread adoption. It will be interesting to monitor how the algorithmic stablecoins and stableassets in this chapter will perform over the coming years.

Recommended Readings

1. Understanding Risk of Rebase Tokens Through Smart Contract Analysis
   https://www.coingecko.com/buzz/understanding-risk-of-rebase-tokens-through-smart-contract-analysis
2. Understanding Fei, Float and Rai
   https://medium.com/float-protocol/float-and-the-money-gods-5509d41c9b3a
3. Exploring the Key Success Factors for Algorithmic Stablecoins
   https://messari.io/article/the-art-of-central-banking-on-blockchains-algorithmic-stablecoins
4. Deeper dive into Rebase and Seigniorage Models
   https://insights.deribit.com/market-research/stability-elasticity-and-reflexivity-a-deep-dive-into-algorithmic-stablecoins/
5. Impact of Uniswap on Algorithmic Stablecoins
   https://medium.com/stably-blog/what-uniswaps-liquidity-plunge-reveals-about-stablecoins-4fcbee8d210c

CHAPTER 7: DECENTRALIZED DERIVATIVES

The acceptance of digital assets have progressed into the creation of sophisticated financial products for users and traders. Currently, the usage of crypto derivatives are more commonplace at the centralized platforms like Binance Futures, Deribit, FTX, and Bybit.

With the growth of decentralized derivatives platforms, traders can now trade crypto derivatives in a trustless manner too. In this chapter, we will be going through decentralized derivatives in three distinct sections - decentralized perpetuals, decentralized options, and synthetic assets.

Decentralized Perpetuals

As one of the most popular derivatives in the crypto-space, perpetual swaps enable users to open a leveraged position on a futures contract with no expiration date. Previously, perpetuals were only available on centralized exchanges, however decentralized platforms such as Perpetual Protocol and dYdX have since paved the way for the wider DeFi community to gain access to leveraged positions while being fully in control of their own funds.

Perpetual Protocol

Perpetual Protocol is a decentralized protocol that offers perpetual contract trading, allowing users to open up to ten times leverage long or short positions on various cryptoassets. To achieve this, Perpetual Protocol uses a unique approach of virtual Automated Market Makers (vAMMs).

Functioning similarly to Uniswap and Balancer's AMMs, traders can execute transactions directly through the vAMMs. The main difference lies with the "virtual" part.

In conventional AMMs, assets are stored within the smart contract, and the exchange price for each asset is determined through a specific mathematical function. vAMMs in Perpetual Protocol do not store any assets whatsoever.

Instead, the real assets are stored in a smart contract vault, denominated in USDC, which becomes the collateral for users to open a leveraged position. The total amount of funds in the vault essentially forms the cap for traders' profits. Each perpetual contract will have its own specific vAMM, but all of them are protected under the protocol's insurance fund.

Perpetual Protocol is able to offer increased trading speed and minimal gas trades with the use of the xDai chain for trade execution. With vAMM, users will have access to high liquidity and low slippage for their trading needs.

As with all forms of perpetual contract trading, funding rates and liquidation ratios are crucial aspects of Perpetual Protocol. Funding rates are settled on an hourly basis, while liquidation ratios are set at 6.25% of posted margin. This means that traders with positions that fall below the 6.25% margin ratio will face the risk of being liquidated by keeper bots. Keeper bots will earn 20% of the liquidated margin, while the remainder will be sent to the protocol's insurance fund.

The protocol has its own native PERP token, which primarily serves as a governance token for the platform. PERP token holders receive voting power in proportion to their holdings. Additionally, they may stake their PERP for a fixed period to receive even more PERP and a share of the protocol's transaction fees in USDC.

This fixed period, known as an epoch, lasts for seven days. Token holders may not withdraw their funds until the end of each epoch. Transaction fees are claimable immediately after, while PERP rewards are locked for up to 6 months. Stakers get to enjoy zero impermanent loss, but they would still be exposed to the price volatility of the PERP token itself.

That's all you need to know about Perpetual Protocol. As of April 2021, trading is live on the Ethereum and xDai mainnet, so you can go ahead and give it a spin.

dYdX

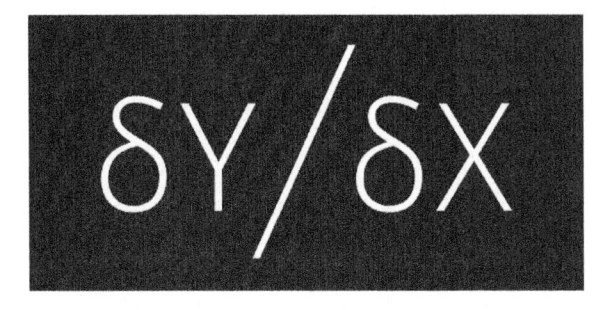

dYdX is a decentralized exchange protocol for lending, borrowing, spot trading, margin trading, and perpetual swap trading. One of the first projects to specialize in decentralized perpetual, dYdX supports three assets for spot and margin trading - ETH, USDC, and DAI. For perpetual swaps, 11 different contracts are available for trading, including BTC, ETH, AAVE and LINK.

dYdX shares some common characteristics with other lending and borrowing platforms such as Aave and Compound - allowing users to deposit their assets to earn interest or use their deposited assets as collateral for borrowing. However, dYdX sets itself apart by incorporating margin trading on ETH, with up to five times leverage, using either DAI or USDC. Users can also utilize up to ten times leverage on perpetual contracts trading on dYdX.

Lending on dYdX is flexible and automatically matched to borrowers, so there is no waiting period before you can start earning interest on deposits. Interest payments are compounded every time a transaction is made using that asset.

Interest rates are dynamically updated based on the level of utilization - higher utilization leads to higher interest rates for lenders. For borrowers, an initial collateralization ratio of 125% is required, while a minimum ratio of 115% needs to be maintained to prevent automatic liquidation.

dYdX offers spot traders similar functions as centralized exchanges such as market, limit, and stop orders. Trading fees for margin or spot positions are limited only to takers, where the amount charged is either 0.3% or the variable gas costs at the time, whichever is higher. To minimize gas cost, traders should pay attention to order size - the platform charges additional fees on smaller orders to pay for gas fees to complete the transaction.

For dYdX's perpetual markets, all contracts are collateralized in USDC. However, each contract uses different oracles, order sizes, and margin requirements. Funding rates are continuously charged each second for as long as a position remains open. The rates are recalculated every hour and are represented as an 8-hour rate, similar to Binance Futures. Unfortunately, perpetual contracts on dYdX are not available for United States residents.

In Q1 2021, dYdX partnered with Starkware to build a Layer-2 trading protocol, allowing for faster and cheaper transactions. Using a scalability engine known as StarkEx, trades will be matched off-chain using zero-knowledge rollups (zK-Rollup) and settled on the Ethereum mainnet. Users can now access the Layer-2 markets by generating a Stark Key, used to identify your Layer-2 account on dYdX and to send a transaction to register the account on-chain.

Comparison between Perpetual Protocol and dYdX (Layer 1)

Factor	Perpetual Protocol	dYdX (Layer 1)
Contracts supported	BTC, ETH, YFI, LINK, DOT, SNX	BTC, ETH, LINK, AAVE, UNI, SOL, SUSHI, YFI, 1INCH, AVAX, DOGE
Exchange Model	Virtual AMM	Orderbook
Maximum Leverage	10x	10x
Initial Margin	10%	10%
Maintenance Margin	6.25%	7.5%
Funding Rate	Every hour	Every second
Transaction Fees	0.1% on notional	Maker: -0.025% Taker: Higher of 0.2% or gas costs

In terms of contract specifications, both platforms offer highly similar leverage options and margin requirements for their respective markets. Perpetual Protocol offers a larger variety of assets and a much forgiving funding rate for open positions, bringing in an average of $60 million in daily trading volume compared to $15 million done by dYdX on Layer 1 in the first quarter of 2021.[38] On the other hand, dYdX takes the "exponential" approach by continuously benefiting its position holders, even if the higher fees may discourage smaller traders.

---

[38] (n.d.). Perpetual Swaps Trade Volume - The Block. Retrieved April 29, 2021, from https://www.theblockcrypto.com/data/decentralized-finance/derivatives/perpetual-protocol-trade-volume

In our view, dYdX may have the potential to compete with Perpetual Protocol after the introduction of both Layer-2 technology and more markets for popular tokens such as Aave and Uni, and on a lower fee basis.[39]

Notable Mentions

- **Futureswap**
  Futureswap is a decentralized perpetual exchange that allows users to trade up to 10x leverage on any ERC-20 pairs.

- **MCDEX**
  MCDEX is an AMM-based decentralized perpetual swap protocol that currently uses the second iteration of their Mai Protocol. Any user can create a perpetual market, as long as there is a price feed for the underlying asset and ERC-20 tokens to use as collateral.

- **Injective Protocol**
  Powered by the Injective Chain, this Layer-2 derivatives platform supports a fully decentralized order book and bi-directional token bridge to Ethereum. As of April 2021, it is still in testnet.

Decentralized Options

Options have long been a staple of traditional finance, offering buyers the opportunity to bet on price movements in either direction to hedge the value of their assets or amplify their returns with minimal capital. As DeFi continues to make waves throughout the crypto industry, it is only natural that decentralized options protocols come about as well.

Crypto users have historically traded options on centralized exchanges such as Deribit, but there is an inherent demand for decentralized options protocols. In this chapter, we will be looking at two leading decentralized options protocols, Hegic and Opyn.

---

[39] (2021, April 12). UNI, AAVE Markets now live - dYdX. Retrieved April 20, 2021, from https://dydx.exchange/blog/markets-01

Hegic

Hegic is a decentralized on-chain protocol that allows users to purchase American call and put options on ETH and WBTC. Users may also sell options by being liquidity providers to earn premiums. Using the platform's interface, users can customize the terms of the options they want to purchase, such as the strike price and expiry date.

Options' prices will be automatically calculated once the terms are selected, including a 1% settlement fee on the option sizes purchased. Although the options are non-tradeable, users can exercise them at any time since liquidity is locked on the option contract.

Hegic operates using a liquidity pool model. In other words, users pool their funds together and use it as collateral for underwriting all options sold. As of April 2021, there are two separate pools for ETH and WBTC. Liquidity providers lock up either ETH or WBTC and receive a certain amount of Write tokens according to the asset provided.

Write tokens represent the provider's claims on the premiums paid by users to purchase options. Although anybody can purchase options from the liquidity pools, the maximum purchase limit for each pool is set at 80% of the total underlying collateral.

An interesting thing to note about Hegic is that you can get rewarded for using the platform. HEGIC has a liquidity mining program that rewards users who stake their Write tokens and rewards option buyers based on option size and duration purchased. These rewards come in the form of rHEGIC tokens, a token claimable for the actual HEGIC token once certain milestones on the Hegic platform are achieved.

HEGIC tokens can also be staked to earn the protocol's fees, where 100% of the settlement fees from both pools are distributed to Hegic Staking Lot owners. To own a lot, you would need 888,000 HEGIC. If that's a little too much, you can delegate any amount you wish at www.hegicstaking.co.

Hegic has amassed more than $50 million in Total Value Locked and has settled more than $22 million of trading volume in a single day.[40,41] With these figures, Hegic remains as one of the top decentralized options protocols.

And that's pretty much it for Hegic! Next, we will be looking at another decentralized options platform called Opyn.

Opyn

Opyn is one of the first decentralized options platforms to launch. The first version, Opyn V1, lets you create tokenized American options in the form of oTokens by locking 100% of the underlying asset as collateral. This ensures that the holders can always exercise the options since it is fully collateralized. Provided there are enough liquidity providers to lock in their collateral, Opyn can offer a wide range of options on assets such as ETH, WBTC, UNI, and SNX, albeit with a fixed duration and strike price. oTokens can be exercised by sending the strike amount of stablecoins and burning the oTokens in

---

[40] (2021, April 10). Hegic Quarterly Report #2. Hegic has achieved steady ... - Medium. Retrieved May 7, 2021, from https://medium.com/hegic/hegic-quarterly-report-2-6c4170ac82e0

[41] (n.d.). Options TVL Rankings - Defi Llama. Retrieved May 7, 2021, from https://defillama.com/protocols/options

exchange for the underlying asset, or it can be resold to other parties via Uniswap. On top of that, Opyn does not charge any additional transaction or settlement fees.

The second version, Opyn V2 was launched with additional features such as auto-exercise and flash minting, an innovative spin on the existing concept of flash loans popularized by Aave. The latest iteration offers European options through an order book system, similar to Deribit, but is currently limited to Wrapped Ether (WETH) and with a smaller range of strike prices and expiry dates.

Comparison between Hegic and Opyn

How do these two protocols stack up against each other? In the table below, we compare both platforms based on several factors.

Factor	Hegic	Opyn V1	Opyn V2
Option Type	American	American	European
Liquidity Model	Single-asset Pool	Uniswap Pool	Order book
Settlement Type	Cash	Cash	Cash
Collateral Assets	ETH, WBTC	ETH, WBTC, UNI, SNX	WETH, WBTC
Premium Payment	ETH	DAI, ETH, USDC	USDC
Collateral Requirement	100%	100%	100%

Here, we can see that both options platforms need to be fully collateralized by the options writers, but are very different in terms of liquidity models and the number of assets supported.

American options seem to be favored by both protocols due to the degree of flexibility it offers in the fast-paced DeFi space. This is in contrast to European options, which is favored by centralized derivative exchanges such as Deribit. In Opyn V2, thin order books with a smaller selection of strike prices indicate lower demand for products with a heavy time constraint, given the volatile nature of the digital asset space.

Notable Mentions

- **FinNexus**

  FinNexus allows users to create options on almost any asset, as long as there is a reliable price feed. The protocol uses a Multi-Asset Single Pool (MASP) system, which allows for positions on different underlying assets while using only a single asset type as collateral.

- **Auctus**

  Auctus is a DeFi protocol that allows users the ability to perform flash exercises, where they do not need to own the strike tokens to exercise their options. They also offer principal-protected yield farming through their Auctus Vaults and a dedicated section for OTC options trading.

- **Premia**

  Premia offers a secondary marketplace for users to purchase and sell their options. Users can mint, transfer and exercise multiple options types with fewer transactions, saving both time and gas costs.

- **Antimatter**

  Antimatter aims to market itself as the Uniswap of options by providing an exchange for their perpetual options products. Users can receive long or short exposure by purchasing these Polarized option tokens, which can be redeemed without worrying about expiry dates.

- **Siren Protocol**

  Through Siren Protocol, users can choose to be a writer or purchaser of options by purchasing either bTokens or wTokens of a particular options series from the SirenSwap Automated Market Maker.

bTokens represent the buyer's side, allowing holders to exercise the options, while wTokens represent the writer's side, which will be used to withdraw the collateral or receive payment upon exercise.

Synthetic Assets

Synthetic assets are assets or a mixture of assets that have the same value or effect as another asset. Synthetic assets track the value of underlying assets and allow exposure to the assets without the need to hold the actual asset itself.

Examples of synthetic assets include virtually any trackable assets, from real-world stocks to Ethereum gas prices and even metrics on the CoinGecko website. Users trading these synthetic assets can have financial exposure in these assets without holding any of the actual assets themselves.

In this chapter, we will be comparing two of the largest protocols in the DeFi synthetic assets sector, namely Synthetix and UMA.

Synthetix

SYNTHETIX

We have covered Synthetix extensively in our *How to DeFi: Beginner*'s book, but here's a little recap.

Synthetix is a decentralized platform for minting and trading synthetic assets known as Synths, backed by collateral provided by the platform's users. Synths allow users to track the value of an underlying asset without holding the actual asset itself. There are two types of Synths - Regular Synths (e.g. sDEFi) and Inverse Synths (e.g. iDEFI). Not all Synths have an inverse counterpart.

Synths can be created for various asset classes such as cryptocurrencies, fiat currencies, commodities, equity indexes, and equities. The prices of the assets are tracked using Chainlink, a decentralized oracle that gathers price feeds from multiple sources.

Synths are created using over-collateralization, a concept similar to Maker in minting Dai. To mint Synths, users would have to stake the Synthetix Network Token (SNX) as collateral. Since the value of SNX can move quickly in either direction, a large collateralization ratio of 500% is required to mitigate liquidation risks.

To maintain a minimum of 500% collateralization ratio, users can burn Synths if they are below the target ratio or mint more Synths if they are above the threshold. Do note that as of January 2021, the only Synth that users can mint is sUSD.

Synths are mainly traded on the Synthetix Exchange, a decentralized exchange that does not rely on order books but on user liquidity. Synthetix Exchange allows users to trade directly against a smart contract that maintains constantly adequate liquidity, which reduces the risk of slippage. This is particularly useful for large transactions that would otherwise incur significant price slippages on other exchanges.

To incentivize staking and minting of Synths, users have the chance to receive exchange fees and SNX staking rewards. Fees generated from trading on the Synthetix Exchange are sent to a pool, where SNX stakers can claim their proportion of the fees collected. Stakers can also claim rewards of SNX tokens as long as their collateralization ratio does not fall below the current threshold.

Now that you have had a refresher on Synthetix, let's dive into what UMA is all about.

UMA

UMA or Universal Market Access is a decentralized protocol for creating and enforcing synthetic assets on the Ethereum network. UMA provides the infrastructure for building secure financial contracts using two core parts of their technology - a framework for building and deploying the derivatives and also an oracle known as the Data Verification Mechanism (DVM) to enforce them.

Unlike Synthetix, these financial contracts are designed to be "priceless", meaning they do not require an on-chain price feed to be properly valued. Instead, the contracts will rely on proper collateralization of the contracts' counterparties. This is incentivized by rewarding users who identify falsely collateralized positions. To further verify improper collateralization, the contracts may employ the use of the DVM.

The DVM is an oracle made to respond to price requests from these contracts and is only used to resolve disputes regarding liquidations and settlement of the contracts. The price requests are derived from UMA token holders, who vote on the most accurate value at a specific time. Token holders commit and reveal their votes over a multi-day process.

Once votes are revealed, the price or value with the most votes is relayed back to the financial contract. Collateral is then distributed to the token holders based on this voted figure. The DVM is built in such a way that there is an economic guarantee regarding the validity of the price requested.

Basically, this means that malicious actors are disincentivized from behaving badly. This is accomplished by ensuring that the cost of corrupting the DVM, taken as the total cost of more than half of the UMA voting tokens, is always greater than the profit from corruption or the total collateral available within the contracts. This inequality is maintained by adjusting the price of the tokens through additional fees on the contracts.

Besides the DVM, there are five other important actors in the UMA ecosystem as well. These include the:

Token Sponsors - Individuals who deposit collateral in a smart contract to mint synthetic tokens. They are responsible for maintaining their own collateralization ratio to prevent liquidation.

Liquidators - Network of monitors that are incentivized to check if a position is properly collateralized through off-chain price feeds. There is a 2-hour delay for disputers to verify the accuracy of the liquidation before it is finalized.

Disputers - Disputers are incentivized users that monitor contracts. They reference their off-chain price feed to validate a liquidation event. If it is invalid, the DVM will be called into action.

DVM - The oracle will aim to resolve the dispute by proposing a vote on the most accurate price of the asset at a given timestamp.

Token holders - UMA token holders collectively vote on the price of an asset at a specific time. Token holders will reference off-chain data to provide information to the DVM. The DVM will then tally the votes and report the most agreed-upon price on-chain.

If the disputer is correct, the disputer and the affected token sponsor are rewarded. If the liquidator is correct, the liquidator will be rewarded, while the disputer would be punished, and the token sponsor loses their funds due to a finalized liquidation.

Some of the products that have been built using UMA's framework include synthetic "yield dollars", which are tokens that approach a specific value upon maturity, as well as uGAS tokens, which can be used to speculate on Ethereum gas prices. UMA has also introduced call options on popular DeFi tokens, such as Sushi and Balancer, as well as their own UMA KPI options.

These KPI options track the TVL of UMA and its price performance, determining the amount of UMA that the option holder can redeem upon redemption.

Now that you know a little more about UMA and how it works, let's compare these two synthetic asset platforms.

Comparison between Synthetic and UMA

Factors	Synthetix	UMA
Synthetic Token	Synths	uTokens
Underlying Assets	Fiat, cryptocurrency, commodities, equity indexes, equities	Virtually anything
Oracle	Chainlink	Data Verification Mechanism
Collateralization Ratio	500%	Depends on token minted
Ability to Stake	Yes	Yes

Both Synthetix and UMA offer over-collateralized synthetic assets, which could serve as proxies for a wide range of asset classes. On Synthetix, the value of Synths and the collateralization ratio are dictated by an on-chain price feed.

On UMA, the settlement of synthetic contracts is maintained by incentivizing network actors to behave. With a much more flexible collateralization requirement, which is based on the Global Collateralization Ratio for all token sponsors, we can see that UMA could be a more capital-efficient platform. However, Synthetix has an advantage with options, as it supports over 50 Synths in its catalog.

Moreover, Synthetix has built an ecosystem around Synths, with dHEDGE and Curve Finance's cross-assets swaps being some of the main drivers of demand. dHEDGE, a decentralized asset management platform, allows users to invest sUSD into different investment portfolios. The chosen portfolio managers would then swap sUSD for other synthetic assets as part of their strategy. On the other hand, Curve Finance's cross-asset swaps make use of Synthetix as a bridge, allowing traders to swap up to 8 figures worth of assets, with zero to little slippage.

In terms of liquidity, it remains to be seen if UMA can compete without having a dedicated platform for trading these assets. Its exchange volumes are also low, recording only around $20 million in daily trading volume. That said, synthetic assets still have a long way to go before we see mass retail and institutional adoption.

Notable Mentions

- **Mirror Protocol**
  Available on both the Ethereum and Terra blockchains, Mirror Protocol issues synthetic assets, called mAssets, that mimic the price of real-world assets such as stocks and indices. Some of the offerings include mAMZN and mQQQ.

- **DEUS Finance**
  A DeFi protocol that lets users source data from oracles and tokenize them as tradeable dAssets. dAssets assets are pegged 1:1 to their real-life counterparts using price oracle data.

Associated Risks

When dealing with decentralized derivatives platforms, it is important to note that leveraged trading and derivatives usage is a highly risky endeavor. Maintaining a healthy collateral ratio and keeping an eye on the liquidation price of your positions are essential to safely navigating this particular section of DeFi.

Since synthetic assets mostly rely on oracles as the primary source of price information, false data may lead to unwanted consequences. Additionally, since synthetic assets are mainly minted by depositing collateral, lack of liquidity for these assets may occur, leading to drastically skewed pricing compared to real-world assets.

In the case of options, do ensure that you can exercise in-the-money positions in a timely manner as some platforms do not offer auto-exercise functions. As open interest continues to build up, one should take note of large option expiration periods, as volatility tends to increase.

Conclusion

Decentralized derivatives and synthetic assets offer regular users the opportunity to participate in previously inaccessible markets or markets that did not exist. These products have been simplified for the user's convenience and are no longer reserved for the elites. Users can also now participate in these derivatives markets without an intermediary.

This particular subset of DeFi is still relatively in its infancy, with a Total Value Locked of less than 10% of the entire space as of 1 April 2021. Indeed, bootstrapping liquidity is a problem faced by almost every up-and-coming DeFi project, and derivatives are no exception. Even with incentives, the very nature of these products with inherently higher volatility may seem to outweigh the rewards for participants to underwrite them.

Although protocols such as Charm and Perpetual Protocol can operate with minimal liquidity, it is still a long way to go before they can compete with big centralized exchanges that can offer larger volumes and higher leverage of up to 125x.

Recommended Readings

Decentralized Perpetuals
1. Documentation and Frequently Asked Questions about Perpetual Protocol
https://docs.perp.fi/
2. Research, Insights, and Announcements from dYdX
https://integral.dydx.exchange

3. The latest news from dYdX
   https://dydx.exchange/blog

Decentralized Options
1. Articles and announcements from Hegic
   https://medium.com/hegic
2. Hegic Protocol - On-chain Options Trading Protocol
   https://defipulse.com/blog/hegic-protocol-on-chain-options-trading-protocol/
3. Opyn Review
   https://defirate.com/opyn/
4. Beginner's Guide to Options: Opyn V2
   https://medium.com/opyn/a-beginners-guide-to-defi-options-opyn-v2-4d64f91acc84

Synthetic Assets
1. Documentation & System Overview of Synthetix
   https://docs.synthetix.io/
2. The latest news and announcements about Synthetix
   https://blog.synthetix.io/
3. What is Synthetix? Everything you need to know about one of the leading DeFi protocols
   https://medium.com/coinmonks/what-is-synthetix-everything-you-need-to-know-about-one-of-the-leading-defi-protocols-bc19bdd2949c
4. UMA Documentation
   https://docs.umaproject.org/
5. List of Projects using UMA
   https://umaproject.org/projects.html
6. UMA: Universal Market Access. Interview with Allison Lu
   https://defiprime.com/uma

CHAPTER 8: DECENTRALIZED INSURANCE

As DeFi projects launch and existing projects continue to innovate rapidly, we see an increasing number of hacks and exploits taking place, resulting in significant losses.

DeFi adoption will inevitably stall if the ecosystem only welcomes high-risk takers. Having a robust insurance system in place is a critical measure in reducing the risks users take on when interacting with DeFi applications, thus attracting more users to this space.

What is Insurance?

Insurance is a big industry, with total premiums underwritten globally reaching $6.3 trillion[42] in 2019. The world is inherently chaotic, and there is always the risk of accidents. Below is a simple risk management framework to show what we should do with different kinds of risks.

---

[42] "World Insurance Marketplace | III - Insurance Information Institute." https://www.iii.org/publications/insurance-handbook/economic-and-financial-data/world-insurance-marketplace. Accessed 6 May. 2021.

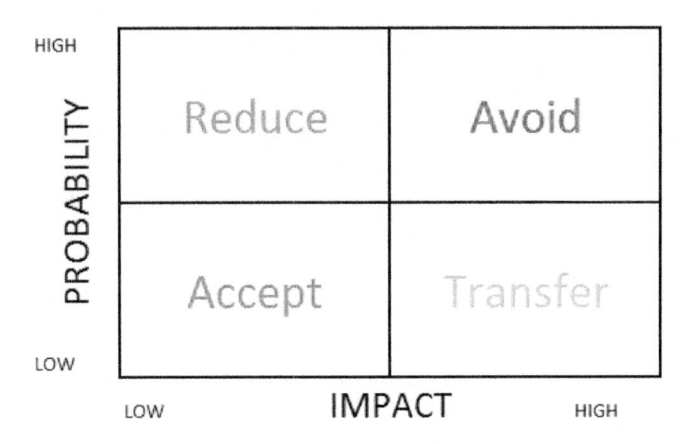

	LOW IMPACT	HIGH IMPACT
HIGH PROBABILITY	Reduce	Avoid
LOW PROBABILITY	Accept	Transfer

In this risk management framework, risks with high impact but with low frequency, such as natural catastrophes and terminal illnesses, should be transferred out. Insurance is created to deal with these types of risks.

How does Insurance work?

Insurance operates based on two main assumptions:

1. **Law of Large Numbers**
   The loss event covered by insurance must be independent. If the event is repeated frequently enough, the outcome will converge to the expected value.

2. **Risk Pooling**
   The loss event has the features of being low frequency and high impact. As such, insurance premiums paid by a large group of people subsidize the losses of several big claims.

Essentially, insurance is a tool to pool capital and socialize large losses so that the participants will not experience financial ruin with a single catastrophic event.

Does Crypto need Insurance?

Insurance empowers individuals to take risks by socializing the cost of any catastrophic events. It is an important risk management tool to encourage more people beyond the current niche user base to participate. The DeFi industry requires insurance products so that institutional players with significant capital to deploy are convinced that it is safe to participate in DeFi.

DeFi Insurance Protocols

We will be looking at three DeFi insurance protocols in detail below - Nexus Mutual, Armor Protocol, and Cover Protocol.

Nexus Mutual

Nexus Mutual
A people-powered alternative to insurance

Nexus Mutual is the largest DeFi insurance protocol in the crypto market by a wide margin. As of 1 May 2021, it has a Total Value Locked (TVL) of $450 million compared to $7 million by the second-largest DeFi insurance protocol, Cover Protocol. Nexus Mutual was founded by Hugh Karp, a former CFO of Munich Re in the U.K.

Nexus Mutual was registered as a mutual in the U.K. Unlike companies that follow a shareholders model, a mutual is governed by its members and only members are allowed to do business with the mutual. It's akin to a company run solely by the members for its members.

Type of Covers

Nexus Mutual offers two types of covers:

1. Protocol Covers

    Cover DeFi protocols that custody users' funds as these smart contracts may experience hacks due to smart contract bugs. Protocol Covers were previously known as Smart Contract Covers and were upgraded on 26 April 2021 to include:

    - Economic design failure
    - Severe oracle failure
    - Governance attacks
    - Protection for assets on Layer-2
    - Protection for non-Ethereum smart contracts
    - Protection for protocols across multiple chains

    Nexus Mutual offers covers for major DeFi protocols such as Uniswap, MakerDAO, Aave, Synthetix, and Yearn Finance.

2. Custody Covers

    Cover the risks of funds getting hacked or when the withdrawal is halted. Nexus Mutual offers covers for centralized exchanges such as Binance, Coinbase, Kraken, Gemini, and centralized lending services such as BlockFi, Nexo, and Celcius.

In total, users can buy covers for 72 different smart contract protocols, centralized exchanges, lending services, and custodians.

Cover Purchase

To buy insurance from Nexus Mutual, users will first have to register as mutual members by going through the Know Your Customer (KYC) process. There is a one-time membership fee of 0.002 ETH. Once approved, users can then purchase cover using ETH or DAI.

Nexus Mutual will convert the payment into NXM, the protocol's token representing the right to the mutual's capital. 90% of the NXM is burned as the cover cost. 10% of the NXM will remain in the user's wallet. It will be used as a deposit when submitting a claim and will be refunded if there are no claims.

Claim Assessment

Users can submit a claim anytime during the Cover Period or up to 35 days after the Cover Period ends. As each claim submission requires users to lock 5% of the premium, users are therefore allowed to submit at most two claims for each policy.

Unlike traditional insurers, the claim result is decided through members voting - members have complete discretion on whether a claim is valid. Members can stake their NXM to participate as a claim assessor, subjected to a seven-day lock-up period.

When the vote is aligned with the result, 20% of the policy's premium will be shared proportionately with these members. However, when the vote is not aligned with the result, members will not receive any rewards, and the locking period will be extended by another seven days.

To be eligible for a valid claim, users will have to prove that they have lost the fund:

- Protocol Covers - lose at least 20% of funds
- Custody Covers - lose at least 10% of funds

Risk Assessment

The pricing of the insurance is decided by the amount of capital staked on a particular protocol. Users can stake NXM on the protocols to become risk assessors - the more NXM staked on the protocol, the lower the cover price will be.

As of April 2021, 50,000 NXM is required to reach the lowest base pricing of 2%. A surplus margin, which is set at 30%, is devised to meet costs and create a surplus for the mutual. Factoring this in, the lowest possible cover cost is 2.6%.

The risk assessor bears the loss when there is a claim. For taking on this risk, 50% of the policy's premium is shared with the risk assessors.

Below is a pie chart showing where the premium flows to:

Pie Chart

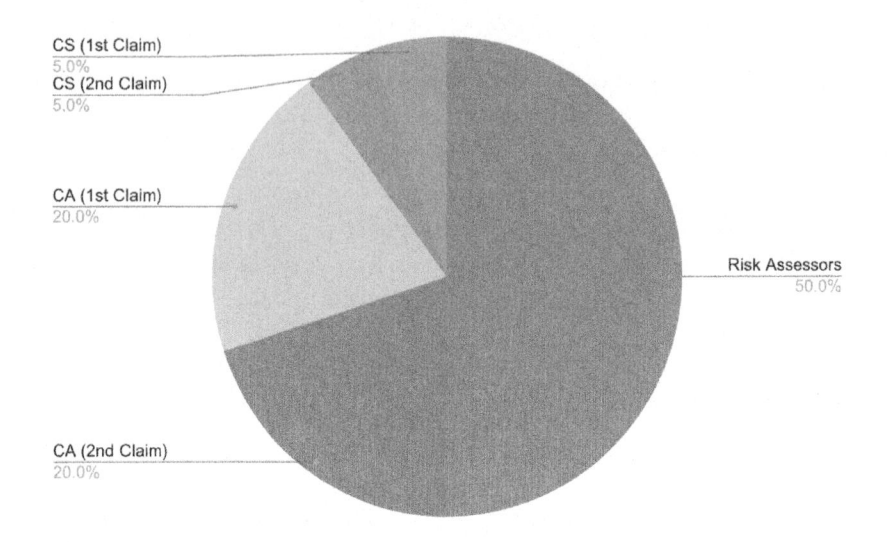

- CS (1st Claim): 5.0%
- CS (2nd Claim): 5.0%
- CA (1st Claim): 20.0%
- CA (2nd Claim): 20.0%
- Risk Assessors: 50.0%

Claim Submission (CS): Fees paid by the user to submit a claim
Claim Assessor (CA): Fees earned by Claim Assessor if there is a claim submission

If no claims are submitted when the policy expires, 10% of the premium will be refunded to the cover buyer, while 40% of the premium will go to the capital pool.

Risk assessors are allowed to stake 15 times the capital available to maximize capital efficiency. For example, if a risk assessor has 100 NXM, he/she can stake 1,500 NXM across multiple protocols, with a maximum stake on any one protocol capped at 100 NXM.

The assumption here is that it will be very unlikely to have multiple protocols hacked at the same time. This practice aligns with how traditional insurance operates, based on the law of large numbers and risk pooling.

If the claim amount is larger than the capital staked by the risk assessors, the mutual's capital pool will pay the remaining amount.

To ensure there will always be enough capital to pay for claims, the mutual needs to have capital above the Minimum Capital Requirement (MCR).

Usually, MCR is calculated based on the risk of the covers sold. But due to the lack of claim data, the mutual follows manual parameters decided by the team.

Token Economics

NXM token economics is a big factor in attracting and retaining capital. It uses a bonding curve to determine NXM's token price. The formula is as follow:

$$\text{Price} = A + \left(\frac{MCR_{ETH}}{C}\right) \times MCR\%^4$$

$A = 0.01028$
$C = 5,800,000$
MCR (ETH) = Minimum Capital Required
MCR% = Available Capital / MCR (ETH)

MCR% is a key factor in determining NXM's token price as it has a power of four in the price formula. When people buy NXM through the bonding curve, available capital will increase, causing MCR% to grow, leading to an exponential increase in NXM's price.

The key thing to note here is that the bonding curve's withdrawal will be halted when MCR% is lower than 100%. This is to ensure there is enough capital to pay claims.

Wrapped NXM (wNXM)

In July 2020, the community members of Nexus Mutual released wrapped NXM (wNXM) as a way for investors to have exposure to NXM without going through the KYC process. When the withdrawal of NXM is halted (MCR% goes below 100%), users can wrap their NXM into wNXM and sell it through secondary markets such as Uniswap and Binance.

wNXM has many shortcomings as it cannot be used in risk assessment, claim assessment, and governance voting. The launch of the Armor protocol helps to solve the above issues by converting wNXM into arNXM.

Further details can be found below in the Armor Protocol's section.

Protocol Revenue

NXM token differs from other governance tokens because a formula controls the token price. So, if the mutual is earning a profit, it will help increase the capital available and increase the price of NXM.

There are three sources of profit:

- Premiums collected - Claims paid - Expenses
- 2.5% spread when users sell NXM from the bonding curve
- Investment earnings from the capital pool

Armor Protocol

INSURANCE EVOLVED

Smart DeFi Asset Coverage

Armor is a decentralized brokerage for cover underwritten by Nexus Mutual's blockchain-based insurance alternative

Read our technical documents to learn more about Armor

Armor makes investing in DeFi as safe as possible with crypto-native, dynamic smart coverage aggregation. As a decentralized smart brokerage, Armor's innovations provide on-demand, real-time coverage and non-custodial security solutions for user assets.

Armor protocol has four main products: arNXM, arNFT, arCORE, and arSHIELD.

arNXM

Nexus Mutual created Wrapped NXM (wNXM) to allow investors to have exposure to NXM without doing KYC. However, as more wNXM were created, less NXM became available for internal functions of the mutual such as staking, claim assessment, and governance voting.

Armor created arNXM to solve this issue by allowing investors to participate in Nexus Mutual's operations without doing KYC. To get arNXM, users can stake wNXM in Armor. Armor unwraps the wNXM, and the NXM token is then subsequently staked on Nexus Mutual. By staking on Nexus Mutual, stakers signal that the smart contracts are safe, opening up more insurance covers for sale.

arNXM can also be referred to as a wNXM vault. Users who deposit wNXM into the vault can expect to receive a higher amount of wNXM in the future.

arNFT

arNFT is the tokenized form of insurance coverage purchased on Nexus Mutual. arNFTs allow users to buy insurance cover without having to do KYC. Since these insurance covers are tokenized, users can now transfer them to other users or sell them on the secondary market. These tokenized covers also allow for further DeFi composability.

arNFTs can be minted for all Nexus Mutual's covers.

arCORE

arCORE is a pay-as-you-go insurance product. Using a streamed payment system, Armor tracks the exact amount of user funds as they dynamically move across various protocols and charges by the second. Underlying arCORE are pooled arNFTs that are broken down and sold at a premium. arCORE allows for much more innovative product design and showcases the composability nature of the DeFi ecosystem.

arCORE's products are charged at a higher premium to compensate arNFT stakers for taking the risk of not fully selling out the cover. As of April 2021, the multiplier is 161.8%, meaning the price would be 61.8% higher instead of purchasing directly from Nexus Mutual.

For the additional premium, 90% is given back to arNFT stakers, and 10% is charged by Armor as an admin fee. At a 1.618 premium multiplier and 90% share of revenue, utilization would have to be greater than 69% for this to be profitable for arNFT stakers. If the covers sold are less than 69% of those staked in the pool, then the stakers will have to foot the cover costs themselves.

arSHIELD

arSHIELD is an insured storage vault for Liquidity Providers (LP) tokens where insurance premiums are automatically deducted from the LP fees earned. arSHIELD essentially creates insured LP tokens where users do not have to pay upfront payments.

arSHIELD only covers the protocol risk of the liquidity pools. For example, insured Uniswap LP tokens only cover the risks of Uniswap's smart contract getting compromised, but not the risks of the underlying assets getting hacked (e.g., a hack of underlying asset protocol).

As such, arSHIELD is just a repackaged version of arCore.

Claim

After a user files a claim, a review process will be triggered and submitted to Nexus Mutual for consideration. Armor token holders will also participate in Nexus Mutual's process for claim approvals and payouts. If a payout is confirmed, the amount will be sent to Armor's payout treasury before being distributed to the affected users.

Protocol Revenue

Armor's focus is on building an ecosystem of interoperable protocols and products to secure and scale mass adoption of DeFi both with institutions and individuals.

Below is the profit-sharing fees table updated as of February 2021:

Product	Stakers' Share	Treasury Share
arNXM	90%	10%
arCore	90%	10%
arNFT	0%	100%

Source: https://armorfi.gitbook.io/armor/products/arcore/model-constants

One thing to note is that 10% of the premium for every cover bought from Nexus Mutual is reserved for claim purposes. As the claim fee is 5% of the premium, every user can claim twice with the same policy. If there are no claims at the end of the policy period, the 10% premium will be refunded. This is the source of arNFT's profit.

Cover Protocol

Cover Protocol was incubated by Yearn Finance, starting as Safe Protocol that offers yInsure. But due to some infighting between the founder, Alan, and a prominent community member, Azeem Ahmed, the project was canceled. Azeem took over the yInsure product and released Armor Protocol, while Alan went on to release Cover Protocol.

Yearn Finance announced a merger with Cover Protocol to insure all of its yVaults with Cover Protocol. However, Yearn Finance ended the partnership on 5 March 2021.[43,44]

Type of Covers

Cover Protocol only offers Smart Contract Covers.

Let's go through an example of how covers are sold. Market makers can deposit 1 DAI, and they will be able to mint one NOCLAIM token and one CLAIM token. Both tokens represent only the risk of a single protocol. The tokens are only valid under a fixed timeframe, such as half a year.

Two scenarios can happen after half-year:

- If there are no valid claim events, NOCLAIM token holders can claim 1 DAI, while CLAIM tokens will have zero value.
- If there is a valid claim event, CLAIM token holders can claim 1 DAI while NOCLAIM token will have zero value.

This is akin to a prediction market where users can bet whether the protocols will get hacked within a fixed timeframe.

Cover Protocol introduced partial claims, so the payout for CLAIM token holders when there is a valid claim event will be decided by the Claim Validity Committee (CVC).

Cover Purchase

Users can buy cover from Cover Protocol's web page with just one Ethereum transaction, without the need to register or do any Know Your Customer (KYC) process.

---

[43] "Yearn & Cover merger. Yearn and Cover Protocol join ... - Medium." 28 Nov. 2020, https://medium.com/iearn/yearn-cover-merger-651142828c45. Accessed 6 May. 2021.
[44] (2021, March 5). yearn.finance on Twitter: "We have decided to end the previously .... Retrieved May 23, 2021, from
https://twitter.com/iearnfinance/status/1367796331507552258

Claim Assessment

There are two options for users to file for a claim:

1. Regular claim: A regular claim costs 10 DAI. COVER token holders will first vote on the validity of the claim. After being validated, it will move to the Claim Validity Committee (CVC) for a final decision.

2. Force claim: A force claim costs 500 DAI. The claim is sent to the CVC directly for a decision.

The CVC consists of external smart contract auditors. Cover Protocol will refund the claim filing cost if the claim is approved.

Risk Assessment

When users buy cover, flash loans are utilized to reduce the gas cost and steps required by the user. In this process, CLAIM and NOCLAIM tokens are minted with borrowed DAI. The NOCLAIM tokens are then sold to a Balancer pool for DAI.

Coupled with the premium paid by the user, the DAI is then used to pay back the flash loan, and users will only receive the CLAIM tokens. The reverse will happen when users sell the CLAIM token back to Cover Protocol.

There are a few benefits under this system:

- Cover cost is expected to reduce as there is only one Balancer pool to conduct yield farming programs. With the right incentives, market makers will buy more NOCLAIM tokens to yield farm or earn trading fees, pushing up the price of NOCLAIM tokens. As such, the price of the CLAIM token will reduce as CLAIM = 1 - NOCLAIM.

- Market Maker is expected to earn more fees as every cover purchase involved selling NOCLAIM tokens into the Balancer pool. Unlike the previous system, market makers only need to provide liquidity for one pool rather than two.

- Cover Protocol is expected to receive higher platform revenue as every purchase involves the CLAIM/NOCLAIM token minting with a 0.1% fee during redemption.

The cover price is decided by the supply and demand of the Balancer pool.

Protocol Revenue

0.1% fees will be charged on CLAIM and NOCLAIM token redemption. COVER token holders have the right to vote on how to use the treasury. As of April 2021, the staking of COVER tokens to earn dividends is being discussed, but details are not finalized.

Comparison between Nexus Mutual and Cover Protocol

	Nexus Mutual	**Cover Protocol**
Token Model	Mutual	Shareholder
Product	Insurance	Prediction Market
Risk Pooling	Yes	No
Capital Efficiency	High	Low
Counterparties covered	72	33
Claims	Voted by members	Voted by auditors
KYC	Not Required (Armor)	Not Required
Proof of Loss	Required	Not Required
Loss Covered	Full	Partial
Total Value Locked	$450 million	$7 million

As of April 2021, Nexus Mutual has a huge lead in the insurance market with seemingly no competitors in sight. But there is plenty of room for competitors to catch up as the insurance penetration rate in DeFi is very low, with roughly only 2% of the total DeFi TVL.[45] In a field where innovations spring up each day, the title of insurance leader is always up for grabs.

---

[45] (n.d.). Nexus Mutual Tracker. Retrieved May 23, 2021, from https://nexustracker.io/

Cover Protocol has been innovating rapidly, even throughout the Safe Protocol fiasco.[46] Even though the product has yet to gain significant traction, zero to one innovation is never easy. We have to remember that the Cover Protocol has been operational for less than a year (as of April 2021).

Capital Efficiency

Nexus Mutual allows capital providers to have 15 times leverage on the capital they stake. This translates into higher premium income for the stakers. Capital providers do have to take on more risks, but this approach is aligned with how the traditional insurance providers spread risk across multiple distinct products with different risk profiles.

In the meantime, capital providers for the Cover Protocol could not leverage their capital as every pool is isolated. As a result, Cover Protocol's covers are more expensive than those from Nexus Mutual due to less capital efficiency. For example, buying cover for Origin Dollar would cost 12.91% annually on Cover Protocol, while it only cost 2.6% on Nexus Mutual. There are plans to bundle different risks together in Cover Protocol Version 2, but details are still scarce.

We can calculate capital efficiency quantitatively by dividing the active cover amount over the capital pool. Nexus Mutual has a capital efficiency ratio as high as 200%, while Cover Protocol, by design, will always be less than 100%.

Covers Available

Cover Protocol only has coverage for 22 protocols, while Nexus Mutual has coverage for 72 counterparties. Nexus Mutual offers more flexibility in cover terms where users can decide to start the cover on any day and have a coverage period up until one year.

Cover Protocol only offers fixed-term insurance where the end date has been decided beforehand. For example, for a particular series, the insurance term is valid until the end of May. Regardless of when the user buys the cover, the

---

[46] "Insurance Mining Hits a Speed Bump with SAFE Drama - DeFi Rate." 16 Sep. 2020, https://defirate.com/safe-insurance-mining/. Accessed 10 May. 2021.

cover will end in May. So as time goes by, CLAIM token will converge to $0 while NOCLAIM token will converge to $1.

Users can find more comprehensive offerings from Nexus Mutual as it has coverage for most of the main DeFi protocols. Even then, many covers are sold out due to the lack of stakers. The launch of Armor Protocol did help to alleviate the issue by attracting more wNXM into arNXM that allows NXM to be staked. As a result, more covers are available.

Cover Protocol can be seen as competing on long-tail insurance because projects can list much faster and do not have to go through cumbersome risk assessments. This is because every risk is isolated and contained within a single pool, unlike NXM, where a claim from any single protocol can eat into the capital pool. However, bootstrapping coverage for lesser-known projects is not an easy task. Other than being constrained by limited capacity, the insurance cost is often too expensive.

Claim Payout Ratio

Yearn Finance suffered an $11 million hack in February 2021.[47] Even though Yearn Finance decided to cover the loss through their fund, insurance protocols have decided to pay out the claims to showcase that their product does work as intended.

Nexus Mutual has accepted 14 claims, amounting to a claim payout of $2,410,499 (1,351 ETH and 129,660 DAI).[48] This resulted in a 9.57% loss to the NXM stakers who staked on Yearn Finance. The losses were fully paid if the claimants can show that they have indeed lost at least 20% of their fund.

Meanwhile, Cover Protocol decided to only have a payout percentage of 36% due to the loss being only 36% of the vault affected. If users held 1,000 CLAIM tokens, they received only $360. Because there was only $409,000

---

[47] "Yearn.Finance puts expanded treasury to use by repaying victims of ...." 9 Feb. 2021, https://cointelegraph.com/news/yearn-finance-puts-expanded-treasury-to-use-by-repaying-victims-of-11m-hack. Accessed 6 May. 2021.
[48] "Paying claims for the Yearn hack | Nexus Mutual - Medium." 24 Feb. 2021, https://medium.com/nexus-mutual/paying-claims-for-the-yearn-hack-693bcfc5cd57. Accessed 6 May. 2021.

worth of CLAIM tokens available for Yearn Finance, market makers only lost $147,240.

Cover buyers should realize that buying insurance from Cover Protocol does not guarantee a full payout in the event of a loss. The way the claim payout is decided is more similar to a prediction market.

Associated Risks

Claim payouts are highly dependent on the agreements set between insurance providers and the buyers. There are always nuances in interpreting agreements, especially in high-stakes scenarios that involve large claims.

Each insurance protocol will have its way of deciding what to pay, which may not necessarily be fair to all buyers. Buyers should be aware of the current limitation offered by the insurance products.

Being a capital provider for insurance protocols is a complicated operation, and users should have a complete understanding of the risks before deciding to get involved. Stakers can incur losses if the probability of claims is higher than expected.

Notable Mentions

- **Unslashed Finance**
  As of April 2021, Unslashed Finance is in private beta mode. Unslashed Finance offers bucket-style risk pooling for capital providers. The first product, named Spartan Bucket, covers 24 different risks covering counterparties such as custodians, wallets, exchanges, smart contracts, validators, and oracles.

Lido Finance purchased $200 million worth of cover[49] from Unslashed Finance for its stETH (ETH 2.0 staking) to cover the risk of slashing penalties. Slashing refers to penalties exerted towards the Proof of Stake (PoS) network's validator when the validators fail to maintain the network consistently.

- **Nsure Network**
Nsure Network raised a $1.4 million seed fund from Mechanism Capital, Caballeros Capital, 3Commas, AU21, Signal Ventures, and Genblock back in September 2020.

Nsure Network is a marketplace to trade risk. It relies on the staking of NSURE tokens to signal the riskiness of a protocol and uses it to price cover. As of April 2021, they are running an underwriting program in Ethereum's Kovan testnet to assess how the pricing will work in mainnet. Participants will receive NSURE tokens as a reward.

- **InsurAce**
InsurAce has raised $3 million[50] from VCs such as Alameda Research, DeFiance Capital, ParaFi Capital, Maple Leaf Capital, Wang Qiao, and Kerman Kohli. It aims to become the first portfolio-based insurance protocol, offering both investment and insurance products to improve capital efficiency.

With InsurAce, users do not have to buy several covers if they are exposed to different protocols while doing yield farming, as it offers a portfolio-based cover covering all the protocols involved in the said investment strategy. It also claims to adopt an actuarial-based pricing model rather than relying on staking or market to price the cover.

---

[49] "Lido and Unslashed Finance Partner to Cover ETH ... - Lido.fi Blog." 23 Feb. 2021, https://blog.lido.fi/lido-unslashed-finance-partner-to-insure-ethereum-staking-service/. Accessed 6 May. 2021.

[50] "$3M Raised during InsurAce Strategic Round | by ... - Medium." 25 Feb. 2021, https://medium.com/insurace/3m-raised-during-insurace-strategic-round-ca94a7296dac. Accessed 6 May. 2021.

As of April 2021, InsurAce has yet to announce its launch date. Due to the lack of claim history, it remains to be seen if InsurAce's portfolio-based insurance protocol and pricing model will work in the DeFi space.

Some derivative protocols also offer interesting insurance products such as:

- Hakka Finance's 3F Mutual - covers the de-pegging risk of DAI.
- Opium Finance - covers the de-pegging risk of USDT.

The adoption of these insurance products offered by the derivative protocols so far has been lackluster.

Unlike other decentralized exchanges and lending/borrowing protocols, insurance protocols seem to receive less attention. Besides being a more capital-intensive operation, the awareness of buying protection is not that prevalent in the crypto field. We may see more users getting onboard to use insurance with more insurance protocols slated to launch in 2021 and beyond.

Conclusion

The insurance market is still underexplored. According to the active cover amount of Nexus Mutual, only around 2% of the DeFi's Total Value Locked is covered. Derivatives products such as Credit Default Swap and options may dilute the need to buy insurance.

However, the construction of those products is usually more capital intensive than the risk pooling method of insurance, leading to more expensive covers. Plus, derivatives are rightfully more costly as they have exposure to price risk.

There is also the possibility that high-risk-takers and retail users dominate the current DeFi market; they may not have a strong emphasis on risk management and therefore do not consider the need for insurance. The insurance market will gain more traction when the crypto space matures and has more involvement with institutional capital.

The underlying business of Nexus Mutual is humming well, with the active cover amount increasing ten times from $68 million in January 2021 to $730 million in February 2021.

Armor Protocol's launch has been a huge boon to Nexus Mutual, cementing Nexus Mutual's lead in the DeFi insurance market. As a wNXM vault, arNXM is intended to replace wNXM. It has attracted so much wNXM that arNXM now contributes 47% of the total NXM staked. This has helped to open up more covers for purchase. arNFTs meanwhile have contributed approximately 70% of the total active cover.

Cover Protocol has been innovating rapidly with new products such as Credit Default Swap, but their business growth has been rather slow. Cover Protocol offers fewer product offerings and has less flexibility in cover terms. But it allows projects to list faster and can offer coverage with relatively less capital.

Recommended Readings

1. Why DeFi insurance needs an Ethereum native claims arbitrator
   https://blog.kleros.io/why-defi-insurance-needs-an-ethereum-native-claims-arbitrator/
2. Why insurance is needed for DeFi and what it looks like
   https://cryptoslate.com/why-insurance-is-needed-for-defi-and-what-it-looks-like/
3. Nexus Mutual is the most undervalued token in digital assets
   https://twitter.com/jdorman81/status/1376920737949184002?s=20

PART THREE: EMERGING DEFI CATEGORIES

CHAPTER 9: DECENTRALIZED INDICES

One way to get cryptocurrency exposure in your investment portfolio without constantly monitoring individual currency's performance is by investing in passively managed portfolios such as decentralized indices. Decentralized indices work similarly to Exchange Traded Funds (ETF) in the legacy financial markets.

An ETF is a type of structured security that can track anything such as an index (e.g., S&P500), commodities (e.g., precious metals), or other assets. It can be purchased or sold on a stock exchange.

Historically, ETFs have a better return than actively managed strategies like mutual funds. In 2020, global ETFs had $7.74 trillion worth of Assets Under Management (AUM), with volume reaching one-third of global equity trading volume.[51,52,53]

---

[51] "Worldwide ETF assets under management 2003-2020 - Statista." 18 Feb. 2021, https://www.statista.com/statistics/224579/worldwide-etf-assets-under-management-since-1997/. Accessed 9 Mar. 2021.

[52] "Institutional investors | iShares - BlackRock." https://www.ishares.com/us/resources/institutional-investors. Accessed 9 Mar. 2021.

[53] "ETF assets reach $7tn milestone | Financial Times." 9 Sep. 2020, https://www.ft.com/content/e59346a7-b872-4402-8943-2d9bdc979b08. Accessed 9 Mar. 2021.

As of 1 April 2021, the decentralized indices sector is growing fast, with on-chain ETF amounting to approximately $234 million in AUM.[54] It is not far-fetched to imagine this figure reaching trillions of dollars in the coming years.

In this chapter, we will be focusing on decentralized indices where you can diversify your portfolios without spending too much time and effort to research, manage, and allocate your investments.

Indices protocols refer to the asset managers, while index tokens refer to the indices' products (equivalent to ETFs). These index tokens represent your share of the index fund and entitle you to receive profits from the capital appreciation of the underlying assets. Additionally, there are governance tokens for some protocols, giving you voting rights in determining the direction of the indices protocols.

First, an overview of the decentralized indices market landscape:

DeFi ETF Landscape

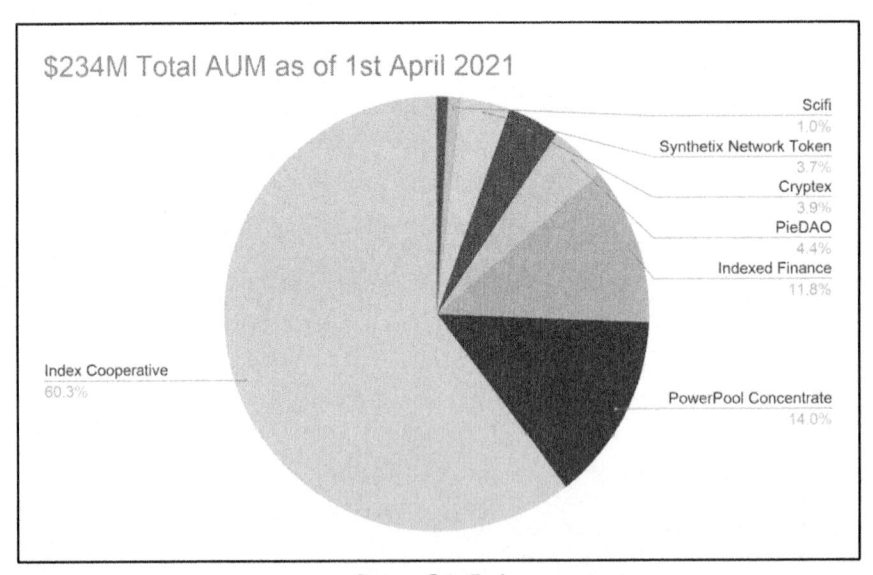

$234M Total AUM as of 1st April 2021

- Index Cooperative: 60.3%
- PowerPool Concentrate: 14.0%
- Indexed Finance: 11.8%
- PieDAO: 4.4%
- Cryptex: 3.9%
- Synthetix Network Token: 3.7%
- Scifi: 1.0%

Source: CoinGecko

---

[54] (n.d.). Top Index Coins by Market Capitalization - CoinGecko. Retrieved May 22, 2021, from https://www.coingecko.com/en/categories/index-coin

As of 1 April 2021, Index Cooperation has the largest market share with 60% of decentralized indices AUM. This is followed by PowerPool (14%) and Indexed Finance (12%).

Despite having over 20 DeFi index tokens in the market, the decentralized indices market is not as crowded and competitive as it seems.[55] The decentralized indices AUM comprises only 0.3% of the DeFi's Total Value Locked.

Let's take a look at the top 3 largest indices protocols - Index Cooperative, PowerPool Concentrated Voting Power, and Indexed Finance.

Index Cooperative (INDEX)

Index Cooperative, also known as Index Coop, is the oldest decentralized indices protocol. It was founded by Set Labs Inc., the same company that built Set Protocol.

Index Coop enables users to gain broad exposure to different protocols of varying themes across the cryptocurrency industry. Indices token holders can own, have exposure to, and can directly redeem the underlying assets that comprise the index.

Index Coop works with various methodologists - data providers that are accountable for the specific indices' strategy to launch its products.

As of April 2021, there are five indices available under Index Coop:

---

[55] "Top DeFi Index Coins by Market Capitalization - CoinGecko." https://www.coingecko.com/en/categories/defi-index. Accessed 11 May. 2021.

- DeFiPulse Index (DPI)
- CoinShares Crypto Gold Index (CGI)
- ETH 2x Flexible Leverage Index (ETH2X-FLI)
- BTC 2x Flexible Leverage Index (BTC2X-FLI)
- Metaverse Index Token (MVI)

Indexed Finance (NDX)

Indexed Finance is a protocol that focuses on portfolio management. Users can mint, swap or burn the indices token and the underlying assets, and the integrated Automated Market Maker (AMM) mechanism forked from Balancer rebalances its indices automatically. Indexed Finance has five team members, one of whom is anonymous.

As of April 2021, there are seven indices available under Indexed Finance:

- DEGEN Index (DEGEN)
- Cryptocurrency Top 10 Tokens Index (CC10)
- Oracle Top 5 Index (ORCL5)
- DEFI Top 5 Tokens Index (DEFI5)
- NFT Platform Index (NFTP)
- 484 Fund (ERROR)
- Future Of Finance Fund (FFF)

PowerPool Concentrated Voting Power (CVP)

PowerPool's indices are smart pools based on Balancer's Automated Market Maker (AMM) with additional functionality. Its main purpose is to pool governance tokens together for lending, borrowing, and executing meta-governance. Additionally, users can directly swap one governance token for another. An anonymous team runs PowerPool.

Currently, PowerPool has four indices:

- Power Index Pool Token (PIPT)
- Yearn Ecosystem Token Index (YETI)
- ASSY Index (ASSY)
- Yearn Lazy Ape (YLA)

Comparing the Protocol Indices

As a protocol investor, there are three primary metrics to look at:

1. Protocol fees
2. Protocol strategies
3. Fund weighting

Protocol Fees

Index Projects	Index Cooperative (INDEX)			Indexed Finance (NDX)						PowerPool Concentrated Voting Power (CVP)			
Index Funds	DPI	CGI	FLI	DEFI5	CC10	DEGEN	ORCL5	NFTP	FFF	PIPT	ASSY	YETI	YLA
Entry fee (mint)	-	-	0.10%	-	-	-	-	-	-	0.10%	0.10%	0.10%	0.10%
Swap fee*	-	-	-	2.00%	2.00%	2.00%	2.00%	2.00%	2.00%	0.20%	0.20%	0.20%	0.20%
Asset Manager Treasury										0.10%	0.10%	0.10%	0.10%
LP return	-	-	-	2.00%	2.00%	2.00%	2.00%	2.00%	2.00%	0.10%	0.10%	0.10%	0.10%
Management Fee**	0.95%	0.60%	1.95%	-	-	-	-	-	-	-	-	-	-
Asset Manager Treasury	0.65%	0.24%	1.17%										
Methodologist	0.30%	0.36%	0.78%										
Exit fees (Burn/Redeem)	-	-	0.10%	0.50%	0.50%	0.50%	0.50%	0.50%	0.50%	0.10%	0.10%	0.10%	0.10%

Source: CoinGecko, Index Cooperation, Indexed Finance, Powerpool, Tokensets. Taken as at 1st April 2021
* When the user swap one of the underlying assets from one to another
** Annualized

Index Cooperative

The management fees of each index are split between Index Coop and the associated methodologist. The fees are as follows - DPI: 0.95%, CGI: 0.60%, FLI: 1.95%. There are no exit fees for DPI and CGI. Only FLI has an exit fee of 0.1%.

Indexed Finance

To cover impermanent loss, a 2% swap fee is charged and distributed to the LP holders in the form of the input token in any swap when you mint or burn an index token from or to one of its component assets. This 2% fee is not charged if you mint using all of the underlyings, or redeem back to all the underlying assets.

However, you will be charged a fixed 0.5% fee when burning any of the index token, which is distributed back to protocol users who have staked the native NDX governance token.

PowerPool Concentrated Voting Power

There are three types of fees: Entry, Swap, and Exit fees. If you were to mint an index token, you would be charged 0.1% as an entry fee. 0.2% swap fees apply to users who swap one governance token for another. The swap fee is then split evenly between the index fund liquidity providers and the treasury. If you exit the indices, there is an additional 0.1% fee.

From the fee comparison above, Index Coop would stand to earn the most revenue as it charges the highest fees. Indexed Finance only has one source of revenue - an exit fee of 0.5%. Powerpool meanwhile has a more diversified income from minting, swapping, and exit fees.

As a fund investor, you are likely to be a long-term holder, thus fees matter.

In this case, the index token PIPT would be the cheapest option relative to DPI and DEFI5. With PIPT and DEFI5, there is no ongoing cost, unlike DPI at 0.95% per annum.

Protocol Strategies

It is important we understand each protocol's strategies to understand their vision and direction on their decentralized indices products.

Index Cooperation

Below is a summary of how the team onboards a product on their protocol:

1. New product ideas are proposed and discussed with their community members
2. Product application is submitted to the community in the governance forum
3. The first snapshot vote is taken to move forward with vetting review
4. The passed proposals are reviewed by Index Coop's team.
5. The second snapshot vote is taken on product release
6. Product launch

Index Coop has a stringent process and needs two stages of community voting for product approval. For example, it took roughly three months to launch the Flexible Leveraged Index (FLI) since the first snapshot vote.

Indexed Finance

Relative to Index Coop, Indexed Finance moves faster.

For example, ORCL5, the first index fund that was up for voting, took a total of 18 days to launch starting from the voting stage.[56,57]

Powerpool Concentrated Voting Power
The latest index product by Powerpool was Yearn Lazy Ape, which was put up for governance voting on 17 January 2021. It was only launched almost three months later, on 3 March 2021.[58,59]

Currently, Index Coop and Powerpool have four index products under them. Indexed Finance has seven indices.

Although Indexed Finance appears to be the fastest one at launching indices, Index Coop and PowerPool teams work with their methodologist to ensure their products are safe and consider all associated factors and risks.

Indexed Finance may start moving slower with the launch of their Sigma program. The Sigma program allows Indexed Finance to collaborate with external partners, which would require a longer time. For instance, the DEGEN index fund, a collaboration with Redphonecrypto was announced in late December 2020 and only went live three months later.

Fund Weighting

Metrics	Index Cooperative (INDEX)		Index Finance (NDX)				PowerPool Concentrated Voting Power (CVP)			
	DPI	CGI	DEFI5	CC10	ORCL5	DEGEN	PIPT	ASSY	YETI	YLA
Fund Weighting	Market Cap-Weighted	A bi-level approach, accounting historical volatility	Sqrt of Market Cap-weighted	Sqrt of Market Cap-weighted	Sqrt of Market Cap-weighted	Sqrt of Market Cap-weighted	Equal-weighted Market Cap	Market Cap-weighted	Market Cap-Weighted	Adaptive weights proportional to vaults TVL

In general, there are three major approaches in weighing tokens in decentralized index tokens:

---

[56] (n.d.). Oracle Top 5 Token Index proposal - Proposals - Indexed Finance. Retrieved May 31, 2021, from https://forum.indexed.finance/t/oracle-top-5-token-index-proposal/89
[57] (2021, February 19). Indexed Finance on Twitter: "The $ORCL5 index is live! The initial .... Retrieved May 31, 2021, from https://twitter.com/ndxfi/status/1362839864106840064
[58] (n.d.). PowerPool - Accumulate governance power in Ethereum based .... Retrieved March 14, 2021, from https://app.powerpool.finance/
[59] (2021, January 16). Power Pool $CVP on Twitter: "Proposal 18: Yearn Lazy Ape Index .... Retrieved March 14, 2021, from https://twitter.com/powerpoolcvp/status/1350658954607509505

I. **Market Cap Weighted (e.g., DPI)**
   This method tracks each asset's market caps dynamically, where the allocation of each asset is proportional to their market capitalization relative to the other assets in the index. Indices using this method will be concentrated towards larger market capitalization coins relative to smaller ones, enabling the index to mimic the actual market performance closely.

II. **Square Root of Market Cap Weighted (e.g., DEFI5)**
   All indices on Indexed Finance are based on the square root of the market capitalization relative to each underlying asset. This approach dampens the effect of market performance skewed towards larger market capitalizations coins.

III. **Equally-Weighted Market Cap Weighted (e.g., PIPT)**
   This method sets asset allocation equally. For example, there are eight underlying assets in PIPT. Hence each of the assets is set to 12.5% weightage. An equal-weighted strategy is driven by price momentum and would favor smaller market capitalization coins. Smaller market capitalization coins are given the same importance as large market capitalization coins.

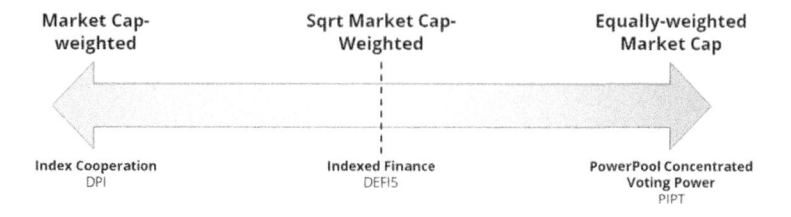

Market Cap-weighted	Sqrt Market Cap-Weighted	Equally-weighted Market Cap
Index Cooperation DPI	Indexed Finance DEFI5	PowerPool Concentrated Voting Power PIPT

Associated Risks

Here are the three big risks when it comes to investing in these DeFi indices protocols and funds:

I.   Code is Law
Although all the top-3 indices protocols have been audited, investors need to keep in mind that audited protocols are not hack-proof.[60,61,62,63] Despite the audit, there have been numerous hacks happening in the crypto space, and more often than not, the funds are irrecoverable.

II.   Mercenary Capital
Most indices protocols have liquidity mining programs to incentivize liquidity providers and bootstrap liquidity for the index tokens. However, much of these capitals are typically known as "mercenary capital". These capital are purely searching for high returns and will exit as soon as another protocol with a higher yield appears. Consequently, once liquidity mining rewards dry up, it may result in mass withdrawals leading to a downward spiral for the indices protocol.

III.   Systemic Risk
In DeFi, protocols can be stacked on top of each other like a money lego. However, composability can be a double-edged sword as it introduces systemic risk. For example, Yearn Lazy APE (YLA) by PowerPool has ten different risk exposures from its five underlying Yearn's stablecoin vaults.

---

[60] (2020, September 4). Set Protocol Audit – OpenZeppelin blog. Retrieved March 17, 2021, from https://blog.openzeppelin.com/set-protocol-audit/

[61] (n.d.). Security Audits - Power Pool. Retrieved March 17, 2021 from https://docs.powerpool.finance/security/security-audits

[62] (n.d.). monoceros-alpha/audit-indexed-finance-2020-10 - GitHub. Retrieved March 17, 2021, from https://github.com/monoceros-alpha/audit-indexed-finance-2020-10

[63] (n.d.). maxsam4/indexed-finance-review - GitHub. Retrieved March 17, 2021, from https://github.com/maxsam4/indexed-finance-review

1. yvCurve-Compound (8.6%) 2. yvCurve-3pool (36%) 3. yCurve-GUSD (17.3%)	4. yUSD (27%) 5. yvCurve-BUSD (11.1%)

These assets interact with ten different protocols and therefore have ten different risks. The ten protocols involved in Yearn's stablecoin vault are:

1. Yearn 2. Curve 3. Compound (cDai & cUSD) 4. Maker (DAI) 5. Tether (USDT)	6. Circle (USDC) 7. Gemini (GUSD) 8. Binance (BUSD) 9. TrustToken (TUSD) 10. PowerPool (YLA)

Notable Mentions

- **BasketDAO - Interest Bearing DPI (BDPI)**
  A product of the BasketDAO team, BDPI is the interest-bearing version of DPI. The difference is that the underlying assets are lent out to lending protocols such as Aave and Compound to earn a yield. As a result, the returns for holding this index fund is expected to be higher than DPI.

- **Cryptex Finance - Total Crypto Market Cap (TCAP)**
  Created by Cryptex Finance, TCAP allows you to have exposure to the entire crypto market. The team also runs Prysmatic Labs, one of the research teams behind ETH 2.0.

Conclusion

We are still very early in the decentralized indices sector, which we expect will grow rapidly in the coming months and years. As a long-term investor, we highly recommend that you look into a fund's past performance, check every chargeable fee, and consider the fund strategy utilized. It is also advisable to choose funds based on your risk appetite, factoring in the asset category you wish to have exposure in.

Recommended Readings

1. DeFi Indices Explained
   https://newsletter.banklesshq.com/p/the-best-defi-indices-for-your-crypto
2. How to buy Indices with Argent
   https://www.argent.xyz/learn/how-to-buy-defi/
3. Dashboard on DeFi Indices
   https://duneanalytics.com/0xBoxer/indices-products

CHAPTER 10: DECENTRALIZED PREDICTION MARKETS

Prediction markets are markets created for participants to bet on the outcomes of future events. A great example of conventional prediction markets is sports betting platforms.

Decentralized prediction markets utilize blockchain technology to create prediction markets on just about anything. For example, prediction markets can be made based on when the Bitcoin price will exceed $100,000 or who the next US president would be.

Proponents of decentralized prediction markets believe that centralized platforms put users at a disadvantage.[64] Standard practices include high transaction fees, delaying withdrawals, and freezing accounts. Moreover, most of today's traditional betting platforms are focused on sports betting, limiting the types of prediction markets available to the general public.

Decentralized prediction market protocols have been designed to empower users by allowing them to create their own markets.

---

[64] Beneš, N. (2018, April 6). *How manipulation-resistant are Prediction Markets?* Medium. https://blog.gnosis.pm/how-manipulation-resistant-are-prediction-markets-710e14033d62

How do Prediction Protocols work?

Unlike conventional prediction markets, prediction protocols are decentralized and have to rely on innovative methods to function. We can roughly break down a prediction's protocol process map into two primary sections:

1. Market-Making
2. Resolution

Market-Making

In market-making prediction protocols, there are two types of shares (outcome tokens) in a basic category-type market: YES (long) shares and NO (short) shares. Payout is determined based on whether an event occurs.

In a simple prediction market, a single YES share (which is often denominated as $1) pays out $1 if the event in question occurs and pays out $0 if the event does not occur. Each NO share pays out $1 if the event does not occur and $0 if it does occur. Category-type markets utilize this basic principle, for example, 'Will BTC surpass $100,000 by 31 December 2021?'

Another example of a question is: 'Who will be the US President in 2025? In this case, there may be more than two options, such as:

A. Joe Biden
B. Kamala Harris
C. Trump

The above functions similarly as a basis category-type market, except three shares have been included to represent the three different answers instead of two. The price of shares is based on how much buyers are willing to pay and how much sellers are willing to accept. In other words, the system is an autonomous bookie whose rates (i.e. price) are determined by the market's weighing of probabilities.

On the other hand, markets with a range of answers and associated rewards will operate differently. Known as scalar markets, outcomes vary within defined parameters.

A good way to envision scalar markets is to think of them as possessing outcomes that set out to determine who is the *most* right/wrong as opposed to who is *definitively* right/wrong.

Let's use an example here with the following assumptions:

"What will the price of Bitcoin be on 10 November 2021?"

Precision = $10k
Range = $0 - $200k

With this setup, a user may choose either $10k, $20k, $30k, and so on.

Unlike YES/NO and Multiple Choice markets, the payout from scalar markets is distributed to all participants. Each payout is based on where the price falls within the range relative to the outcome. So if on the closing date, the price of BTC is $198k, then the pot will be split between all purchasers. However, the closest answer to the $200k strike price will receive the highest payoff amount in proportion to the size of their bets.

For a scalar market, price per share translates to a particular strike price in the underlying asset, or whatever is being predicted.

Resolution

Using the same example as before, how does one determine whether Bitcoin surpasses $100,000 by 31 December 2021? Do I refer to Coinbase, or do I refer to the aggregate prices of all exchanges on CoinGecko? In practice, the market maker will specify the resolution source before its creation. So in this scenario, one may establish Coinbase as the resolution source.

The real issue is who provides this information, and how is that information validated? For price-based markets, public APIs can be drawn and extracted from online sources. Oracles can also be used but may not cover all market types, such as "Will Vitalik Buterin marry before 2022?"

Considering the size and scope of prediction markets, purely relying on tech is impossible. Prediction protocols recognize this and rely on humans to ensure that the information is accurate.

However, how does one ensure that bad actors do not manipulate the market by supplying false information? Unlike conventional prediction markets, prediction protocols are decentralized and do not have the resources to monitor and regulate every market. To resolve this issue, prediction protocols have come up with different solutions. We will cover two examples in this chapter.

Prediction Market Protocols

Augur

Augur operates on the Ethereum network and uses a resolution model which incentivizes users to report information accurately through rewards and penalties.[65] After the market has closed, it will enter a reporting period where either the market creator or someone else (depending on who the market creator specified as the Designated Reporter) may supply the information to validate the results.

---

[65] Augur. *The Ultimate Guide to Decentralized Prediction Markets*. Augur. (n.d.). https://augur.net/blog/prediction-markets.

During the reporting period, the Designated Reporter (DR) will have 24 hours to submit a report on the market's outcome. The catch is that the DR must stake the protocol's native token before reporting their findings.

There are two versions of the native tokens: REP and REPv2. REPv2 tokens only apply for Augur's v2 protocol update, whereas REP is migratable and redeemable for REPv2 tokens.

The key difference is that REP holders may not participate in a fork, should there be a substantial dispute over an outcome. However, we will collectively refer to them as REP tokens for simplicity's sake because they are functionally similar.

Whichever outcome the DR selects becomes the Tentative Winning Outcome (TOR). Once a DR submits the TOR, it is open to dispute. Contested results will open up the dispute period for one week, where anyone with REP can stake on the answer that they believe is correct. One round lasts for one week but can reach up to sixteen rounds.

If there is no dispute, a portion of the winnings is used to compensate the DR. This fee rate is variable and determined based on all REP tokens' total aggregate value in circulation.

If there is a dispute, users who staked on the winning outcome will get a share of the REP that was staked on the losing outcome. This is on top of the fee that reporters will receive. Users who staked on the losing outcome will not receive any fees and lose all their REP tokens.

Omen

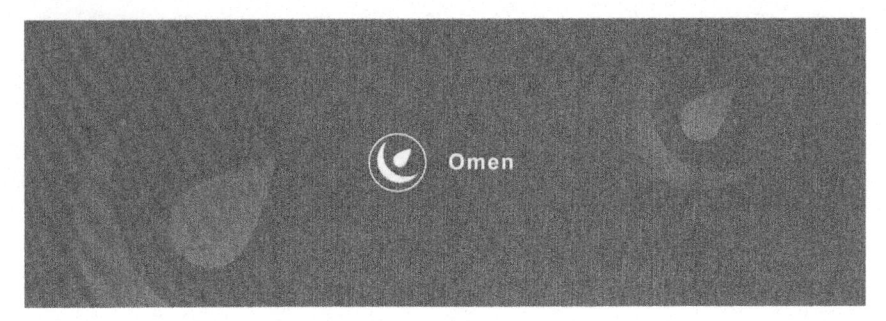

Omen is a prediction protocol developed by DXdao and powered by the Gnosis protocol - it operates on Ethereum and the xDai sidechain.[66] Gnosis allows Omen users to engage with their token framework, an event-based asset class that comprises the building blocks of prediction markets.

Unlike Augur, Omen does not incentivize the community to report and resolve markets. Instead, they rely on a decentralized community-driven oracle known as Reality.eth which verifies real-world events for smart contracts.

Most markets will be resolved following through Reality.eth where the community members will decide on topics based on fees. Users on Reality.eth post bonds for their chosen outcomes, and they can be challenged by someone posting a new answer and doubling the bond. This may happen for several cycles until the posting stops, where the answer is determined by the last person posting their bond.

Once Reality.eth has internally completed their resolution obligations, they will supply the outcome to the respective Omen market. If an Omen user is unhappy with the findings, he/she may (through Reality.eth) appeal to an external arbitrator, Kleros.

Kleros randomly selects jurors from a juror pool and offers game-theory based incentives to ensure the anonymous voters reach consensus. Those who stake on the correct outcomes collect from those who staked on the incorrect outcomes (much like Augur).

---

[66] *Omen Prediction Markets*. Omen. (n.d.). https://omen.eth.link/.

Notably, DXdao, the self-governing organization behind Omen, may also decide to function as a competent arbiter in the future.

What are the other key differences between Augur and Omen?

As we have just discussed, both Augur and Omen have very different approaches to the resolution process. Augur addresses the oracle problem by creating an ecosystem of incentives and penalties which regulate the reliability of reporting information. Omen outsources their reporting needs to an external DAO (using similar principles as Augur's approach). In that sense, Augur is more self-sufficient.

In terms of liquidity, markets on Augur v2 use 0x's off-chain order book - orders are collected off-chain, and settled on-chain. In contrast, Omen's Automated Market Makers operate similarly to DEXs like Uniswap, which creates large liquidity pools for token pairs.

Although both outcome tokens use the ERC-1155 standard, Omen's tokens may be wrapped into the ERC-20 standard and accessed outside their network - this allows Omen to access DEXs and tap into larger liquidity pools. On the other hand, Augur's outcome tokens are confined to their protocol's internal liquidity pools.

For a concise comparison of Augur and Omen, you can refer to the table below:[67]

---

[67] Gnosis. (2020, July 5). *Omen and the Next Generation of Prediction Markets*. Medium. https://blog.gnosis.pm/omen-and-the-next-generation-of-prediction-markets-2e7a2dd604e

	Augur	**Omen**
Information Validation System	Uses internal rewards and penalties to control	Outsourced to external DAO-type arbitrators
Liquidity	Traditional order book + 0x protocol for decentralized implementation	Automated Market Maker
Governance	Admin key that are burned means there are no further updates	DAO
Tokens	REP (REP + REPv2)	-
Outcome Tokens	ERC-1155	ERC-1155 but may be wrapped into ERC-20 tokens to access liquidity pools from other DEXs
Market Pairs	DAI	30 pairs
Supported Blockchains	Ethereum	Ethereum and xDai

We do not have access to either protocol's market data, but an arbitrary scan (conducted on 28 April 2021) of both protocol's websites will show that there is very little activity going on.

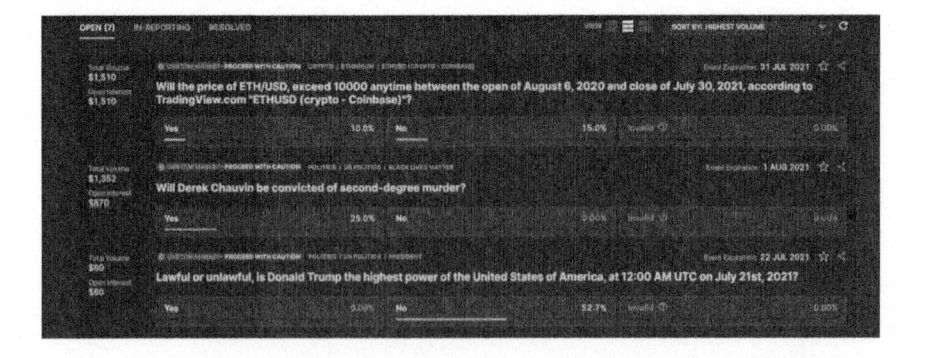

For Augur, there are only seven markets created. Only the top three have actual trading volume which collectively add up to just shy of $3,000.

> What will Joe Biden's Presidential Job Approval Rating be after 100 days in office? (Source: Gallup)
>
> ⭐ 54.00 %   6 days remaining   3.25K xDAI - Liquidity
>
> What will the average USD price of CTX be on May 1st, 2021? (REF: most liquid of Uniswap, Sushiswap, or Swapr pools)
>
> ⭐ 18.50 USD   5 days remaining   2.19K xDAI - Liquidity
>
> Will Compound Chain be launched and usable by the end of Q2 2021?
>
> ⭐ No (73.40%)   2 months remaining   1.63K xDAI - Liquidity
>
> Will EIP-1559 be deployed on Mainnet before August 2021?
>
> ⭐ Yes (75.33%)   3 months remaining   1.13K xDAI - Liquidity

And as for Omen, there are only four markets but have a combined trading volume of roughly $7,200 (not reflected in the image but is shown on another webpage).

Associated Risks

The biggest concern with prediction markets is the reliability of data. While there are multiple profit-based incentives to minimize data manipulation, irrational actors could try to jeopardize outcomes. Furthermore, challenged outcomes could lead to situations that are time-consuming and costly.

Notable Mentions

- ◰ **Polymarket**
  As of April 2021, Polymarket has a beta product that is live on Ethereum. The whitepaper for the protocol has yet to be published, but they appear to be a hybrid between centralized and decentralized

structures. The protocol seems far more popular than Augur or Omen - our quick scan on 28 April 2021 showed a booming market activity with over sixty prediction markets. The most popular market alone reached about $2 million in trading volume.

Conclusion

Prediction markets is an interesting space because there are implications beyond betting - it allows users to hedge risks. Traditional derivatives allow buyers and sellers to hedge against particular outcomes by holding the right to trade a specific good in the future at a particular price. For example, a rice farmer may enter into a derivative contract to sell 1,000 kilograms of rice on 31 December 2021 for $5,000 if he expects the price to be lower during that time.

Prediction markets can be based on anything and not just rice. Rather than hedge against the price of rice, the rice farmer may decide to hedge against the weather instead. In other words, prediction markets allow users to hedge against more specific risks.

Prediction protocols provide a platform for anyone to hedge against anything. Not only that, but prediction markets can also act as "de facto" polls. Participants in prediction protocols effectively share their opinions on different matters, which can be extrapolated for general insights on a wide range of topics.

The future for prediction protocols is exciting because their principles could be the foundation for real-life use cases. One could imagine using similar resolution systems to bring legal contracts on-chain, as the arbitration methods function very similarly to the juror-based justice system. However, in the near term, we expect more protocols to leverage the power of prediction protocols and utilize them to create innovative hedging instruments.

Recommended Readings

1. Prediction Market Basics
   https://augur.net/blog/prediction-markets
2. Pricing in Prediction Markets
   https://medium.com/veil-blog/a-guide-to-augur-market-economics-16c66d956b6c
3. How resistant Prediction Markets are to Market-Manipulation
   https://blog.gnosis.pm/how-manipulation-resistant-are-prediction-markets-710e14033d62
4. Key differences between Augur and Omen
   https://blog.gnosis.pm/omen-and-the-next-generation-of-prediction-markets-2e7a2dd604e

CHAPTER 11: DECENTRALIZED FIXED-INTEREST RATE PROTOCOLS

If we look at traditional finance, where most financial consumers reside, globalization has led to an increased demand for stable financial ecosystems. Indeed, it has been over 20 years since the European Parliament first acknowledged the need for more price stability in their working paper entitled "The Determination of Interest Rates":

> "The integration of the world's financial markets is increasing the pressure of external factors in the determination of domestic monetary policies. In addition, though the approaches of the world's major central banks towards the conduct of monetary policy differ in detail, there is broad agreement on fundamentals: the **pursuit of price stability and the stability of financial markets**."[68]

The key point here is integration. Analogous to how the crypto industry operates, the space has matured to a point where DeFi has become the industry standard for protocols. Often referred to as financial Legos, blockchain technology has allowed developers to integrate with other protocols and build innovative financial products. However, such progress does not change the fact that the crypto industry is unpredictable and highly volatile.

---

[68] Patterson, B., & Lygnerud, K. (n.d.). *The Determination of Interest Rates*. https://www.europarl.europa.eu/workingpapers/econ/pdf/116_en.pdf.

Stable interest rates are an important facet of every financial ecosystem. Although there is an abundance of lending protocols and yield aggregators that offer interest rates to lenders in the crypto industry, relatively few of them offer fixed interest rates.

With the growing popularity of yield farming and the demand for more stable lending and borrowing rates, several DeFi protocols have attempted to address the ever-increasing demand for stable interest rates and become the hallmark for reliability. This has bred a new class of protocols known as Fixed-Interest Rate Protocols (FIRPs).

Compared to traditional finance, where fixed interest rates come in the form of fixed deposits (or bonds), FIRPs leverage their underlying tokenomics structure and offer different incentives to maintain their interest rates. At this point, the FIRP ecosystem can be broadly classified into two categories:

1. Lending/Borrowing
2. Yield Aggregators

Even under this umbrella classification, FIRPs come in many shapes and sizes. Each protocol has its method of "fixing" interest rates which leads to different use-cases. Some offer a "fixed interest rate" or a "fixed interest-earning ratio". Moreover, some FIRPs do not offer fixed interest rates at all but rather create an environment that facilitates fixed-interest rates.

We will cover three examples in this chapter.

Overview of Fixed Interest Rates Protocols

Yield

YIELD

Yield is a decentralized lending system that offers fixed-rate lending and interest rate markets using a new kind of token called "fyTokens". The current iteration (Version 1) includes fyTokens for the DAI stablecoin. Called "fyDai", this new class of tokens enables fully collateralized fixed-rate borrowing and lending in DAI.[69]

fyDai tokens are Ethereum-based tokens (ERC20) that may be redeemed for DAI after a predetermined maturity date. fyDai are analogous to zero-coupon or discount bonds.

To mint or sell fyDai, borrowers will have to put up ETH collateral that currently follows the same collateralization ratio as MakerDao (150%). Lenders buy fyDai, which will typically be priced at a discount to DAI. The difference between the discounted value and 1 DAI (the maturity value) represents the lender's lending rate or the borrower's borrowing rate.

Although the value of fyDai reflects the borrowing/lending interest rate, it could also be traded in the market as a bond instrument on its own. This is possible because there are several "series" of fyDai, each with a different maturity date.

The system is tightly integrated and complementary to Maker. Maker users can "migrate" their DAI vaults into fyDai vaults, locking in a fixed interest rate for a period and converting back to a Maker vault after maturity.

Interest rates are determined by the market's valuation of fyDai (with each series having its own maturity date). For lenders, a higher valuation of fyDai will lower the interest rates earned once it reaches maturity.

---

[69] *Introduction.* Introduction · GitBook. (n.d.). https://docs.yield.is/.

Conversely, a higher valuation of fyDai will lower the borrowing rate for borrowers as it would be sold off to purchase the respective stablecoin (e.g., DAI). This means that depending on the time of purchase of fyDai tokens, both borrowers and lenders can determine their borrowing/lending interest rate.

Example:

Assume that a borrower deposits 1.5 ETH as collateral and intends to borrow 900 DAI at an annual borrowing rate of 10%. Once executed, the borrower will receive 1000 fyDai with a value of 900 DAI - this will be automatically sold off in the marketplace by the protocol, and the borrower will receive 900 DAI. At the end of the one year maturity period, the borrower will have to repay 990 DAI if they wish to withdraw their collateral.

For lenders, assume that a lender lends 1000 Dai. In return, the lender receives 1000 fyDai which will accrue value as it approaches maturity. Initially, 1 fyDai received is worth 1 Dai, but after one year has lapsed, 1 fyDai will be worth 0.909 Dai. The lender may then redeem 1000 fyDai for 1100 Dai. This effectively puts the lending interest rate at 10%.

In practice, users can only select fyDai series that have been pre-programmed by Yield. This is similar to how regular bond instruments function, where there are different bond rates and maturity periods.

In Q1 2021, Yield has proposed integration with the MakerDao protocol that would permit MakerDao to be a fixed-rate Dai lender to Yield borrowers. The proposal has been accepted by MakerDao governance and is in the process of being integrated into the MakerDao protocol.

Yield is also expecting to launch version 2 of their protocol in Summer 2021. It will include new collateral types and permit borrowing of assets beyond Dai, like USDC and Tether.

> **Did you know?**[70]
>
> In January 2021, an anonymous individual paid off his mortgage loan with a bank and is now paying down his refinanced home loan through DeFi protocol Notional Finance. Notional has similar functionalities as Yield as they also use a zero-coupon bond system via the introduction of a novel financial primitive called fCash.

Saffron.Finance

![saffron.finance]

Saffron Finance is a decentralized yield aggregator for liquidity providers and was one of the first protocols to utilize a tranche-based system.[71] Tranches are segments created from liquidity pools that are divided by risk, time to maturity, or other characteristics to be marketable to different investors.

With the various tranches, Saffron Finance users can select different portfolios based on their preferred risk appetite. More importantly, the Saffron Finance ecosystem creates an internal insurance system where investors in the higher-risk tranches insure investors in the lower-risk tranches.

Saffron Finance's native token, SFI, is primarily used as a utility token to access tranche A, the higher-earning tranche. However, SFI can also be staked to earn pool rewards and vote on protocol governance.

A tranche system allows one to divide up the earnings and create different earning rates for different pools. In Saffron Finance's case, the A tranche makes ten times the earnings of tranche AA. Tranche S offers a variable

---

[70] Fernau, O. (2021, February 2). *Engineer Becomes His Own Lender in First DeFi Mortgage*. The Defiant - DeFi News. https://thedefiant.io/engineer-becomes-his-own-lender-in-first-defi-mortgage/.

[71] *saffron.finance*. Saffron. (n.d.). https://app.saffron.finance/#docs.

interest rate that balances the A and AA tranches; they are always in a perfect equilibrium to maintain the fixed-interest earning ratio of ten times between tranche A and tranche AA.

> **Example**
>
> If Tranche AA earns 100 DAI:
>
> 1) Tranche A will earn 1,000 DAI
> 2) Tranche S will earn DAI at a rate that ensures Tranche A pays off 10 times more than Tranche AA
>
> If, however, there is a platform risk (e.g., black swan event), Tranche AA will get their deposited assets and earnings first - this is taken from Tranche A's principal and interest earnings.

Horizon Finance

HORIZON

Unlike conventional yield aggregators, Horizon allows users to create their own markets based on game-theory principles.[72] Game theory envisions an environment where there are only rational actors. In such a hypothetical situation, buyers and sellers will make optimal decisions based on the available information.

Horizon allows users to submit their collateral into a liquidity pool, which is then lent to lending protocols such as Compound. To provide fixed interest rates to users, Horizon invites users to submit their sealed bids for fixed interest rates (acting as yield caps) or floating interest rates in each round.

---

[72] *Whitepaper*. Horizon. (n.d.). https://docs.horizon.finance/general/whitepaper.

The bids are revealed after each round, thus creating an order book of bids. The protocol will rank the bids from the lowest interest rate to the highest interest rate. The lending protocol's variable earnings are then distributed from the lowest interest rate bids to the highest interest rate bids, with any excess income spilling over into the floating pool.

One notable feature is that all bids will be displayed on Horizon's website. The displayed bids allow users to actively compete and ascertain which interest rates are the most popular. On top of that, users can freely amend their bids, including switching to the floating rate. Horizon essentially doubles up as an interest prediction protocol.

Example

To illustrate this, let's say that the round for Pool X lasts from 1 May 2021 - 14 May 2021:

On 1st May,
- Participant A deposits 100,000 DAI and bids that he will earn a 20% interest rate.
- Participant B deposits 100,000 DAI and bids the floating rate.

On 7th May,
- Participant C deposits 100,000 DAI and bids that he will earn a 10% interest rate.

At this point, Participant A reconsiders his bid as Participant C submitted a much lower bid. If Pool X earns too little, he may not get anything at all.

On 13th May,
- Participant A amends his bid to a 5% interest rate.

After the round ends, let's say the 300,000 DAI in Pool X managed to earn an interest rate of 4% for a total of 461 DAI, therefore:

> - Participant A fulfills his bid and gets 192 DAI, earning 5% interest rate.
> - Participant C partially completes his bid and gets the remainder 269 DAI, which is a 7% interest rate. His original bid of 10%, if fully fulfilled, would have generated 383 DAI during the two weeks period if Pool X had earned sufficient interest.
> - Participant B fails in his bid and does not get anything.

As you can see, there are a lot of mind games involved! Moreover, interest rates are not technically fixed. However, the system rewards users who can gauge the amount of interest they should earn from their bids. This incentivizes users to conform to a 'safe' bid if they are uncertain about the amount they could earn. Bidding too high or bidding the floating rate could result in lesser gains or none at all. Thus 'safe' bids effectively become the 'de facto' fixed interest rate over time.

Which FIRP should I use?

FIRPs cannot be lumped into a single basket and compared side-by-side. For one, lending protocols are very different from yield aggregators.

Before even looking at more profit-oriented metrics like the competitiveness of interest rates, we should be looking at the FIRP's ability to maintain their "fixed interest rate", which is effectively their functionalities. And if we were to breakdown how FIRPs operate, there are essentially three defining characteristics that revolve around their promise of fixed-interest rates:

I. **What kind of promises are they making?**
Different protocols make different promises. For example, Saffron Finance promises that if you participate in Tranche A, you will earn 10 times more than Tranche AA. Horizon does not even make any promises as to how much you would earn. Understanding the type of promise made allows users to decide which protocol offers their preferred product.

II. **How do they intend to maintain that promise?**
Each type of promise requires a different methodology. For example, Saffron Finance offers insurance to Tranche AA users by giving them the earnings first, in the event of a deficit. Understanding how each promise is maintained allows users to determine which protocol is more reliable.

III. **How dependent are they on external agents to maintain that promise?**
Developing protocol mechanisms that influence user behavior are essential to all FIRPs. For example, Yield requires relatively even ratios of lenders and borrowers to maintain fixed interest rates. Identifying such traits allows users to determine how exposed the protocol's promise is to factors outside their direct control.

If we consider these criteria, it is impossible to say which would be the best fit for you. Ultimately, it boils down to each individual's preferred risk appetite, the type of financial instrument required, and the belief in the underlying protocol's mechanisms. And perhaps more importantly, the industry is still nascent because many protocols are still getting established - they have yet to prove themselves, especially during difficult market conditions which threaten their ability to offer fixed-interest rates.

Associated Risks

One of the most significant risks is a FIRP's ability to provide fixed-interest rates. Most of these protocols rely on external agents or other users to actively participate in the protocol to drive market functionality.

If there is an inactive community or a disproportionate amount of user profiles and liquidity (e.g., more lenders than borrowers for Yield, or more participants in Tranche A than Tranche AA for Saffron Finance), FIRPs may not be able to back their fixed-interest rates.

Notable Mentions

- **Notional**

  Notional facilitates fixed-rate, fixed-term lending and borrowing of crypto-assets. Much like Yield Protocol, both protocols have very similar functionalities as Notional creates a zero-coupon bond system via the introduction of a novel financial primitive called fCash. There are, however, some key differences. In particular, Notional has a different Automated Market Maker and different collateral options.

- **BarnBridge**

  BarnBridge leverages a tranche system (similarly to Saffron Finance) for yield-based products. However, BarnBridge also has another product (SMART Alpha) that offers exposure to market prices through tranched volatility derivatives.

- **88mph**

  88mph is a yield aggregator which offers fixed-interest rates. They are able to maintain their rates through the introduction of floating-rate bonds and a unique tokenomics structure that helps influence market behavior.

- **Pendle**

  Pendle is an upcoming protocol that allows users to tokenize future yield, which can then be sold for upfront cash. Essentially, Pendle will calculate your expected yield, effectively locking in your interest rates.

Conclusion

FIRPs are a new suite of protocols that are bound to become a staple in the DeFi scene. We highlighted three examples because they are innovative and able to showcase DeFi's potential when combined with traditional fixed-income instruments.

There are a lot of exciting developments in this space that offer unique products and services. We already have protocols combining price prediction and yield aggregation; imagine if a bank offered competitive betting services on fixed deposit yields? We have not even discussed protocols that tokenize future yields, which essentially allow anyone to create their own bonds and sell them off for upfront cash.

As this area develops further, we expect more institutional interest in FIRP products. Fixed-income instruments have always been commonplace in traditional finance. However, as aggregate debt levels and inflation continue to rise, and the value of the US dollar continues to fall, FIRPs may offer more reliable yields.

Recommended Readings

1. Report on Tranche-based Lending in DeFi
   https://consensys.net/blog/codefi/how-tranche-lending-will-bring-fixed-interest-rates-to-defi/
2. Fixed-Interest Rate Protocol Highlights
   https://messari.io/article/fixed-income-protocols-the-next-wave-of-defi-innovation
3. Why Fixed-Interest Rates are Important
   https://medium.com/notional-finance/why-fixed-rates-matter-1b03991275d6

CHAPTER 12: DECENTRALIZED YIELD AGGREGATORS

Crypto gave birth to the activity of yield farming, where users can earn yields just by allocating capital in DeFi protocols. Many crypto natives have since become yield farmers, searching for farms that offer the most attractive yields.

Due to the sheer number of new yield farms being released each day, no individual can be aware of every opportunity. With sky-high returns, the opportunity cost of missing out on new yield farms is increasingly high.

Yield aggregators are born to serve the need of automating users' investment strategies, sparing them the trouble of monitoring the market for the best yield farms. Below we are going to look into several decentralized yield aggregator protocols.

Yield Aggregators Protocols

Yearn Finance

ABOUT
yearn.finance
yearn.finance defi made simple

Yearn Finance started as a passion project by Andre Cronje to automate capital-switching between lending platforms to search for the best yield offered by DeFi lending platforms. This is needed as most DeFi lending platforms provide floating rather than fixed rates. Funds are automatically shifted between dYdX, Aave, and Compound as interest rates change between these protocols.

The service includes major USD stablecoins such as DAI, USDT, USDC, and TUSD. For example, if a user deposits DAI into the Yearn Finance, the user will receive a yDAI token in return, a yield-bearing DAI token.

Later on, Yearn Finance collaborated with Curve Finance to release a yield-bearing USD token pool named yUSD. Curve Finance is a decentralized exchange that focuses on trading between assets with roughly similar value, such as USD stablecoins. yUSD is a liquidity pool that includes four y-tokens: yDAI, yUSDT, yUSDC, and yTUSD.

Holding yUSD allows users to have five sources of yields:

1. Lending yield of DAI
2. Lending yield of USDT
3. Lending yield of USDC
4. Lending yield of TUSD
5. Swap fees earned by providing liquidity to Curve Finance

yUSD is thus promoted as a superior crypto USD stablecoin than just holding the underlying stablecoins.

Vaults

Yearn Finance debuted the vault feature after its token launch, igniting a frenzy on automated yield farming, and is considered the initiator of the category of yield farming aggregator. The vaults will help users to claim liquidity mining rewards and sell the protocol's native tokens for the underlying assets.

Vaults benefit users by socializing gas costs, automating the yield generation and rebalancing process, and automatically shifting capital as opportunities arise. Users also do not need to have proficient knowledge of the underlying protocols involved. Thus the vaults represent a passive investing strategy for users. It is akin to a crypto hedge fund, where the goal is to increase the number of assets that users deposited.

Besides simple yield farming, Yearn Finance also integrated various novel strategies to help increase the vaults' return. For example, it can use any assets as collateral to borrow stablecoins and recycle the stablecoins into a stablecoin vault. Any subsequent earnings are then used to buy back the asset.

Yearn version 2 was launched on 18 January 2021.[73] Version 2 vaults can employ multiple strategies per vault (up to 20 strategies simultaneously), unlike version 1 vaults that only employ one strategy per vault.

Strategies

As a yield aggregator, Yearn Finance has leveraged the composability feature of Ethereum to the maximum extent possible. Below, we will examine how Curve Finance's liquidity mining program plays a role in Yearn Finance's vault strategy.

Curve Finance is a decentralized exchange that focuses on stablecoins pairs. It utilizes a fairly complicated governance system - veCRV is used to measure the governance voting power, which users can get by locking their CRV tokens.

---

[73] (2021, January 18). Yearn Finance Launches v2 Vaults, YFI Token Jumps ... - BeInCrypto. Retrieved May 24, 2021, from https://beincrypto.com/yearn-finance-v2-vaults-yfi-token/

- 1 CRV locked for 4 years = 1 veCRV
- 1 CRV locked for 3 years = 0.75 veCRV
- 1 CRV locked for 2 years = 0.50 veCRV
- 1 CRV locked for 1 year = 0.25 veCRV

veCRV can be used to vote for enlisting new pairs and decide how much CRV yield farming rewards will be given to each pair. More importantly, veCRV is used to determine the boosted yield farming reward available for the liquidity providers.

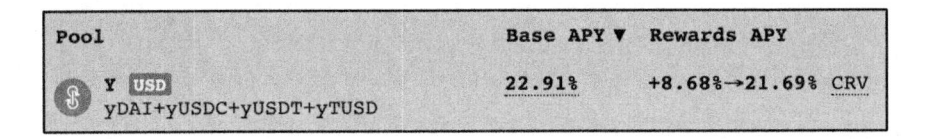

Pool	Base APY ▼	Rewards APY
Y USD yDAI+yUSDC+yUSDT+yTUSD	22.91%	+8.68%→21.69% CRV

By referring to the image above, yUSD is a pool of yield-bearing stablecoins. Users can deposit yUSD into Yearn Finance to obtain yCRV, where the CRV rewards will be harvested and sold to get more yUSD.

The Base Annual Percentage Yield (Base APY) refers to the swap fee earned by being a Liquidity Provider of the Curve pool. Rewards APY refers to the liquidity mining program rewards in the form of CRV tokens. With the use of veCRV, the base rewards of 8.68% can be scaled up to 21.69%, or 2.5 times from the base. In total, the expected return is roughly 31.59% to 44.60%.

By depositing your USD stablecoins into Yearn Finance, you will benefit from the maximum 2.5 times boosted yield farming rewards instead of having to lock your CRV to gain the boost.

Yearn Finance Partnerships

From 24 November 2020 until 3 December 2020, Yearn Finance announced a series of partnerships (dubbed Mergers and Acquisitions) of several protocols, essentially forming an alliance revolving around YFI.[74]

---

[74] (2020, December 4). Defi Lego connects as Yearn Finance announces five mergers in a .... Retrieved May 24, 2021, from https://bravenewcoin.com/insights/defi-lego-connects-as-yearn-finance-announces-five-mergers-in-a-week

- SushiSwap joined as its Automated Market Maker (AMM) arm
- Cover joined as its insurance arm
- CREAM joined as its lending arm
- Akropolis joined as its institutional service provider for vaults and upcoming lending products.
- Pickle joined as one of its strategists.

Yearn Finance has chosen to end the partnership with Cover Protocol on 5 March 2021.[75]

Yearn Finance's version 2 also incentivizes contributions from the community by sharing a percentage of profits to community strategists. Yearn Finance has also established an affiliate program with other protocols that are willing to form synergistic relationships whereby the protocols stand to receive up to 50% of revenue generated. In other words, Yearn Finance has become a large ecosystem that offers a range of yield-farming products and services.

Alpha Finance

Alpha Finance introduced leveraged yield farming through their first product Alpha Homora, allowing users to use borrowed capital to increase their exposure in their yield farming activities. Essentially, it is acting as both a lending and yield aggregator protocol.

---

[75] (2021, March 5). yearn.finance on Twitter: "We have decided to end the previously .... Retrieved May 24, 2021, from
https://twitter.com/iearnfinance/status/1367796331507552258

In Alpha Homora version 2, users can lend (to earn lending interest rate) and borrow many assets (to leverage their yield farming position), including ETH, DAI, USDT, and USDC, YFI, SNX, sUSD, DPI, UNI, SUSHI, LINK, and WBTC.

> **Example**
>
> Using the example of SUSHI/ETH as mentioned in Chapter 2, rather than yield farming with only $1,000 capital, with Alpha Homora, you can now choose to leverage two times your capital by borrowing $1,000 worth of ETH.
>
> By borrowing $1,000, you will now participate in yield farming by providing $1,000 worth of ETH and $1,000 worth of SUSHI, totaling $2,000. This strategy will only yield a profit when the swap fees and yield farming rewards are greater than the borrowing cost on Alpha Homora.
>
> Also, note that since both ETH and SUSHI are available as borrowable assets, you can yield farm on leverage by borrowing both ETH and SUSHI to minimize swapping fees.

The borrowing cost on Alpha Homora is calculated at a variable rate, affected by supply and demand. If the borrowing cost spikes suddenly due to increased borrowing, then the leveraged position may incur a loss. Another risk is when the borrowed asset increased in price as compared to the yield farming position. Using the example above, if ETH increases rapidly in price while SUSHI drops in price, the leveraged position may experience a liquidation.

Besides earning higher returns, having a leverage position on the yield farms will also expose users to higher Impermanent Loss. The profit earned is highly influenced by the choice of asset borrowed to yield farm. For example, borrowing ETH vs. USD stablecoins will result in a completely different return profile. For more details about Impermanent Loss, do refer to Chapter 5.

Alpha Homora V2 also supports Liquidity Provider (LP) tokens as collateral. For instance, users with liquidity providing position on ETH/SUSHI pool on Sushiswap will be able to deposit ETH/SUSHI LP token as collateral on

Alpha Homora V2 and borrow more ETH and SUSHI tokens to leverage yield farm.

Badger Finance

Badger DAO aims to create an ecosystem of DeFi products with the ultimate goal of bringing Bitcoin into Ethereum. It is the first DeFi project that chose to focus on Bitcoin as the main reserve asset rather than using Ethereum.

A Sett is a yield farming aggregator focused on tokenized BTC. Setts can be categorized into three main categories.

   a) Tokenized BTC Vaults
      - Inspired by Yearn Finance's vaults, initial products include Bitcoin vaults that farm CRV tokens such as SBTCCURVE, RENBTCCURVE, and TBTC/SBTCCURVE metapool.
      - They also collaborate with Harvest protocol to farm CRV and FARM tokens with RENBTCCURVE deposited in Harvest itself.

   b) LP vaults
      - To attract more users, there is a Sett for WBTC/WETH that farms SUSHI rewards.
      - Other than that, four Setts are created to bootstrap liquidity for BADGER and DIGG.
         1) WBTC/BADGER UNI LP
         2) WBTC/DIGG UNI LP

            3) WBTC/BADGER SUSHI LP
            4) WBTC/DIGG SUSHI LP

    c) Protocol Vaults
        - Users can choose to avoid Impermanent Loss and tokenized BTC risks just by staking the native BADGER and DIGG tokens into bBADGER and bDIGG vaults, earning protocol fees and yield farming rewards.

Trivia: The word Sett is chosen as it refers to a badger's home.

Harvest Finance

Starting as a Yearn Finance fork, Harvest Finance has since adopted a fast-mover strategy. It has been releasing new strategies faster than other yield aggregator protocols, even those deemed high risk.

As of April 2021, it supports an astounding 63 different farms in Ethereum alone, with categories covering stablecoins, SushiSwap, ETH 2.0, BTC, NFT, 1inch, algorithmic stablecoins, and mAssets by Mirror Protocol.

It has also recently expanded into Binance Smart Chain, offering farms on Ellipsis, Venus, Popsicle Finance, PancakeSwap, Goose Finance, and bDollar.

Harvest Finance team has released an interest-bearing FARM (iFARM) token where users can stake their FARM to earn the protocol fees.

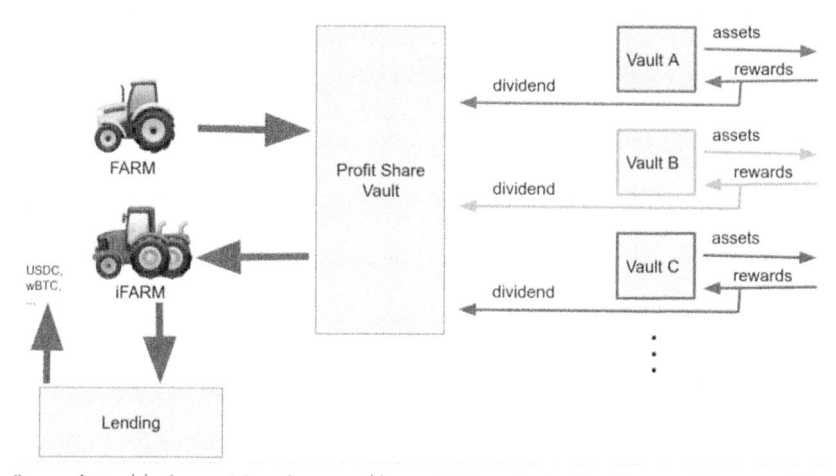

Source: https://mbroome02.medium.com/harvest-101-understanding-ifarm-and-its-potential-54d9cfe305e5

Comparison of Yield Aggregators

	Yearn Finance	Alpha Finance	Badger DAO	Harvest Finance
Management Fee	2%	-	-	-
Performance Fee	20%	-	20%	30%
Borrowing Fee	-	10%	-	-

One of the important factors to consider when deciding which yield aggregators to use is the fees charged. Yearn Finance follows the standard hedge fund model, where it charges a 2% management fee and 20% performance fee. Badger DAO and Harvest Finance charge only a performance fee of 20% and 30%, respectively. Alpha Finance's Alpha Homora v1 on Ethereum and BSC collect 10% of the interest charged based on the amount borrowed for leverage and collects 20% on Alpha Homora V2.

The fee structure suggests that users may have to pay the highest fees by investing with Yearn Finance - 2% of the amount invested is taken away annually regardless of whether the strategies deployed are earning a return or not.

Charging performance fees can be considered fairer as it just means a lower return for the users. Yearn Finance can charge a premium due to its industry-leading position, with a lot of its vaults being integrated with other protocols such as Alchemix, Powerpool, and Inverse Finance.

	Yearn Finance	Alpha Finance	Badger DAO	Harvest Finance
TVL ($ Mil)	2,000	936	1,140	527
Market Cap ($ Mil)	1,305	434	287	113
FDV ($ Mil)	1,348	1,810	975	180
Market Cap/TVL	0.65	0.46	0.25	0.21
FDV/TVL	0.67	1.93	0.86	0.34

Data taken as of 1 April 2021

Yearn Finance still maintains the lead in terms of Total Value Locked (TVL), while Harvest Finance seems to be the most undervalued among the Yield Aggregators. Meanwhile, Alpha Finance is the most overvalued, based on the ratio of Fully Diluted Valuation against Total Value Locked (FDV/TVL).

Associated Risks

Yield aggregators are exposed to a high risk of hacks due to their nature of seeking high yields from riskier protocols. Out of the four protocols, only Badger DAO has yet to be hacked (as of April 2021).

Integration with insurance protocols is still lackluster, which may be the biggest bottleneck to further growing the sector's Total Value Locked. With the launch of more insurance protocols, we may see the launch of insured yield aggregator products in the future.

Notable Mentions

- **Pancake Bunny**
    Pancake Bunny is the biggest yield aggregator in the Binance Smart Chain ecosystem. It only provides farms that are based on PancakeSwap. The low gas fee on Binance Smart Chain allows for a

more frequent re-staking strategy, thereby compounded yield and resulting in higher APY. The offered farms consistently provide yields that are higher than 100%.

- **AutoFarm**
  AutoFarm is a cross-chain yield farming aggregator, supporting Binance Smart Chain and Huobi ECO Chain. Like Pancake Bunny, AutoFarm offers a higher frequency of compounding and thus higher APY for its farms. It is the second-largest yield aggregator in the Binance Smart Chain ecosystem.

Conclusion

Yield aggregators have a similar role to actively managed funds or hedge funds. Their job is to find the best investment opportunities and earn fees from them.

In DeFi, liquidity mining programs have given birth to a specialized way of earning returns. With DeFi composability being utilized in increasingly creative ways, we predict the strategies employed by yield aggregators will get more complicated.

Most yield farming programs only live for roughly three to four months and can be changed anytime by governance. Yield aggregators help users find high-yielding farms, but new farms usually have increased risk of being hacked. It is challenging to balance the search for high yields with risks.

There is also the worry that the high yield offered by the yield aggregators may not be sustainable. As of April 2021, the high yields are partly supported by the speculative market environment. For example, a high CRV token price translates into high yield farming rewards. No one knows for sure how yields may behave in a bear market, but it has a high chance of compressing to zero. That will not be a good sight for the yield aggregators.

Recommended Readings

1. Yearn Improvement Proposal (YIP) 56 - Buyback and Build
   https://gov.yearn.finance/t/yip-56-buyback-and-build/8929
2. Yearn Improvement Proposal (YIP) 61: Governance 2.0
   https://gov.yearn.finance/t/yip-61-governance-2-0/10460
3. Upcoming Alpha Homora V2 Relaunch! What Is Included?
   https://blog.alphafinance.io/upcoming-alpha-homora-v2-relaunch-what-is-included/

PART FOUR: TECHNOLOGY UNDERPINNING DEFI

CHAPTER 13: ORACLES AND DATA AGGREGATORS

DeFi is powered by smart contracts. Sometimes, the inputs required to produce an output consist of real-world data not stored on the blockchain, such as weather conditions or traffic information. There is a need for protocols to bridge the gap by relaying off-chain data onto the blockchain for smart contracts to interact with the data.

Off-chain information is an integral part of DeFi and should always be valid and accurate. Having false data will completely misrepresent a particular project and cause major problems for DeFi. However, how do we ensure that the data provided is always accurate and can be trusted?

Some protocols aim to achieve this by transmitting and broadcasting data onto the blockchain without being manipulated or tampered with. This is usually done through a voting or consensus mechanism where validators agree on the most accurate data. Without oracles or data aggregators as the main "source of truth", bad actors can make use of false information to take advantage of unsuspecting users.

In this chapter, we will take a closer look at some of the oracles and data aggregators available such as Chainlink, Band Protocol, Graph Protocol, and Covalent. We will see how these oracles and data aggregators bridge the gap between blockchains and real-world data.

Oracle Protocols

Oracles act as a bridge between off-chain data and the blockchain, or between protocols that do not have internal data feeds to reference on-chain data. These oracles seek to relay external information to the blockchain to be verified and executed upon by smart contracts or Dapps in the DeFi ecosystem.

Chainlink

Chainlink is a framework and infrastructure for building decentralized oracle networks that securely connect smart contracts on any blockchain network to external data resources and off-chain computation. Each oracle network is secured by independent and Sybil-resistant node operators that fetch data from a multitude of off-chain data providers, aggregate the information into a single value, and deliver it on-chain to be executed upon by smart contracts.

One of the main functions of Chainlink is to deliver the most accurate asset prices through its price feeds, which can be integrated into blockchain protocols for specific use cases. For example, asset prices are very important when settling options and futures contracts upon maturity and when the assets are used as collateral for loans. Chainlink's services also include a 'Proof-of Reserve' reference feed for cross-chain tokens and a Verifiable Random Function for on-chain gaming applications.

In order to dive deeper into how Chainlink interacts with and processes data, we will look at some of the methods used by Chainlink oracles to bridge real-world data onto the blockchain.

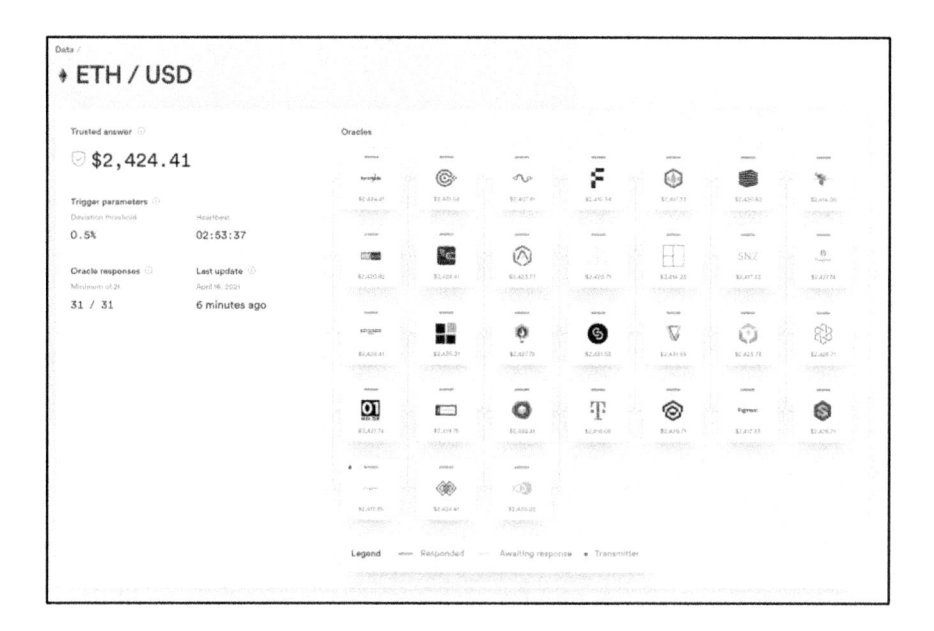

The most common method that Chainlink oracles use to bring external data on-chain is the Decentralized Data Model, a continuously updated on-chain smart contract representing a specific piece of data (e.g., the price of ETH against BTC) that can be queried on-demand in a single transaction.

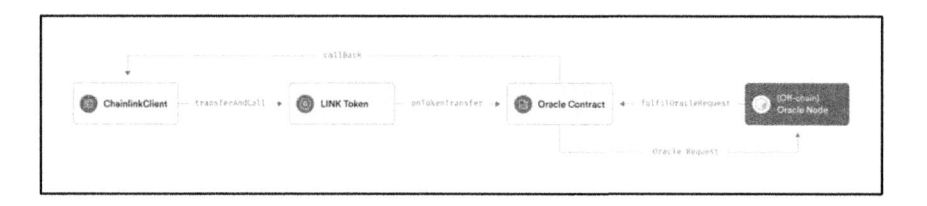

The Basic Request and Receive Model is another method where a user's smart contract requests data directly from one or multiple Chainlink nodes and the reported value is received in the next transaction. This model is used to fetch random values or more unique datasets. Chainlink nodes are paid in LINK tokens as a fee for their services in both of these oracle network models.

Anybody can become a Chainlink node operator and start providing data to the network. Chainlink's Price Feed networks are secured by nodes operated by a combination of traditional enterprises like Deutsche Telekom's T-systems, data providers, and professional DevOps firms. Data providers who operate their own Chainlink node cryptographically sign their data directly at the source, providing smart contracts with greater security guarantees.

In April 2021, the Chainlink 2.0 whitepaper was released, introducing a new architecture for Decentralized Oracle Networks. Decentralized Oracle Networks functions similarly to Layer-2 solutions, significantly increasing the speed of data delivery and boosting security. Furthermore, Chainlink introduced its super-linear staking model, a crypto-economic security mechanism that incentivizes nodes to deliver accurate oracle reports and significantly increases the cost of attack for malicious actors.

That's a quick overview of Chainlink and decentralized oracle networks! You may have noticed: some of the top DeFi protocols introduced in this book, such as Synthetix and Aave, are also powered by Chainlink.

Band Protocol

Similar to Chainlink, Band Protocol is a cross-chain oracle platform that connects smart contracts with external data and APIs. Decentralized applications that have been integrated with Band Protocol receive data through Band Protocol's smart contract data points instead of directly from off-chain oracles.

A unique aspect of Band Protocol is that they utilize BandChain, a separate blockchain to handle and relay information that can handle thousands of transactions. Data can be sent to other blockchains via Cosmos' Inter-Blockchain Communication (IBC) protocol.

Data sourced from Band Protocol are curated and verified by the community, ensuring that they are reliable enough to be referenced by Dapp users and developers alike. These data sources can be aggregated from various on-chain feeds and data aggregators using different statistical methods such as mean, median, or mode, as well as any additional data-cleansing methods such as normalization or time-weighted averages.

To retrieve data from Band Protocol, the requester will need to specify several parameters: the oracle script ID the requester wants to call, the parameters for the oracle script, and the number of validators required. Once the request has been made and verified on BandChain, the oracle script will begin the first phase of execution, known as the preparation phase, by emitting the data sources required to fulfill the request.

Validators will be chosen to handle the request based on a randomized stake-weighted algorithm. The validators will attempt to retrieve the requested data from all the specified sources and submit a raw data report, with the retrieved results, to the BandChain for confirmation.[76]

Once the minimum number of validators have successfully submitted their reports, the BandChain will proceed with the second phase, also known as the aggregation phase. All collected reports are compiled into a single result stored on BandChain, which can be accessed and sent to other blockchains for future use.

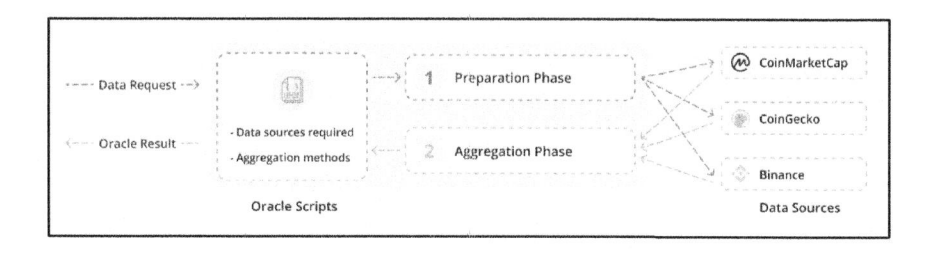

The BandChain network relies on multiple participants, the most important being validators and delegators. The top 100 validators with the most staked BAND tokens are responsible for creating and confirming new blocks on the BandChain network. On the other hand, delegators can delegate their BAND tokens to any validators to earn block rewards.

---

[76] (2020, July 20). Understanding Band Oracle #2 — Requesting Data on BandChain .... Retrieved April 29, 2021, from https://medium.com/bandprotocol/understanding-band-oracle-2-requesting-data-on-bandchain-b3fde67072a

Whenever requested, validators on BandChain have the duty of fetching data from specified data providers. Validators are economically incentivized to provide accurate data since the provision of false data will result in the slashing or confiscation of staked BAND tokens. Subsequent counts of misinformation will result in lower trust scores and user count, further decreasing the value of the staked tokens and compounding the losses.

On top of that, the data request process along with the validator's execution is publicly available for all to see and verify, further mitigating the risk of transmitting false or tampered data. Validators have served approximately 4.3 million requests for data in the first six months since oracle functionality went live on BandChain's mainnet in October 2020.

To become a validator on BandChain, you will need to own some BAND tokens or have other users delegate BAND tokens to you. Validators are chosen at random using a stake-weighted algorithm based on their share of staked tokens. The larger the proportion, the higher the chances of getting selected.

Data Aggregators

If oracles bridge real-world data to the blockchain, then data aggregators help users to read it. These protocols compile blockchain data into a simplified format, making it easier for projects and individual users to create their analytics dashboard.

The Graph Protocol

The Graph is a decentralized protocol for querying and receiving data from blockchains such as Ethereum, Polkadot, and Solana. Although it is simpler to answer queries directly retrieved by reading a contract address on the blockchain, data with higher specificity and granularity is much more difficult to find. The Graph solves this problem by indexing blockchain data into "subgraphs", or open APIs that can be queried using a standard GraphQL API.

The Graph works by Well indexing diverse types of data based on the subgraph's description, also known as the subgraph manifest. The manifests define the relevant smart contracts and the contract's key events to focus on. It also figures out how to map the event data to the stored data in The Graph's database.

Once a subgraph manifest is created, The Graph CLI stores it in the InterPlanetary File System (IPFS), a decentralized storage solution, and begins indexing information for that subgraph.

Here is a basic flow on how data is detected and stored by Graph Nodes:

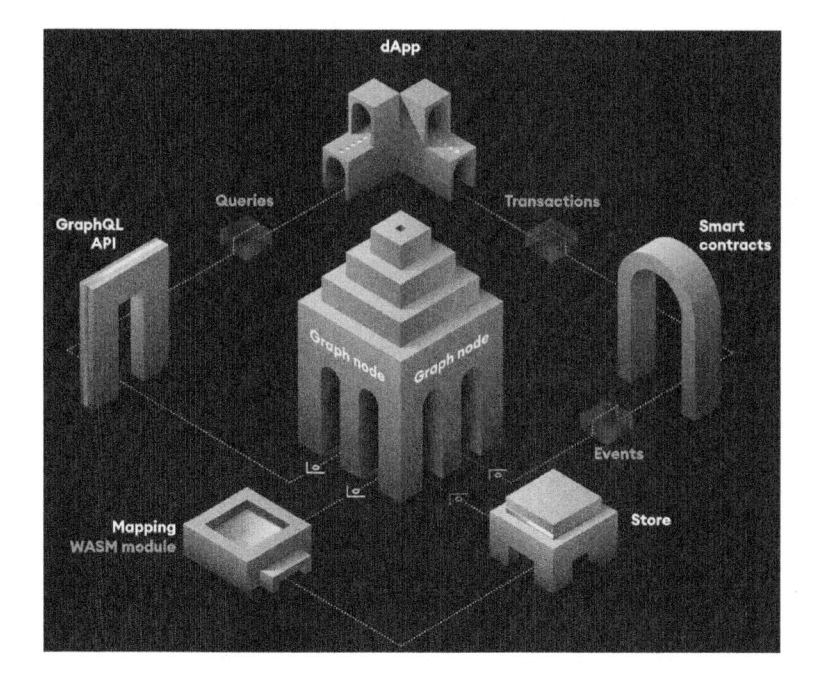

1. Decentralized applications (Dapps) add data from a smart contract transaction to the blockchain.

2. The smart contract emits events while processing the transaction.

3. Graph Nodes continuously scan the blockchain for new blocks and data for subgraph manifests.

4. The Graph Nodes find the events and run the mapping handlers provided. The WASM module generates and updates the data stored within the nodes.

5. Dapps query Graph Nodes for indexed data using the GraphQL endpoint.

6. GraphQL queries are translated by the nodes before they are retrieved by the dApp.

7. The dApp displays this data via its user interface to be used as reference when issuing new transactions on the blockchain.

The Graph is used by many dApps in the DeFi and Web3 space, including Uniswap, Aave, Balancer, and Synthetix. It provides the proper infrastructure to service data-intensive protocols. As of Q1 2021, over 10,000 subgraphs have been deployed by approximately 16,000 developers and over 100 billion queries processed in less than a year.[77]

---

[77] (2021, February 24). The Graph's Indexing and Querying is now live on the Fantom Layer .... Retrieved March 4, 2021, from https://thegraph.com/blog/graph-fantom

Covalent

Covalent

Covalent is a blockchain data provider that provides a unified API for accessing the seemingly endless rows of on-chain data. Detailed information for token balances and wallet activity from various blockchains can be retrieved using a single API, making it much easier for developers to create analytics dashboards or gather insights on blockchain activity.

Covalent's functions may seem quite similar to The Graph, but it differentiates itself in a few ways. For instance, the Graph requires a subset of data to be converted into a subgraph before it can be queried. Covalent, meanwhile, will index the blockchain in its entirety, resulting in larger quantities of granular data for users. Furthermore, Covalent has expanded beyond Ethereum. As of April 2021, Covelant supports data from four other blockchains, including Fantom, Binance Smart Chain, Polygon, and Avalanche.

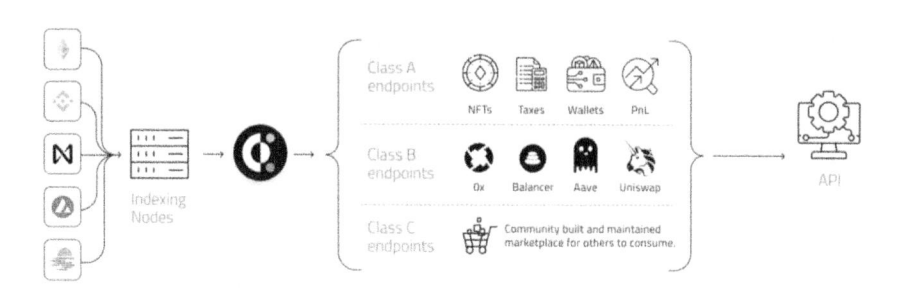

Source: https://www.covalenthq.com/blog/beginners-guide-to-covalent/

To access the Covalent API, you will need to first obtain a free API key by creating an account on Covalent. There are two classes of Covalent API - Class A and Class B.

You may use Class A endpoints to retrieve blockchain data that are network-agnostic. In short, this is general data that applies to all networks, such as balances, transactions, and token holders. On the other hand, you may use Class B endpoints to return values from specific protocols on a blockchain. For example, you may query data from Uniswap or PancakeSwap, both decentralized exchanges isolated on their respective networks.

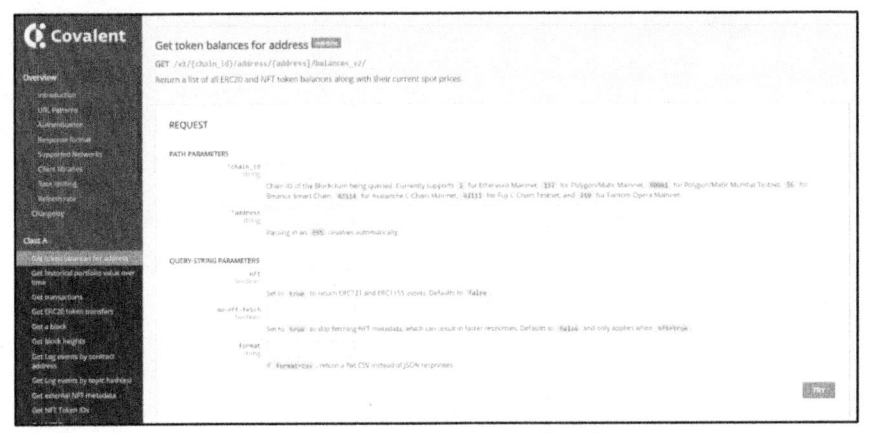

Source: https://www.covalenthq.com/docs/api/

Notable mentions

- **DIA**

    DIA, short for Decentralized Information Asset, is an open-source oracle that provides data for many DeFi applications. They provide price feeds for popular DEXs such as Uniswap and Sushiswap on other chains such as Binance Smart Chain and Polygon.

- **API3**

    API3 provides information to projects via decentralized APIs or dAPI. The data feeds are overseen by a DAO which includes project partners and industry experts. They also allow dAPI users to obtain on-chain insurance in the event that the API does not work as intended.

Associated Risks

As more protocols start to rely on long-standing products that have been battle-tested in the harshest environments, it is also important to remember that these products may not be completely foolproof. If black swan events were to happen, the oracles might not be able to provide data efficiently, causing inaccurate decisions to be made.

In March 2020, otherwise known as Black Thursday, oracles such as Chainlink and MakerDAO's 'Medianizer' failed to update their price feeds quickly enough, resulting in grossly incorrect prices. MakerDAO's price failure kickstarted a chain of catastrophic events, leading to over $8 million worth of ETH collateral lost for CDP owners.

Conclusion

Oracles and data aggregators form the backbone of many DeFi protocols. The need for extreme speed and accuracy in querying and relaying data is of utmost importance for future projects seeking to change the data provision game. Currently, Chainlink is dominating the space with over 400 integrations, including more than 200 DeFi projects.

However, the DeFi scene is constantly on the bleeding edge of innovation, with better oracle and data collection mechanisms coming into play on a regular basis. Ultimately, the goal of DeFi is to have an oracle service that is reliable, internally secure, and well-protected from negative externalities. Additionally, the robust indexing protocols that have been built and continuously improved will serve to bring more clarity and insight into the behavior of users on the blockchain, allowing projects to provide better products and services with greater product-market fit.

Recommended Readings

1. Documentation and Additional Information on Chainlink
   https://docs.chain.link/docs
2. Chainlink Whitepaper
   https://link.smartcontract.com/whitepaper
3. What Is Chainlink and Why Is It Important in the World of Cryptocurrency?
   https://finance.yahoo.com/news/chainlink-why-important-world-cryptocurrency-110020729.html
4. Documentation on Band Protocol
   https://docs.bandchain.org/
5. What is Band Protocol and How to Buy BAND
   https://decrypt.co/resources/what-is-band-protocol-defi-oracle
6. Documentation on The Graph Protocol
   https://thegraph.com/docs/
7. The Graph - Google on Blockchains?
   https://finematics.com/the-graph-explained/
8. Documentation on Covalent API
   https://www.covalenthq.com/docs/api/#overview
9. Here's a Quick Look at the Role of 'Covalent Blockchain Data API'
   https://newspi.site/heres-a-quick-look-at-the-role-of-covalent-blockchain-data-api-in-terms-of-data-gathering-e-hacking-news/
10. Blog Post on Covalent Network Launch
    https://www.covalenthq.com/blog/covalent-network-blog/

CHAPTER 14: MULTI-CHAIN PROTOCOLS & CROSS-CHAIN BRIDGES

Ethereum is undoubtedly the go-to home for many DeFi projects. However, the spikes in gas fees due to the high usage levels and the run-up of Ether to its All-Time High have served as a wake-up call for users and developers to explore other blockchains with lower transaction fees.

Many DeFi projects found a second home in other blockchain networks to service even more users and scale more efficiently. Although exchanges usually offer the ability for users to transition easily between various blockchain networks, it can still restrict the movement of funds.

From this dilemma, several projects such as Ren, THORChain, and Anyswap have grown to allow users to seamlessly connect and move funds between blockchains in a trustless manner. Centralized exchanges such as Binance have also tried to bridge Ethereum and other blockchains by introducing the Binance Bridge.

Protocols and Bridge Overview

Ren Project

Ren Project is a permissionless protocol that allows users to interact and transfer tokens between blockchains anonymously. Ren Protocol does this via RenBridge, an offering powered by the Ren Virtual Machine (RenVM).

RenBridge allows for the easy representation of cryptocurrencies on other networks. For example, Bitcoin can be represented on the Ethereum Network as an ERC-20 token by having it wrapped into renBTC. Using RenVM, the assets are converted based on the format of its destination network at a 1:1 ratio, ensuring that the wrapped versions are always fully backed by the underlying asset.

While you explore other blockchains with your newly wrapped tokens, RenVM acts as a decentralized custodian of your original assets, with the value of the bonded REN maintained at three times the total value of the locked assets via minting and burning. The Darknodes are continuously shuffled to maintain the smooth operation of RenVM, and additional levels of security such as the implementation of the RPZ MPC algorithm and algorithmically adjusted fees make it extremely challenging for hackers to attack. In the unlikely event that an attack happens, RenVM can restore the stolen funds.

RenVM works by running on a decentralized network of computers known as Darknodes, which help verify transactions and maintain the security of the Ren network. To operate a Darknode, users need to stake 100,000 REN tokens as collateral, which amounts to approximately $103,000 (7 May 2021).

The Darknodes collect a portion of the trading fees from RenVM transactions in the form of wrapped assets.

The Ren Virtual Machine supports three types of cross-chain transactions - lock-and-mint, burn-and-release, and burn-and-mint.

Lock-and-mint

Lock-and-mint occurs when the user sends funds from the original chain to a destination chain. Tokens sent to RenVM are "locked" in custody. Once the assets are confirmed to be locked, RenVM will release a minting signature to the user, which allows the user to mint a 1:1 tokenized version of the asset on the destination chain. The minted assets are redeemable at any time with no minimum quantity.

Burn-and-release

To complement the first transaction, burn-and-release allows users to send their tokens from the destination chain back to the original chain by burning the tokenized version of the asset on the destination chain and receiving the locked assets on a chosen address. As the name suggests, the pegged tokens are "burned" while the RenVM "releases" an equal amount of the underlying asset on the original chain.

Burn-and-mint

Burn-and-mint combines both transactions above. Users can directly move their assets between host chains by burning the pegged assets from one host chain and minting the same amount of pegged assets on another host chain. However, this will require multiple payments and confirmations through the RenVM, making it a slow and costly process.

ThorChain

ThorChain is a decentralized liquidity network with an interoperable blockchain that allows cross-chain token swaps in a non-custodial manner. It does not peg or wrap assets but enables users to swap tokens across various Layer 1 blockchains. For instance, traders on ThorChain can seamlessly move their assets from Bitcoin to Ethereum without registering or going through the KYC process of a centralized exchange.

The attraction of ThorChain is that its chain-agnostic feature allows it to swap assets without undergoing some form of conversion. Unlike Ren, there is no 1:1 wrapped Bitcoin (renBTC) created. Instead, we would be able to swap ETH for actual Bitcoin. This is a milestone as previously, the closest representation of Bitcoin in DeFi is in its wrapped form. Thus, ThorChain brings Bitcoin much closer to the heart of the DeFi ecosystem.

Furthermore, as the number of new smart contract platforms grows, such as Solana and Polkadot, the variety of projects and protocols that exist on these blockchains continue to expand at a parabolic rate. The diversity of chains induces the need for a trust-minimized and decentralized way to exchange tokens across different chains.

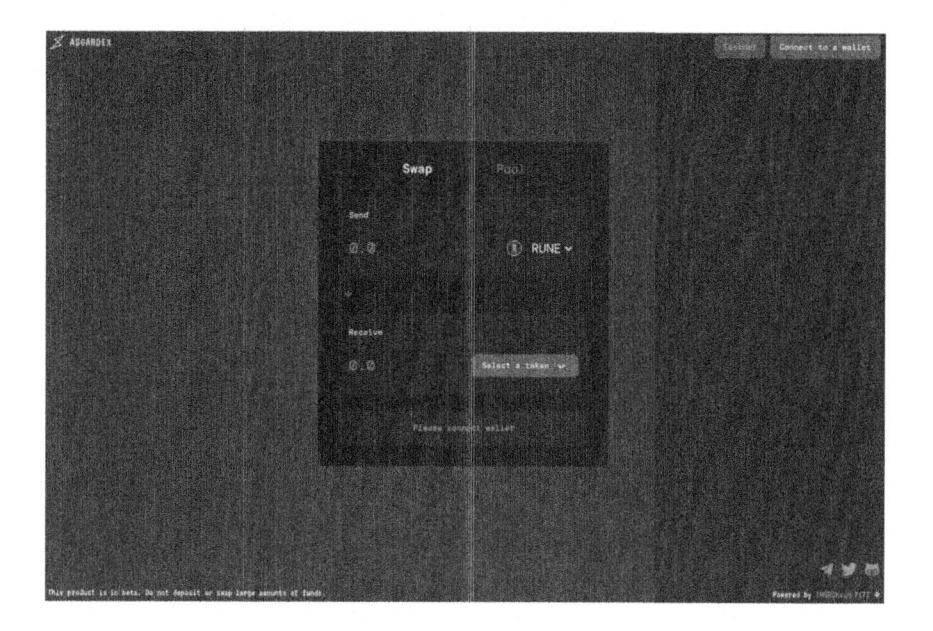

ThorChain uses the Proof-of-Stake consensus mechanism. It is built on Tendermint where network validators or nodes are required to bond the native token, RUNE. RUNE has a token model that increases in value as the utilization of the network grows. This means that as more liquidity is deposited into ThorChain liquidity pools, RUNE will become more valuable.

RUNE is needed for two fundamental reasons:

I. In liquidity pools, RUNE acts as a base pair where a 1:1 ratio of ASSET:RUNE is required for staking (e.g., BNB-RUNE or ETH-RUNE). ThorChain does not operate by direct asset transfer; instead, it needs RUNE to move from one asset to another. RUNE is also required to activate ThorChain's Bifrost Protocol, which acts as the bridge that enables multi-chain connectivity. The protocol also tracks the ratio of RUNE to the assets in their Continuous Liquidity Pools (CLP), meaning they also inherit a trustless on-chain price feed for digital assets without relying on third-party oracles.

II. RUNE is bonded as collateral by node operators to disincentivize malicious actors following a 2:1 bond:stake ratio. RUNE is not intended to be a governance token; ThorChain will be governed more like Bitcoin, where node operators can determine its future direction. This also means that ThorChain is not limited only to traders but is also used by liquidity providers and node operators.

With a 2:1 bond:stake ratio, combined with the 1:1 pool stake ratio, the amount of RUNE needed would be three times the amount of the non-RUNE assets locked. In other words, this 3:1 ratio represents the intrinsic or minimum value of the RUNE tokens required for the protocol to operate.

Users who utilize ThorChain's cross-chain services between the pools will need to pay fixed network fees and a variable slip fee, to cover gas fees on external services and fast execution. Besides offering a seamless service to traders, users can also become liquidity providers on ThorChain.

Liquidity providers on ThorChain can add liquidity to various pools, which are tied to RUNE in a separate vault. The liquidity pools incentivize any ThorChain participant to supply liquidity in exchange for RUNE rewards, equal to twice the amount of gas used.

As mentioned on ThorChain's website, "liquidity is provided by stakes who earn fees on swaps, turning their unproductive assets into productive assets in a non-custodial manner. Market prices are maintained through the ratio of assets in the pool which traders can arbitrage to restore correct market prices".

What sets ThorChain apart is its cross-chain feature – it enables users to swap any asset and create a liquidity pool around it, opening a whole new world of possibilities for the DeFi ecosystem.

As of 13 April 2021, THORChain multi-chain Chaosnet is live, along with their decentralized exchange, Asgardex[78]. Users can perform transactions across five active blockchain networks - Bitcoin, Bitcoin Cash, Litecoin, Ethereum, and Binance Chain.

---

[78] (2021, April 13). THORChain launch multichain chaosnet | by THORChain ... - Medium. Retrieved May 24, 2021, from https://medium.com/thorchain/thorchain-launch-multichain-chaosnet-bb9f60008a03

Binance Bridge

Using the Binance Bridge, users can transfer funds to and from various blockchains such as the Ethereum, Tron, or Binance Smart Chain (BSC) network. Only specific blockchains are supported for each particular asset. For example, native tokens for other blockchains such as Cosmos (ATOM) and Ontology (ONT) are limited to transfers between either Binance Smart Chain, Binance Chain, or their native network. There is a daily limit for how much you can transfer for each asset.

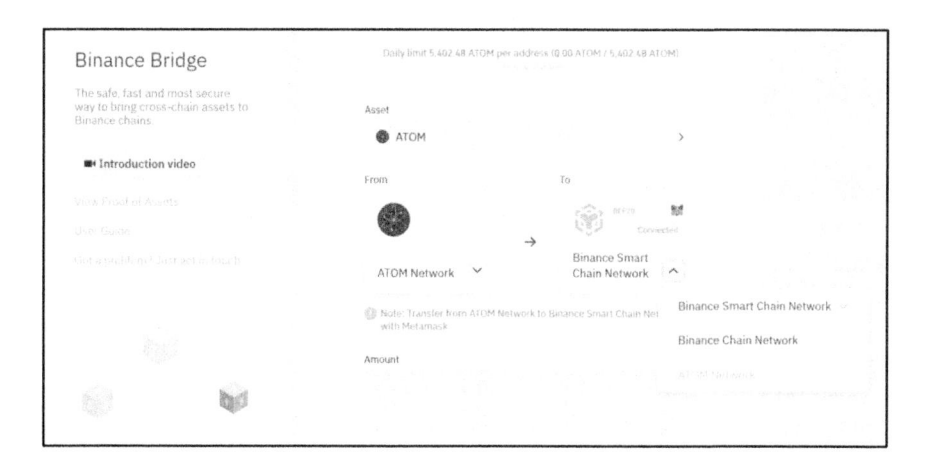

If you are moving assets to the Binance Smart Chain network, you can also opt to swap for some Binance Coin (BNB) as well. Similar to how Ether is used to pay for transaction fees on the Ethereum network, BNB is used to pay for transaction fees on the Binance Smart Chain network. As such, it is advisable to select the option to swap for some BNB, especially if you are a newcomer to the Binance Smart Chain blockchain.

How to DeFi: Advanced

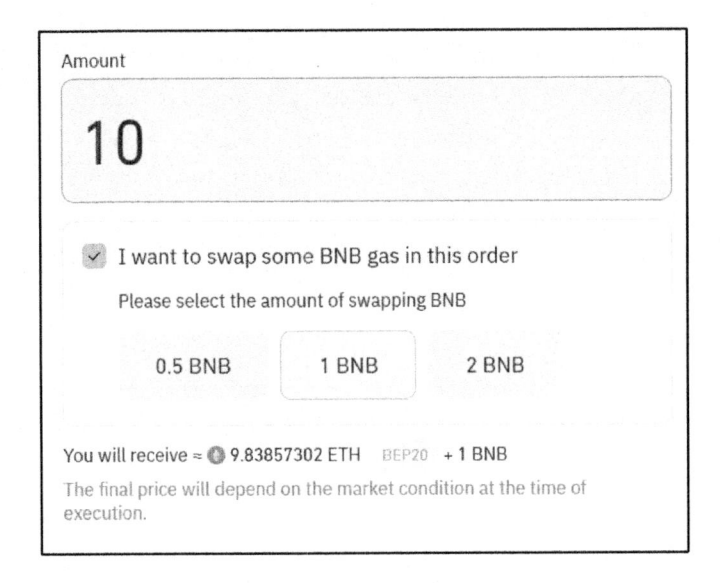

```
Amount
10
☑ I want to swap some BNB gas in this order
      Please select the amount of swapping BNB
        0.5 BNB      1 BNB      2 BNB

You will receive ≈ 9.83857302 ETH   BEP20  + 1 BNB
The final price will depend on the market condition at the time of execution.
```

Anyswap

Anyswap is a decentralized cross-chain exchange that supports eight different blockchains such as Ethereum, Binance Smart Chain, and Fantom. It offers an all-in-one platform for users to swap or convert their assets onto other blockchains. Users can opt for the conventional method of depositing their assets to mint wrapped tokens or directly perform cross-chain swaps to trade their tokens for another token on a different blockchain.

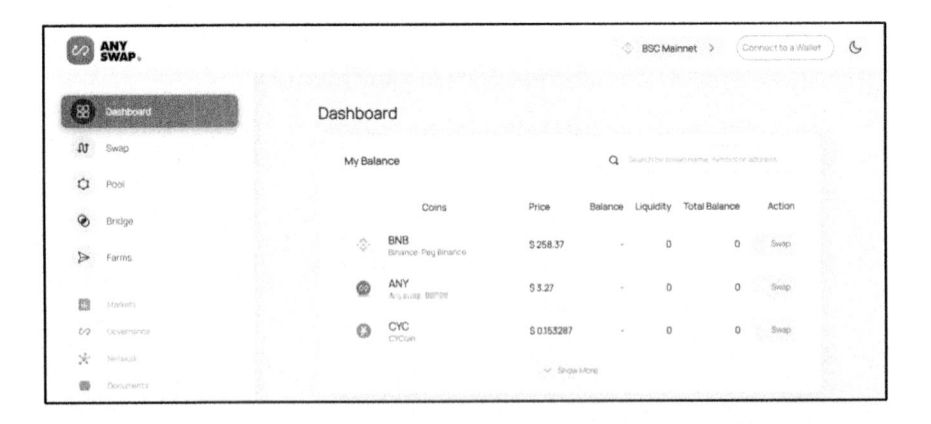

For each blockchain, the Anyswap DEX supports different token pairs, which, as of version 1, are always paired to the network's native token. For example, on the Fantom network, tokens are paired to the FTM token.

The fees charged to use the exchange vary based on the amount of gas used and the type of assets used in the swap. Essentially, users have to pay a 0.4% swap fee in addition to the network's transaction fees. 75% of the fees go to the liquidity providers, and the remainder is sent to Anyswap. Users who perform a transaction between any two non-native assets of their choice are charged the 0.4% fee twice.

Anyswap has risen in popularity ever since Andre Cronje shared his interests and admiration for the cross-chain project. With Total Value Locked of more than $620 million across their supported blockchains (as of May 2021)[79], there is still much room for the protocol to grow as more users are willing to embrace and explore other networks. Inspired by Anyswap, Andre Cronje has also released multichain.xyz, a cross-chain protocol that functions similarly with customized pairs for each network.

Terra Bridge

The Terra Bridge is an application for users to send supported Terra assets on the Terra blockchain to and from the Ethereum and Binance Smart Chain networks. Among these assets are LUNA (Terra's native token), Terra stablecoins such as UST (Terra USD), and mirrored assets such as mTSLA (Tesla) and mAAPL (Apple Inc.).

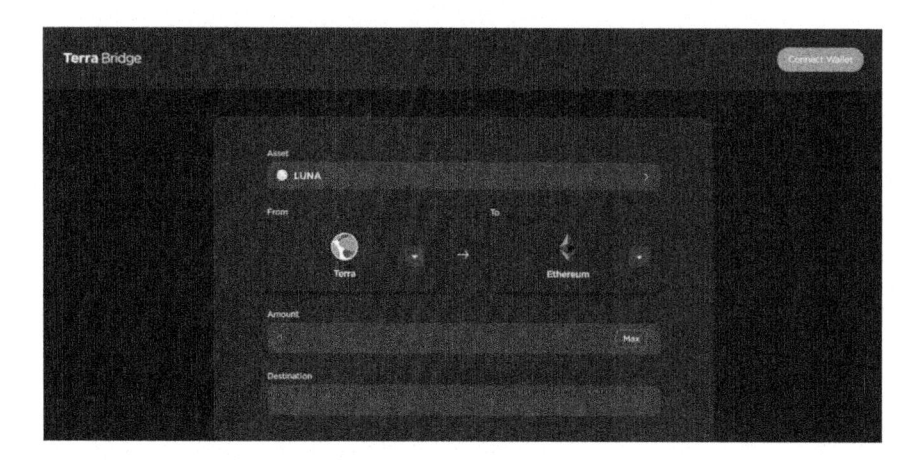

---

[79] (n.d.). Network: AnySwap. Retrieved May 24, 2021, from https://anyswap.net/

Notable mentions

- **Multichain.xyz**

  Supporting 10 different blockchains, Multichain.xyz allows you to swap a variety of assets such as BNB, ETH and USDC. As of May 24, 2021, it has a Total Value Locked of over $200 million and supports over 280 tokens[80].

- **Matic Bridge**

  The Matic Web Wallet Bridge allows users to transfer funds to and from the Polygon network, using Plasma or Proof-of-Stake (PoS) bridge. Depending on the bridge used, only certain assets can be transferred. Withdrawal times may vary.

- **APYSwap**

  APYSwap is a decentralized protocol for exchanging assets across different blockchains with a unique feature - it functions for non-EVM compatible blockchains as well, allowing users to transfer funds from Ethereum, Binance Smart Chain and Huobi ECO Chain to Solana and vice versa.

Associated Risks

Although bridges and cross-chain protocols are becoming a vital step in improving the connectivity between different blockchain networks, users should also be aware of the existing problems that may occur when interacting with these protocols.

Besides the inherent risks that come with the nature of smart contracts and their exposure to faulty code and exploits, users have to ensure that their original assets are truly locked on the native chain before minting pegged assets on other chains. If the original tokens could be freely unlocked and

---

[80] (n.d.). Multichain.xyz Stats. Retrieved May 24, 2021, from https://multichain.xyz/stats

used by others, the minted assets will become worthless since they cannot be used for redemption back on the original chain.

Users also need to be aware of the varying smart contracts of the tokens for different networks. Although most tokens have the same contract address across multiple blockchains, it is still important to check that you are indeed getting the same version of the token or a pegged equivalent when attempting to perform transfers or cross-chain deposits.

Conclusion

As alternative chains are beginning to see more and more traction, bridges and multi-chain protocols will be more important than ever before. Whether through proxy tokens or seamless swapping between native tokens, it is clear that more users will continue to experiment and cross over into blockchains that may offer different services or lower fees. As such, improving the safety and user experience of these protocols is critical to ensure that DeFi is truly for everyone, on every network.

Recommended Readings

1. Ren Protocol Review
   https://defirate.com/ren-protocol/
2. An In-depth Guide to Thorchain's Liquidity Pools
   https://medium.com/thorchain/an-in-depth-guide-to-thorchains-liquidity-pools-c4ea7829e1bf
3. Documentation on Binance Bridge v2
   https://docs.binance.org/smart-chain/guides/bridge-v2.html
4. Anyswap DEX User Guide
   https://anyswap-faq.readthedocs.io/en/latest/
5. User Guide for Interchain Transfers on Terra's Shuttle Bridge
   https://docs.anchorprotocol.com/user-guide/interchain-transfers
6. Guide to use Matic Bridge by Matic Network
   https://blog.matic.network/deposits-and-withdrawals-on-pos-bridge/
7. How to Add Networks Using Chainlist.org
   https://metamask.zendesk.com/hc/en-us/articles/360058992772-Add-Network-Custom-RPC-using-Chainlist-in-the-browser-extension

CHAPTER 15: DEFI EXPLOITS

Exploring DeFi is risky; smart contract hacks happen all the time. In 2020 alone, there were at least 12 high-profile DeFi hacks, draining away no less than $121 million in funds from DeFi protocols.

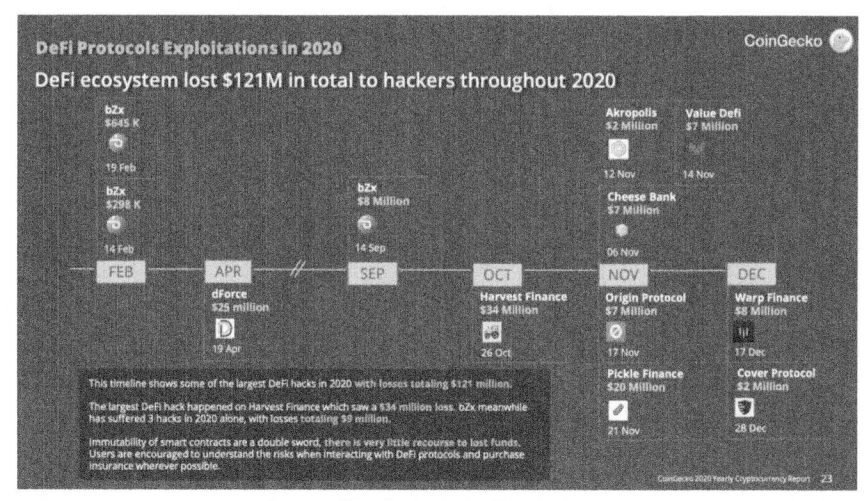

Source: CoinGecko 2020 Yearly Report

No one - not even the best smart contract auditors - can fully predict what will happen with deployed smart contracts. With billions of dollars of funds sitting on smart contracts, you can be sure that the most brilliant hackers are constantly looking to exploit and profit from security weaknesses.

The big risk for DeFi is that as projects leverage the composable nature of DeFi and build on top of one another, the complexity of DeFi applications increases exponentially, making it harder for smart contract auditors to spot weaknesses. DeFi application developers have to ensure that cybersecurity auditors constantly check their codes to reduce any possibility of exploits because the consequences of mistakes will be huge financial losses.

In this chapter, we will look at the causes of hacks, flash loans, potential solutions to reduce losses from hacks, and some tips for individuals to avoid losing funds in DeFi exploits.

Causes of Exploits

Below we will look at some common causes of exploits. The list is not meant to be exhaustive.

1. **Economic Exploits / Flash Loans**

    Flash loans allow users to leverage nearly limitless capital to carry out a financial transaction as long as the borrower repays the loan within the same transaction. It is a powerful tool that allows one to maneuver economic attacks that used to be constrained by capital requirements. With flash loans, having the right strategy is the only requirement to exploit opportunities.

    Almost all DeFi hacks utilized flash loans. We will look into it with more details in the next section.

2. **Code in Production Culture**

    Spearheaded by Andre Cronje, the founder of Yearn Finance, many DeFi projects follow the ethos of test-in-production instead of maximizing security and testing to speed up the pace of product development. Having audits on every release will significantly extend the time required to bring any product updates to market.

    One of the main competitive advantages of DeFi is that developers can iterate much faster, pushing the boundaries of financial innovations. However, not every project can afford to have audits, especially when the project has yet to achieve any traction. Despite having multiple audits, hackers still manage to exploit some projects, suggesting that having audits may not be sufficient to prevent all hacks.

3. **Sloppy Coding and Insufficient Audits**

   In a bull market, many project teams feel pressured to move fast and take shortcuts to release their products quicker. Some may decide to skip audits altogether to have the first-mover advantage and only conduct audits several months after the products are live.

   There are also plenty of "forks" - new projects that use the same code as other established projects. Launched without a complete understanding of how the code works, they are treated as a quick cash grab, resulting in many exploits.[81]

4. **Rug Pull (Inside Jobs)**

   In the DeFi space, it is not uncommon for projects to launch with anonymous teams. Some do so to avoid the scrutiny of regulators due to an uncertain regulatory climate. However, others chose to be anonymous as they have bad intentions. There have been many instances where anonymous teams conducted an inside job and intentionally left a bug, which is exploited to steal from unsuspecting users.

   The crypto community does not alienate projects launched by anonymous founders, seeing how the first cryptocurrency, Bitcoin, was also founded by an unknown person. Users evaluate projects based on the code produced, not who or where the developers are from. This is aligned with the decentralization ethos of open software.

---

[81] "Saddle Finance - REKT - Rekt News." 20 Jan. 2021, https://www.rekt.news/saddle-finance-rekt/. Accessed 4 May. 2021.

Ideals aside, if an exploit were to occur on a protocol launched by an anonymous team, the chances of no recourse are high as it is hard to find the real-world identity of the developers.

5. Oracle Attacks

DeFi protocols need to know asset prices to function correctly. For example, a lending protocol needs to know the asset price to decide whether to liquidate the borrowers' position.

Therefore, as an indispensable part of DeFi infrastructure, oracles may be subject to heavy manipulation. For example, we mentioned in Chapter 12 how the exploit of MakerDao's vault caused unnecessary vaults' liquidation that totaled more than $8 million worth of ETH in losses.

6. Metamask Attack

As the main interface to every Ethereum application, it is no surprise that Metamask has become a primary attack target. The Consensys team has been thorough in security, and to date, there have been no widespread exploits.

However, there were a few high profile attacks:
- $59 million loss through the EasyFi project's admin MetaMask account[82]
- $8 million loss through the personal wallet of Nexus Mutual's founder[83]

---

[82] "EasyFi - REKT - Rekt News." 20 Apr. 2021, https://www.rekt.news/easyfi-rekt/. Accessed 4 May. 2021.
[83] "Rekt - Nexus Mutual - Hugh Speaks Out - Rekt News." 23 Dec. 2020, https://www.rekt.news/nxm-hugh-speaks-out/. Accessed 4 May. 2021.

Flash Loans

What are Flash Loans?

Flash loans are loans where users can borrow funds without any collateral so long as the user pays back the loan in the same transaction. If the user does not repay the flash loan in the same transaction, the transaction will automatically fail, incurring a loss in the transaction fee and ensuring that the flash loan will not take place.[84] Flash loans are offered by various DeFi protocols such as Aave and dYdX.

Flash loans have three main characteristics that make them stands out as compared to a normal loan:[85]

- **No default risk**: Flash loans are repaid within the same transaction. Therefore there is no risk of getting defaulted.

- **No collateral**: Borrowers can take the loan without posting any collateral or credit check as long as they can repay the loan within one transaction.

- **Unlimited loan size**: Users can borrow any amount up to the total liquidity available from the DeFi protocols.

As of April 2021, the execution of flash loans is not user-friendly, as you must execute it by writing a smart contract code. Thus, it is more accessible to software programmers rather than the average layman.

Indeed, some programmers often exploit this factor and launch what we call a "flash loan attack", especially when no collateral is needed. One of the most famous flash loan attacks occurred on Harvest Finance, resulting in a $24 million loss.[86]

---

[84] "Open Source DeFi Protocol | FlashLoan - Aave." https://aave.com/flash-loans/. Accessed 4 May. 2021.
[85] Qin, K., Zhou, L., Livshits, B., & Gervais, A. (2021, March 20). Attacking the DeFi Ecosystem with Flash Loans for Fun and Profit. https://arxiv.org/pdf/2003.03810.pdf
[86] "Harvest Finance: $24M Attack Triggers $570M 'Bank Run' in Latest ...." 26 Oct. 2020, https://www.coindesk.com/harvest-finance-24m-attack-triggers-570m-bank-run-in-latest-defi-exploit. Accessed 4 May. 2021.

The table below shows the fees incurred on the major protocols that offer flash loans:

Protocols	Flash Loan Fee
Aave	0.09%
dYdX	1 Wei (10^{-18}) ETH
bZx	None
Uniswap v2	0.3%

Usage of Flash Loans

The following chart shows the composition of all the Flash Loans usage from Aave[87]:

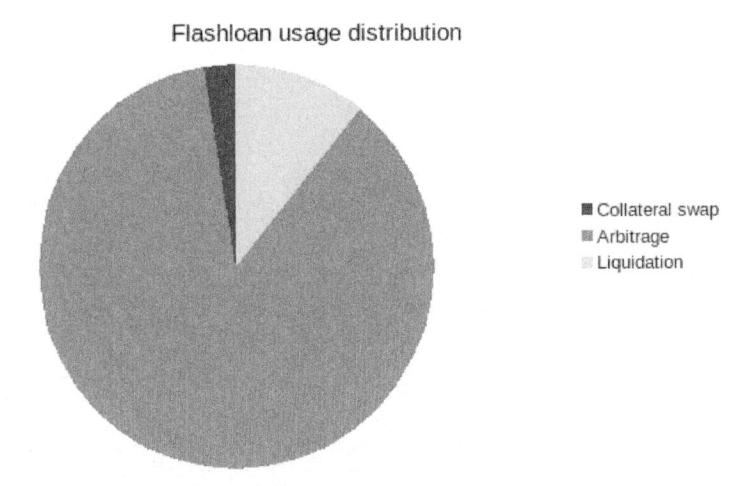

Flashloan usage distribution

- Collateral swap
- Arbitrage
- Liquidation

We can see that flash loans are mainly used for arbitrage purposes. Arbitrage is the act of exploiting price differences between markets to make a profit. For instance, let's say we discover a considerable price difference for WBTC on two different decentralized exchanges. We can use a flash loan to borrow a substantial amount of WBTC without any collateral to profit from the price difference.

---

[87] "Flash Loans, one month in. Balancing fees and first usage ... - Medium." 12 Feb. 2020, https://medium.com/aave/flash-loans-one-month-in-73bde954a239. Accessed 12 May. 2021.

The second usage of flash loans is for loan liquidation. There is usually a penalty for the borrowers if they let the protocol liquidate their position. When the market has substantial price actions, borrowers can choose to obtain flash loans and self-liquidate their positions, avoiding the penalty fees.

Let's look at an example where we borrow DAI from Maker with ETH as collateral. When the price of ETH falls significantly, it may get near the liquidation level for our DAI loan. We may not have ETH to increase our collaterals nor DAI to repay the loan. What we can do is take a DAI flash loan to repay the Maker loan. We can then swap a portion of the withdrawn ETH collateral to DAI to repay the flash loan instantly. Using this method, we will keep the remaining ETH without paying the liquidation penalty.

Lastly, flash loans can also be used to execute a collateral swap. For instance, if we have a DAI loan in Compound with ETH as collateral, we can swap the ETH collateral to WBTC collateral using a flash loan. This allows us to change our risk profiles easily without having to go through multiple transactions.

Executing flash loans still requires considerable technical knowledge and has high entry barriers to those who do not know how to code. However, there is a third-party app that makes the execution of flash loans accessible for average users – this platform is called Furucombo.

Flash Loan Protocol: Furucombo

Furucombo is a platform that allows anyone to create arbitrage strategies using flash loans. Thanks to its drag-and-drop tool that enables end-users to build and customize different DeFi combinations, the barriers to entry for assembling money-legos are lowered. Do note that Furucombo does not find arbitrage opportunities for you.

To use Furucombo, users need to set up input/outputs and the order of the transactions, and it will bundle all the cubes into one transaction for execution. An example of how an arbitrage transaction can be carried out is shown below:

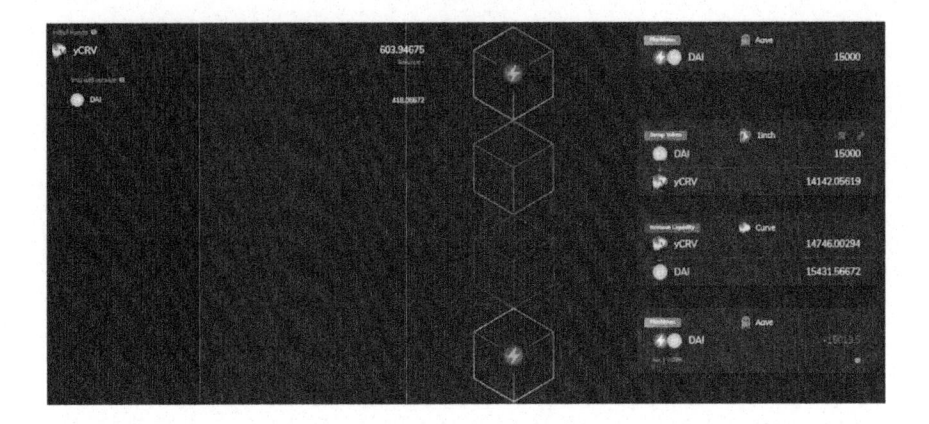

1. Obtain a 15,000 DAI flash loan from Aave.

2. Swap DAI to yCRV using 1inch.

3. Exchange yCRV back to DAI using Curve. Due to price differentials, you end up with 15,431 DAI, more DAI than before.

4. The loan amount of 15,013 DAI including Aave's flash loan fee is repaid to Aave. The user is left with a profit of 418 DAI. All of these steps are executed within one transaction.

Furucombo does not require any upfront funds nor charge fees for users to build "combos" and make arbitrage trades using flash loans on the platform. All you need is ETH in your wallet to pay for the gas fee.

Users are advised to trade at their own risk as arbitrage opportunities are not always available on Furucombo, and a combo may fail if the price difference no longer exists. Users face the risk of paying for the transaction fees regardless of the outcome.

Case Study: bZx Flash Loans Hack

On 15 February 2020, a transaction took place on the Ethereum blockchain that was considered unique at the time. A profit of approximately $360,000 was achieved within one block and in one transaction in just under a minute.

This transaction caught the crypto community's attention and was widely analyzed.[88] The gain was achieved via an initial nearly-risk-free loan in the form of a flash loan, subsequently followed by a series of arbitrage between different decentralized exchanges.

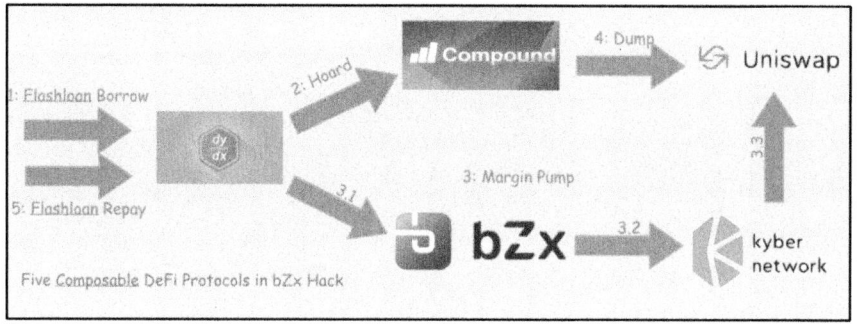

Source: Peckshield[89]

1. Flashloan Borrow
   First, a flash loan of 10,000 ETH was taken from dYdX.

2. Hoard
   Half of those ETH (5,500 ETH) were staked as collateral in Compound to borrow 112 WBTC.

3. Margin Pump
   1,300 ETH is deposited into bZx to short ETH in favor of WBTC using 5x leverage. 5,637 ETH loaned from bZx was used to swap for 51 BTC using KyberSwap. According to the KyberSwap algorithm, the best price was offered by Uniswap. However, due to the low liquidity, the swap drove up the exchange rate of 1 WBTC to around 109.8 WETH, roughly triple the normal conversion rate during the period.

4. Dump
   The attacker sold the borrowed 112 WBTC in Uniswap after the price increase, yielding 6,871 ETH with a conversion rate of 1 WBTC = 61.2 WETH.

---

[88] "Exploit During ETHDenver Reveals Experimental Nature ... - CoinDesk." 15 Feb. 2020, https://www.coindesk.com/exploit-during-ethdenver-reveals-experimental-nature-of-decentralized-finance. Accessed 4 May. 2021.

[89] "bZx Hack Full Disclosure (With Detailed Profit Analysis ... - PeckShield." https://peckshield.medium.com/bzx-hack-full-disclosure-with-detailed-profit-analysis-e6b1fa9b18fc. Accessed 4 May. 2021.

5. Flash Loan Profit
    With an unused 3,200 ETH and 6,871 ETH from the sale, the attacker paid back the 10,000 ETH flash loan with a profit of 71 ETH.

Protocol	Amount	Asset	Type
dYdX	-10,000	ETH/WETH	Debt
Compound	+5,500	ETH/WETH	Collateral
Compound	-112	WBTC	Debt
bZx	+1,300	ETH/WETH	Collateral
bZx	-5,637	ETH/WETH	Debt
bZx	+51	WBTC	Collateral
Accounts	Amount	Asset	Type
-	+3,200	ETH/WETH	Balance
-	+6,871	ETH/WETH	Balance

6. Total Profit
    The Compound position was still in profit. As the average market price of 1 WBTC was 38.5 WETH, the attacker can get 112 WBTC with roughly 4,300 ETH. In total, the attacker gained 71 WETH + 5,500 WETH - 4,300 ETH = 1,271 ETH, roughly $355,880 (assuming the ETH price of $280).

The event above not only demonstrates the possibility of extreme capital gains by manipulating the price of other assets but that there were also no other costs for the borrower besides a relatively low protocol fee. The only condition faced by the borrower was that the loan was to be repaid within the same transaction. Thus, the very concept of uncollateralized loans opens up a wide range of opportunities in the space.

Flash Loan Summary

Flash loans can be a double-edged sword. On one hand, its novel use of smart contracts brings convenience and advancements to the DeFi ecosystem - traders without much capital can launch arbitrage and liquidation strategies with flash loans without the need for a large capital base.

On the other hand, hackers can use flash loans to launch flash loan attacks, vastly enhancing their profits since no collateral is required. Just like any tool, flash loans can be used for both good and bad purposes.

In our view, flash loan attacks utilized for ill-purposes have strengthened the whole DeFi ecosystem as projects improve their infrastructure to prevent future attacks from occurring. As flash loans are still at a nascent stage, the attacks can be seen as a silver lining that mitigates the kinks in the DeFi ecosystem and makes it more antifragile.

Solutions

Having only smart contract audits is not enough to prevent exploits. Projects need to do more, and they are now looking for alternatives to ensure the safety of funds deposited in their protocols. Below are some of the possible solutions:

Internal Insurance Fund

Several projects have decided to use their native token as the risk backstop. Examples include:

- Maker minted MKR back on Black Thursday to cover for liquidation shortfall in DAI.
- Aave rolled out stAAVE to cover any potential shortfall for the depositors.
- YFI collateralized their token and borrowed DAI to pay back hacked funds.[90]

Insurance

Being one of the new kids on the block, Unslashed Finance offered protocol-level covers to LIDO and Paraswap for their users. This opens up the possibility for protocols to buy covers for their users.

---

[90] "Yearn.Finance puts expanded treasury to use by repaying victims of ...." 9 Feb. 2021, https://cointelegraph.com/news/yearn-finance-puts-expanded-treasury-to-use-by-repaying-victims-of-11m-hack. Accessed 12 May. 2021.

Bug Bounty

Projects are increasingly leveraging Immunefi to list bug bounties,[91] encouraging hackers to claim rewards for finding bugs rather than exploiting them. The highest bounties offer up to $1.5 million. However, with higher potential rewards from hacking, whether this will deter the hackers remains to be seen.

Other Possible Solutions

- Industry-wide insurance pool
  There can be an industry-wide insurance pool where every DeFi protocol chips in part of their earnings or pays a fixed fee. The pool is expected to pay out claims when one of the members experiences a hack. This is similar to the idea of the Federal Deposit Insurance Corporation (FDIC).

- Auditors to have skin in the game
  This idea proposed auditors to stake on DeFi insurance platforms such as Nexus Mutual. As stakers, if the protocols are hacked, then the auditors will experience loss. This implementation is expected to align the interest of auditors and the project.

Tips for Individuals

Besides smart contract hacks, you may also be exposed to various hacking attempts. Below are some steps you can take to minimize risks and reduce the chances of getting hacked.

Don't Give Smart Contracts Unlimited Approval

Interacting with DeFi protocols usually requires you to give smart contracts access and consent to spend your wallet's funds. Usually, for convenience purposes, DeFi protocols request that the default approval be set as infinity, meaning the protocol has unlimited access to the approved asset on your wallet.

---

[91] (n.d.). Immunefi. Retrieved May 23, 2021, from https://immunefi.com/

Giving unlimited approval to spend approved assets on your wallet is usually a bad idea because a malignant smart contract may exploit this to drain funds from your wallet.

On 27 February 2021, a hacker used a fake smart contract and tricked Furucombo into thinking that Aave v2 had a new implementation. The attack exploited large wallets with unlimited token approvals and drained these wallets by transferring funds to a hacker-controlled address.

This attack saw Furucombo users experiencing losses totaling up to $15 million.[92] Even the lending protocol, Cream Finance, made the mistake of having unlimited approvals and lost $1.1 million from their treasury in this attack.[93]

Thus, it is a good idea to manually change the approved amount for each transaction to prevent giving DeFi protocols unlimited spending permission during token approvals. Even though this will result in an additional transaction for each subsequent DeFi interaction and incur higher transaction fees, you can reduce the risk of wallets being drained in a smart contract exploit attack.

To manually change the approved amount, follow the step-by-step guide below.

---

[92] "Furucombo Post-Mortem March 2021. Dear Furucombo ... - Medium." 1 Mar. 2021, https://medium.com/furucombo/furucombo-post-mortem-march-2021-ad19afd415e. Accessed 12 May. 2021.

[93] "defiprime on Twitter: "⚠ Just in: Furucombo exploited ⚠ If you ...." 27 Feb. 2021, https://twitter.com/defiprime/status/1365743488105467905. Accessed 12 May. 2021.

Don't Give Smart Contracts Unlimited Approval: Step-by-Step Guide

Step 1
- One of the most common instances that require approvals is swapping.
- In the example, we plan to swap 15.932 SNX to 0.0834 ETH on Uniswap.
- Click "Approve SNX"

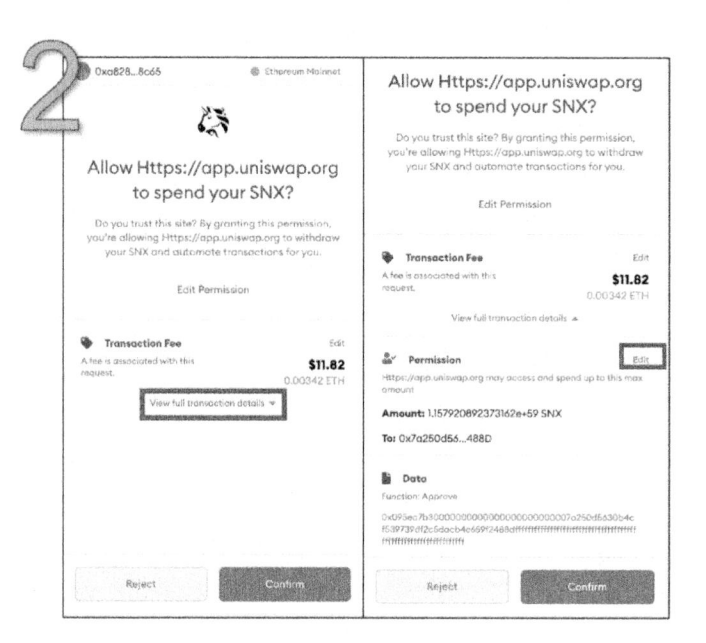

Step 2
- The left image is the default window that we will see.
- Click "View full transaction details"
- Then we will be presented with the right image. Click "Edit".

How to DeFi: Advanced

Step 3
- Choose "Custom Spend Limit".
- A lot of applications choose the "Unlimited" option in default.
- Key in the amount that we want to spend, in this example, that's 15.932 SNX.

Step 4

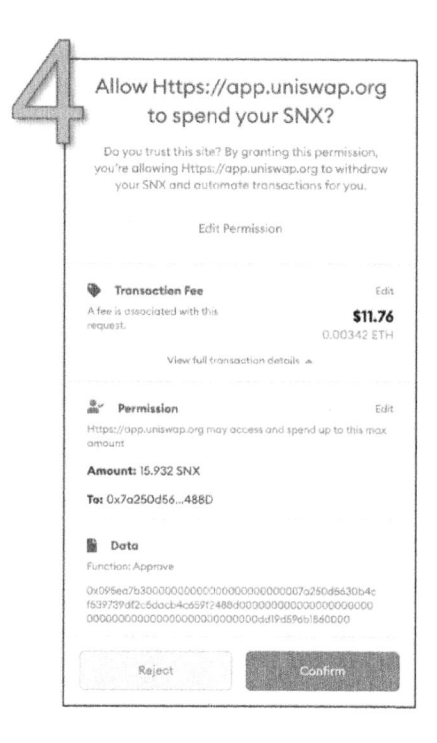

- Under the "Permission" section we can see that the figures are updated.
- Click "Confirm" and pay the transaction fee.

Revoking Unlimited Approvals from Smart Contracts

If you have previously given DeFi protocols unlimited spending approvals, there are two options for you. The easier option is to move all your funds to a new Ethereum address, and you will get a fresh restart without taking on any of the risks associated with your previous Ethereum address.

However, if moving funds out of your existing Ethereum address is not possible, you can check the list of all previous approvals using the Token Approval tool provided by Etherscan.[94]

---

[94] (n.d.). Token Approvals @ etherscan.io. Retrieved May 23, 2021, from https://etherscan.io/tokenapprovalchecker

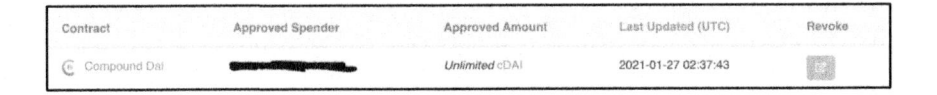

Contract	Approved Spender	Approved Amount	Last Updated (UTC)	Revoke
Compound Dai	▓▓▓▓▓▓▓▓▓▓	Unlimited cDAI	2021-01-27 02:37:43	

On this page, you can see all the approvals that you have previously granted to smart contracts. You should revoke all approvals with Unlimited approved amounts, especially protocols that you no longer interact with. Do note that revoking each approval requires a smart contract interaction itself and will incur transaction fees.

Use a Hardware Wallet

A hardware wallet is a physical device used solely for storing cryptocurrencies. Hardware wallets keep private keys separate from internet-connected devices, reducing the chances of your wallet being compromised.

In hardware wallets, the private keys are maintained in a secure offline environment, even if the hardware wallet is plugged into a computer infected with malware. While hardware wallets can be physically stolen, it is not accessible if the thief does not know your passcode. In the unfortunate event that your hardware wallet is damaged or stolen, you will still be able to recover your funds if you had created a secret backup code prior to the loss.

The top hardware wallets manufacturers are Ledger and Trezor, though more have entered the industry.

Use a Separate Browser Profile

Although browser extensions are helpful and make you more effective and productive in your work, you should always be worried about malicious browser extensions causing trouble with your cryptocurrency experience.

If you accidentally installed a malicious browser extension, it may snoop on your Metamask keys and become an attack vector on your funds. One method to improve your security is to create a separate browser profile on your Google Chrome or Brave browser. In that new browser profile, install only the Metamask extension. By doing so, you reduce the risk of a malicious browser extension siphoning out funds from your wallet.

Here is a step-by-step guide to creating a new browser profile on Google Chrome.

Separate Browser Profile: Step-by-Step Guide

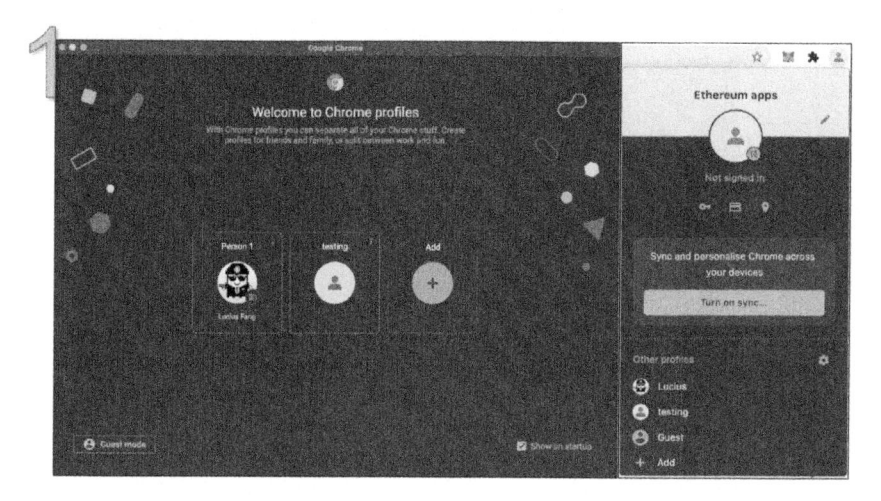

Step 1

- Opening the Chrome browser will lead to the above page. Click "Add".
- Alternatively you can go to the upper right-hand corner and click on the profile icon. Click "+ Add" at the very bottom.

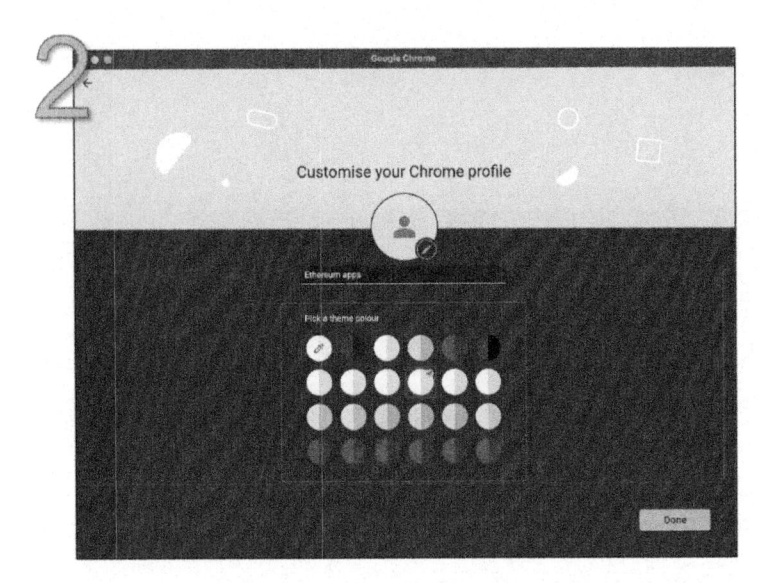

Step 2
- Pick the name and color. Then click "Done"

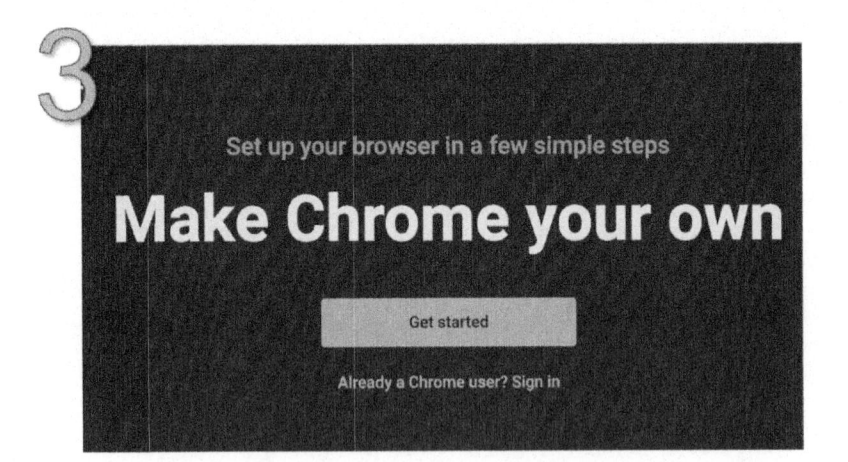

Step 3
- Sign in a different Chrome account if you have one. If not, just click "Get started".

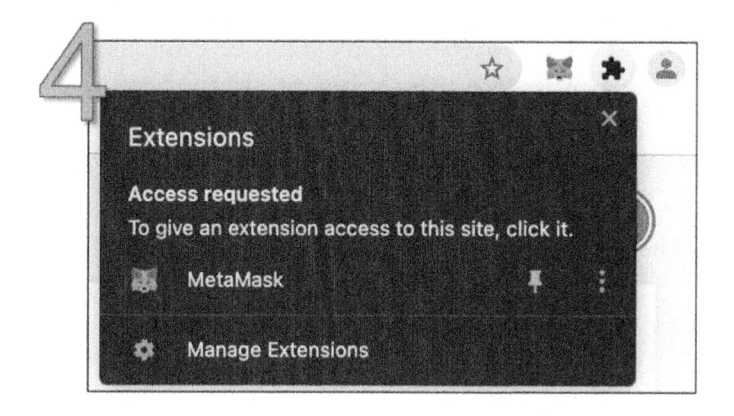

Step 4

- Download the Metamask extension and make it the only extension in this profile.

Conclusion

The DeFi space is still very much an experimental ground for various financial innovations. As such, things may and can go wrong. Do be aware of the risks of using new DeFi applications, especially those that are not battle-tested.

Always do your research before using any DeFi protocols. In most cases, once a mistake takes place, there is no recourse to the losses incurred. Even in the event of remuneration by the protocol, the losses usually exceed the amount of compensation received.

That said, because of the risks involved, the returns from participating in DeFi activities are high. To not miss out on the high returns offered by DeFi, you can opt to hedge some risks by buying insurance or put options.

The DeFi space is still maturing. As we go along, we expect more DeFi protocols to launch with better safeguards and insurance funds incorporated into their operating models.

Recommended Readings

1. To be your own bank with Metamask
   https://consensys.net/blog/metamask/metamask-secret-seed-phrase-and-password-management/
2. How (Not) To Get Rekt – DeFi Hacks Explained
   https://finematics.com/defi-hacks-explained/
3. DeFi Security: With So Many Hacks, Will It Ever Be Safe?
   https://unchainedpodcast.com/defi-security-with-so-many-hacks-will-it-ever-be-safe/
4. News on hacks and exploits
   https://www.rekt.news/

CHAPTER 16: THE FUTURE OF FINANCE

DeFi's mission is clear: reinventing traditional finance's infrastructure and interface with greater transparency, accessibility, efficiency, convenience, and interoperability.

As of April 2021, the Total Value Locked (TVL) in DeFi applications has reached $86 billion - 86 times larger since we last published our *How to DeFi: Beginner* (First Edition) in March 2020. Back then, the TVL within DeFi just hit $1 billion.

Here is a quick summary of DeFi milestones:

- 2018: TVL increased 5 times from $50 million to $275 million
- 2019: TVL increased 2.4 times to $667 million
- 2020: TVL increased 23.5 times to $15.7 billion
- 2021: TVL increased 5.5 times to $86.05 billion (as of April 2021)

Through both of our How to DeFi books, you can see that DeFi, in itself, is reimagining the way global financial systems operate. As we covered in all our chapters, various financial primitives are already live, such as decentralized exchanges, lending, insurance, and derivatives. Regardless of location and status, DeFi has made it possible for anyone in the world to access financial services as long as they have Internet access.

Although most of the DeFi protocols we covered are Ethereum natives, we already see the exponential growth of users and projects on other blockchain networks like Binance Smart Chain, Solana, Polygon, and Fantom.

Reinventing legacy finance is about more than just the tech. It also means reinventing the culture. At its heart, DeFi represents a transparent and open-source movement with an extremely powerful culture that continues its mission to create tens of trillions of dollars in value. This culture is what helps to shape and legitimize DeFi.

Great minds have come together and attempted to solve some of the most pressing issues that plague traditional finance. The result combines traditional finance principles, innovation, and blockchain technology while offering superior financial products and services.

How Long Before Institutions Build on These Networks?

We have already seen instances of institutions building on DeFi. For example, Visa announced in the first quarter of 2021 that it will soon start settling transactions with USDC on Ethereum.[95] In May 2021, Aave built a private pool for institutions as a practice ground before entering the DeFi ecosystem.[96] Both are excellent examples of collaborative learning between the two financial systems and acts as a precursor to institutions' direct involvement with DeFi.

---

[95] (2021, March 29). Visa Will Start Settling Transactions With Crypto Partners In USDC .... Retrieved May 24, 2021, from https://www.forbes.com/sites/ninabambysheva/2021/03/29/visa-to-start-settling-transactions-with-bitcoin-partners-in-usdc/

[96] (2021, May 12). DeFi lending platform Aave reveals 'permissioned pool' for institutions. Retrieved May 24, 2021, from https://cointelegraph.com/news/defi-lending-platform-aave-reveals-private-pool-for-institutions

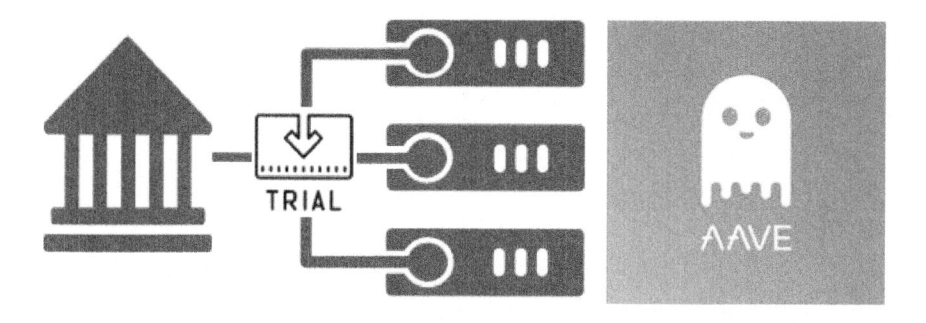

A screenshot of lines of code on Aave Pro's smart contract.
Source: https://twitter.com/StaniKulechov/status/1394390461968633859/photo/1

Where Does This Take Us in the Next 5 to 10 Years?

It is difficult to say how things will be in the future, but we would like to think of DeFi as a technological movement that challenges the status quo of traditional finance. Similar to how the Internet has made many inventions obsolete by revolutionizing the way we communicate and share information, DeFi will do the same for finance and take advantage of a global network to create a more transparent and efficient financial system.

Development takes time, but the pace of innovation in DeFi has been moving at breakneck speed. As of April 2021, the Total Value Locked in DeFi has grown over 1,700 times larger than what it was four years ago in 2018.

One of the big reasons we got here is thanks to the DeFi developers and community who have been relentlessly building, building, and building despite the competitive environment in the space. For that, we want to say thank you all for making open finance possible.

CLOSING REMARKS

Congratulations on making it this far! From the current state of DeFi to decentralized exchanges and exploits, our journey through DeFi in this book has come to a close. However, this is not the end, as there will always be new things to learn and new protocols to explore.

By now, you should have a deeper understanding of DeFi and how it works. You should know that DeFi moves very fast and is infinitely complex. By the time we publish this book, some of the information might already be outdated!

Nevertheless, we hope that *How to DeFi: Advanced* book will be a core reference point in your DeFi journey. May it guide you on your never-ending quest to explore the many rabbit holes of DeFi.

APPENDIX

CoinGecko's Recommended DeFi Resources

Analytics

DefiLlama - https://defillama.com/home
DeBank - https://debank.com/
DeFi Prime - https://defiprime.com/
DeFi Pulse - https://defipulse.com/
Dune Analytics - https://duneanalytics.com/home
LoanScan - http://loanscan.io/
Nansen - https://www.nansen.ai/
Token Terminal -https://www.tokenterminal.com/
The Block Dashboard - https://www.theblockcrypto.com/data

News Sites

CoinDesk - https://www.coindesk.com/
CoinTelegraph - https://cointelegraph.com/
Decrypt - https://decrypt.co/
The Block - https://www.theblockcrypto.com/
Crypto Briefing - https://cryptobriefing.com/

Newsletters

CoinGecko - https://landing.coingecko.com/newsletter/
Bankless - https://bankless.substack.com/
DeFi Tutorials - https://defitutorials.substack.com/
DeFi Weekly - https://defiweekly.substack.com/
DeFi Pulse Farmer - https://yieldfarmer.substack.com/
Delphi Digital - https://www.delphidigital.io/research/
Dose of DeFi - https://doseofdefi.substack.com/
Ethhub - https://ethhub.substack.com/
Deribit Insight - https://insights.deribit.com/
My Two Gwei - https://mytwogwei.substack.com/
Messari - https://messari.io/
The Defiant - https://thedefiant.substack.com/
Week in Ethereum News - https://www.weekinethereumnews.com/

Podcast

CoinGecko - https://podcast.coingecko.com/
BlockCrunch - https://castbox.fm/channel/Blockcrunch%3A-Crypto-Deep-Dives-id1182347
Chain Reaction - https://fiftyonepercent.podbean.com/
Into the Ether - Ethhub - https://podcast.ethhub.io/
PoV Crypto - https://povcryptopod.libsyn.com/
Uncommon Core - http://uncommoncore.co/podcast/
Unchained Podcast - https://unchainedpodcast.com/
Wyre Podcast - https://blog.sendwyre.com/wyretalks/home

Youtube

Bankless - https://www.youtube.com/channel/UCAl9Ld79qaZxp9JzEOwd3aA
Chris Blec - https://www.youtube.com/c/chrisblec
DeFi Dad - https://www.youtube.com/channel/UCatItl6C7wJp9txFMbXbSTg
Economics Design - https://www.youtube.com/c/EconomicsDesign
The Defiant - https://www.youtube.com/channel/UCL0J4MLEdLP0-UyLu0hCktg

Yield TV by Zapper - https://www.youtube.com/channel/UCYq3ZxBx7P2ckJyWVDC597g

Bankless Level-Up Guide

https://bankless.substack.com/p/bankless-level-up-guide

Projects We Like Too

Dashboard Interfaces

Zapper - https://zapper.fi/dashboard
Frontier - https://frontierwallet.com/
InstaDapp - https://instadapp.io/
Zerion - https://zerion.io/
Debank - https://debank.com/

Decentralized Exchanges

Uniswap - https://uniswap.org/
SushiSwap - https://sushi.com/
Balancer - https://balancer.exchange/
Bancor - https://www.bancor.network/
Curve Finance - https://www.curve.fi/
Kyber Network - https://kyberswap.com/swap
Dodo - https://dodoex.io/

Exchange Aggregators

1inch - https://1inch.exchange/
Paraswap - https://paraswap.io/
Matcha - https://matcha.xyz/

Lending and Borrowing

Maker - https://oasis.app/
Compound - https://compound.finance/
Aave - https://aave.com/
Cream - https://cream.finance/

Oracle and Data Aggregrator

Covalent - https://www.covalenthq.com/
The Graph - https://thegraph.com/

Prediction Markets

Augur - https://www.augur.net/

Taxes

TokenTax - https://tokentax.co/

Wallet

Metamask - https://metamask.io/
Argent - https://argent.link/coingecko
Dharma - https://www.dharma.io/
GnosisSafe - https://safe.gnosis.io/
Monolith - https://monolith.xyz/

Yield Optimizers

APY Finance - https://apy.finance/
Yearn - https://yearn.finance/
Alpha Finance - https://alphafinance.io/

References

Chapter 1: DeFi Snapshot

Bambysheva, N. (2021, March 29). *Visa Will Start Settling Transactions With Crypto Partners In USDC On Ethereum*. Forbes. https://www.forbes.com/sites/ninabambysheva/2021/03/29/visa-to-start-settling-transactions-with-bitcoin-partners-in-usdc/.

Emmanuel, O. (2021, April 16). Citibank Demystifies MakerDAO and DeFi for Fund Managers. BTCManager. https://btcmanager.com/citibank-makerdao-defi-fund-managers/.

Franck, T. (2021, March 26). *Fidelity to launch bitcoin ETF as investment giant builds its digital asset business*. CNBC. https://www.cnbc.com/2021/03/24/fidelity-to-launch-bitcoin-etf-as-investment-giant-builds-its-digital-asset-business-.html.

Kharpal, A. (2021, April 19). *After a bitcoin crackdown, China now calls it an 'investment alternative' in a significant shift in tone*. After a bitcoin crackdown, China now calls it an 'investment alternative' in a significant shift in tone. https://www.cnbc.com/2021/04/19/china-calls-bitcoin-an-investment-alternative-marking-shift-in-tone.html.

Manning, L. (2021, April 19). *Coinbase IPO Exceeds All Expectations, Showing More Promise For Bitcoin*. Nasdaq. https://www.nasdaq.com/articles/coinbase-ipo-exceeds-all-expectations-showing-more-promise-for-bitcoin-2021-04-19

Schär, F. (2021, February 5). Decentralized Finance: On Blockchain- and Smart Contract-Based Financial Markets. https://research.stlouisfed.org/publications/review/2021/02/05/decentralized-finance-on-blockchain-and-smart-contract-based-financial-markets.

Schmitt, L. (2021, April 22). *DeFi 2.0-First Real World Loan is Financed on Maker*. Medium. https://medium.com/centrifuge/defi-2-0-first-real-world-loan-is-financed-on-maker-fbe24675428f.

Chapter 2: DeFi Activities

Cryptopedia, S. (2021, April 17). Airdrops: Crypto Airdrops and Blockchain Airdrops. Gemini. https://www.gemini.com/cryptopedia/airdrop-crypto-giveaway-uniswap.

Etherscan. (n.d.). Airdrops List. https://etherscan.io/airdrops.

Etherscan (n.d) Ethereum Activities Stats. https://etherscan.io/charts.

How to add tokens to SushiSwap Exchange as an LP. SushiSwap. (n.d.). https://help.sushidocs.com/guides/how-to-add-tokens-to-sushiswap-exchange-as-an-lp.

Liquidity Bootstrapping FAQ. Balancer. (n.d.). https://docs.balancer.finance/smart-contracts/smart-pools/liquidity-bootstrapping-faq.

Xie, L. (2021, March 13). A beginner's guide to DAOs. Mirror. https://linda.mirror.xyz/Vh8K4leCGEO06_qSGx-vS5lvgUqhqkCz9ut81WwCP2o.

Zapper: Dashboard for DeFi. (n.d.). https://zapper.fi/dashboard.

Chapter 3: Decentralized Exchanges

Balancer Whitepaper. (2019, September 19). https://balancer.fi/whitepaper.pdf.

Bancor. (2021, February 17). Using Bancor Vortex. Medium https://blog.bancor.network/using-bancor-vortex-46974a1c14f9.

Chainlink. (2020, June 29). DeFi Series: More Capital & Less Risk in Automated Market Makers. Chainlink. https://blog.chain.link/challenges-in-defi-how-to-bring-more-capital-and-less-risk-to-automated-market-maker-dexs/.

FAQ. Balancer. (n.d.). https://docs.balancer.finance/getting-started/faq.

Hasu. (2021, April 19). Understanding Automated Market-Makers, Part 1: Price Impact. Paradigm Research. https://research.paradigm.xyz/amm-price-impact.

Kohli, K. (2020, June 1). How AMMs Work (Explainer Video). DeFi Weekly. https://defiweekly.substack.com/p/how-amms-work-explainer-video.

Kohli, K. (2020, June 25). The State of AMMs. DeFi Weekly. https://defiweekly.substack.com/p/the-state-of-amms-3ad.

Kozlovski, S. (2021, March 31). Balancer V2- A One-Stop-Shop. Medium. https://medium.com/balancer-protocol/balancer-v2-a-one-stop-shop-6af1678003f7.

Krishnamachari, B., Feng, Q., & Grippo, E. (2021). Dynamic Curves for Decentralized Autonomous Cryptocurrency Exchanges.

Martinelli, F. (2021, April 19). Balancer V2: Generalizing AMMs. Medium. https://medium.com/balancer-protocol/balancer-v2-generalizing-amms-16343c4563ff.

Naz. (2020, February 24). Crypto Front Running for Dummies. Medium. https://nazariyv.medium.com/crypto-front-running-for-dummies-bed2d4682db0.

Pintail. (2020, August 30). Uniswap: A Good Deal for Liquidity Providers? Medium. https://pintail.medium.com/uniswap-a-good-deal-for-liquidity-providers-104c0b6816f2.

Powers, B. (2020, December 30). New Research Sheds Light on the Front-Running Bots in Ethereum's Dark Forest. CoinDesk. https://www.coindesk.com/new-research-sheds-light-front-running-bots-ethereum-dark-forest.

Understanding Returns on Uniswap. Uniswap Blog RSS. (n.d.). https://uniswap.org/docs/v2/advanced-topics/understanding-returns/

Uniswap Info DAI/ETH. Uniswap Info. (n.d.). https://info.uniswap.org/pair/0xa478c2975ab1ea89e8196811f51a7b7ade33eb11.

Uniswap. Uniswap Blog RSS. (n.d.). https://uniswap.org/blog/uniswap-v3/.

Xu, J., Vavryk, N., Paruch, K., & Cousaert, S. (2021). SoK: Decentralized Exchanges (DEX) with Automated Market Maker (AMM) Protocols.

Younessi, C. (2019, March 7). Uniswap-A Unique Exchange. Medium. https://medium.com/scalar-capital/uniswap-a-unique-exchange-f4ef44f807bf.

Chapter 4: DEX Aggregators

1inch Network, (2021, March 16). *Introducing the 1inch Aggregation Protocol v3*. Medium. https://blog.1inch.io/introducing-the-1inch-aggregation-protocol-v3-b02890986547.

1inch Network. (2020, December 25). *1INCH token is released*. Medium. https://blog.1inch.io/1inch-token-is-released-e69ad69cf3ee.

Balakrishnan, A. (2021, March 22). *DeFi Aggregators*. Delphi Digital. https://www.delphidigital.io/reports/defi-aggregators/.

Gonella, T. (2021, January 27). *Say hello to 0x v4*. Medium. https://blog.0xproject.com/say-hello-to-0x-v4-ce87ca38e3ac.

Hemricourt, P. de. (2020, August 24). *DeFi, DEXes, DEX Aggregators, AMMs, and Built-In DEX Marketplaces, Which is Which and Which is Best?* Medium. https://medium.com/2key/defi-dexes-dex-aggregators-amms-and-built-in-dex-marketplaces-which-is-which-and-which-is-best-fba04ca48534.

Kalani, C. (2020, June 30). *Say hello to Matcha!* Matcha. https://matcha.xyz/blog/say-hello-to-matcha.

Kalani, C. (2020, October 2). *How Matcha is taking DEX aggregation to a whole new level.* Matcha. https://matcha.xyz/blog/trading-on-matcha-keeps-getting-better.

Paraswap. (2021, January 28). *Introducing ParaSwap's new UI & a significant upgrade for our contracts.* Medium. https://medium.com/paraswap/introducing-paraswaps-new-ui-a-significant-upgrade-for-our-contracts-ed15d632e1d0.

Paraswap. (2020, September 17). *Towards a community-owned & driven DeFi middleware.* Medium. https://medium.com/paraswap/towards-a-community-owned-driven-defi-middleware-b7860c55d6a6?source=collection_home---6------1----------------------.

Chapter 5: Decentralized Lending & Borrowing

Aave: Open Source DeFi Protocol. Aave. (n.d.). https://aave.com/.

Compound Markets. Compound. (n.d.). https://compound.finance/markets.

Cream: DeFi Lending Protocol. cream. (n.d.). https://cream.finance/.

DeBank | DeFi Wallet for Ethereum Users. DeBank. (n.d.). https://debank.com/ranking/lending?chain=eth&date=1Y&select=borrow.

Lending Protocol Revenue. The Block. (n.d.).
https://www.theblockcrypto.com/data/decentralized-finance/protocol-revenue.

Maker Market. Oasis.app. (n.d.). https://oasis.app/borrow/markets.

Maker: An Unbiased Global Financial System. MakerDAO. (n.d.). https://makerdao.com/en/.

Protocol Revenue. The Block. (n.d.).
https://www.theblockcrypto.com/data/decentralized-finance/protocol-revenue.

Token Terminal Dashboard on Lending Protocols. Token Terminal. (n.d.). https://terminal.tokenterminal.com/dashboard/Lending.

Chapter 6: Decentralized Stablecoins and Stableassets

Tether's Credibility And Its Impact On Bitcoin (Cryptocurrency:BTC-USD). SeekingAlpha. (n.d.). https://seekingalpha.com/article/4403640-tethers-credibility-and-impact-on-bitcoin.

Eva, Matti, Koh, N., & Wangarian. (2021, March 20). *Stability, Elasticity, and Reflexivity: A Deep Dive into Algorithmic Stablecoins.* Deribit Insights. https://insights.deribit.com/market-research/stability-elasticity-and-reflexivity-a-deep-dive-into-algorithmic-stablecoins/.

Empty Set Dollar. (n.d.). *Empty Set Dollar - ESD.* Empty Set Dollar - ESD – Empty Set Dollar. https://docs.emptyset.finance/.

Fei Protocol. (2021, January 11). *Introducing Fei Protocol.* Medium. https://medium.com/fei-protocol/introducing-fei-protocol-2db79bd7a82b.

Float Protocol. (2021, March 22). *Announcing Float Protocol and its democratic launch.* Medium. https://medium.com/float-protocol/announcing-float-protocol-and-its-democratic-launch-d1c27bc21230.

Float Protocol. (2021, March 22). *FLOAT and the Money Gods*. Medium. https://medium.com/float-protocol/float-and-the-money-gods-5509d41c9b3a

Frax Finance. *Frax: Fractional-Algorithmic Stablecoin Protocol*. Frax ¤ Finance. (n.d.). https://docs.frax.finance/.

Ionescu, S. (2020, October 29). *Introducing Proto RAI*. Medium. https://medium.com/reflexer-labs/introducing-proto-rai-c4cf1f013ef.

McKeon, S. (2020, August 12). *The Rise and Fall (and Rise and Fall) of Ampleforth-Part I*. Medium. https://medium.com/collab-currency/the-rise-and-fall-and-rise-and-fall-of-ampleforth-part-i-cda716dea663.

Schloss , D., & McKeon, S. (2020, August 12). *The Rise and Fall (and Rise and Fall) of Ampleforth-Part II*. Medium. https://medium.com/collab-currency/the-rise-and-fall-and-rise-and-fall-of-ampleforth-part-ii-6c0f438e8129.

Stably. (2021, February 19). *What Uniswap's Liquidity Plunge Reveals about Stablecoins*. Medium. https://medium.com/stably-blog/what-uniswaps-liquidity-plunge-reveals-about-stablecoins-4fcbee8d210c.

Watkins, R. (2021, March 3). The Art of Central Banking on Blockchains: Algorithmic Stablecoins. https://messari.io/article/the-art-of-central-banking-on-blockchains-algorithmic-stablecoins.

Chapter 7: Decentralized Derivatives

dYdX: Leverage, decentralized. (n.d.) https://dydx.exchange/

Hegic: On-chain options trading protocol on Ethereum. (n.d.) https://www.hegic.co/

Opyn: Trade Options on Ethereum. (n.d.) https://www.opyn.co/#/

Perpetual Protocol: Decentralized Perpetual Contract for every asset. (n.d.) https://perp.fi/

Perpetual Protocol Exchange. (n.d.) https://perp.exchange/

Synthetix: The Derivatives Liquidity Protocol. (n.d.) https://synthetix.io/

Synthetix Staking Page. (n.d.) https://staking.synthetix.io/

UMA: UMA enables DeFi developers to build synthetic assets. (n.d.) https://umaproject.org/

UMA KPI Options. (n.d.) https://claim.umaproject.org/

Chapter 8: Decentralized Insurance

Armor.Fi: Smart DeFi Asset Coverage. (n.d.). https://armor.fi/.

Cover Protocol: A peer-to-peer coverage market. (n.d.). https://www.coverprotocol.com/.

InsurAce DeFi Insurance. (n.d.). https://landing.insurace.io/.

Nexus Mutual Tracker. (n.d.). https://nexustracker.io/.

Nexus Mutual: A decentralised alternative to insurance. (n.d.). https://nexusmutual.io/.

Nsure.Network: Experience DeFi, Risk Free. (n.d.). https://nsure.network/#/home.

Unslashed Finance: The Insurance Products that crypto needs. (n.d.). https://www.unslashed.finance/.

Chapter 9: Decentralized Indices

Campbell, L. (2020, November 11). The best DeFi indices for your crypto portfolio. Bankless. https://newsletter.banklesshq.com/p/the-best-defi-indices-for-your-crypto.

Dune Analytics. (n.d.). https://duneanalytics.com/0xBoxer/indices-products.

Governance on Index Coop. Snapshot. (n.d.). https://snapshot.org/#/index.

Governance on Indexed Finance. Snapshot. (n.d.). https://gov.indexed.finance/#/ndx.eth/proposal/QmdVmMefXUAUqU1xgfjeUie4o4Ud4cqFKwyABaQSBnQNG9.

Inc., M. S. C. I. (2010). Update on Msci Equal Weighted Indices. SSRN Electronic Journal. https://doi.org/10.2139/ssrn.1729770

Index Cooperative Website. Index. (n.d.). https://www.indexcoop.com/.

Indexed Finance Official Documentation. Indexed Finance. (n.d.). https://docs.indexed.finance/.

Indexed Finance Official Website. Indexed. (n.d.). https://indexed.finance/.

McKee, S. L. (2016, July 18). Cap Weighted Versus Equal Weighted, Which Approach Is Better? Forbes. https://www.forbes.com/sites/investor/2016/07/18/cap-weighted-versus-equal-weighted-which-approach-is-better/?sh=727e63e847c3.

PowerPool Official Blog. Medium. (n.d.). https://medium.com/@powerpoolcvp.

PowerPool Official Website. PowerPool. (n.d.). https://powerpool.finance/.

PowerPool. (2021, January 24). PowerIndex v2: Unlimited ETFs & Automated Portfolio Strategies. Medium. https://medium.com/powerpool/powerindex-v2-unlimited-etfs-automated-portfolio-strategies-6086917e6348.

pr0, G2theM, Norsefire, Tai, John, RickieJean, ... Noice. (2021, January 30). Oracle Top 5 Token Index proposal. Indexed Finance. https://forum.indexed.finance/t/oracle-top-5-token-index-proposal/89.

Chapter 10: Decentralized Prediction Markets

Augur. *The Ultimate Guide to Decentralized Prediction Markets*. Augur. (n.d.). https://augur.net/blog/prediction-markets.

Beneš, N. (2018, April 6). *How manipulation-resistant are Prediction Markets?* Medium. https://blog.gnosis.pm/how-manipulation-resistant-are-prediction-markets-710e14033d62

Fletcher-Hill, P. (2019, February 7). *A guide to Augur market economics*. Medium. https://medium.com/veil-blog/a-guide-to-augur-market-economics-16c66d956b6c.

Gnosis. (2020, July 5). *Omen and the Next Generation of Prediction Markets*. Medium. https://blog.gnosis.pm/omen-and-the-next-generation-of-prediction-markets-2e7a2dd604e.

Omen Prediction Markets. Omen. (n.d.). https://omen.eth.link/.

The World's Most Accessible, No-Limit Betting Platform. Augur. (n.d.). https://augur.net/.

Chapter 11: Decentralized Fixed-Interest Rate Protocols

Horizon. (n.d.). https://horizon.finance/#/.

How Tranche Lending Will Bring Fixed Interest Rates to DeFi. ConsenSys. (2021, February 4). https://consensys.net/blog/codefi/how-tranche-lending-will-bring-fixed-interest-rates-to-defi/.

Introduction. Introduction · GitBook. (n.d.). https://docs.yield.is/.

Rai, R. (n.d.). *Fixed Income Protocols: The Next Wave of DeFi Innovation*. Messari Crypto News. https://messari.io/article/fixed-income-protocols-the-next-wave-of-defi-innovation.

saffron.finance. Saffron. (n.d.). https://saffron.finance/.

Woodward, T. (2020, November 19). *Why Fixed Rates Matter*. Medium. https://medium.com/notional-finance/why-fixed-rates-matter-1b03991275d6.

Chapter 12: Decentralized Yield Aggregators

Alpha Finance Lab. (2021, April 19). https://alphafinance.io/.

Badger Finance: Community Rules Everything. (2020, December 27). https://badger.finance/.

Defi Lego connects as Yearn Finance announces five mergers in a week. Brave New Coin. (n.d.). https://bravenewcoin.com/insights/defi-lego-connects-as-yearn-finance-announces-five-mergers-in-a-week.

Harvest Finance. (n.d.). https://harvest.finance/.

yearn.finance. (n.d.). https://yearn.finance/.

Yearn.finance. (2021, March 5). We have decided to end the previously announced merger process of Yearn and Cover. Both protocols will continue to operate independently. yVault depositors who have previously purchased Cover protection are unaffected by this. Twitter. https://twitter.com/iearnfinance/status/1367796331507552258.

Yearn Finance Launches v2 Vaults, YFI Token Jumps 15%. BeInCrypto. https://beincrypto.com/yearn-finance-v2-vaults-yfi-token/.

Chapter 13: Oracles and Data Aggregators

Band Protocol: Secure, Scalable Blockchain-Agnostic Decentralized Oracle. (n.d.) https://bandprotocol.com/

BandChain. (n.d.) https://bandprotocol.com/bandchain

Chainlink: Connect your smart contract to the outside world. (n.d.) https://chain.link/

Chainlink. (2021, April 30). Chainlink 2.0 Lays Foundation for Adoption of Hybrid Smart Contracts.Chainlink.https://blog.chain.link/chainlink-2-0-lays-foundation-for-adoption-of-hybrid-smart-contracts/.

Covalent: One unified API. One billion possibilities. (n.d.). https://www.covalenthq.com/

The Graph: APIs for a vibrant decentralized future. (n.d.) https://thegraph.com/

Chapter 14: Multi-Chain Protocols & Cross-Chain Bridges

An Introduction to Binance Bridge. (n.d.) https://academy.binance.com/en/articles/an-Introduction-to-binance-bridge

AnySwap Dashboard. (n.d.) https://anyswap.exchange/dashboard

Binance Bridge. (n.d.) https://www.binance.org/en/bridge

Chainlist: Helping Users Connect to EVM powered networks. (n.d.) https://chainlist.org/

Documentation on Terra Bridge. (n.d.) https://docs.mirror.finance/user-guide/terra-bridge

Terra Bridge. (n.d.) https://bridge.terra.money/

ThorChain Technology. (n.d.). https://thorchain.org/technology#how-does-it-work

Chapter 15: DeFi Exploits

Etherscan Information Center. (n.d.). https://info.etherscan.com/.

Flash Loans. Aave FAQ. (n.d.). https://docs.aave.com/faq/flash-loans.

Furucombo: Create all kinds of DeFi combo. (n.d.). https://furucombo.app/.

Immunefi: DeFi's leading bug bounty platform. (n.d.). https://immunefi.com/.

rekt. (n.d.). https://www.rekt.news/.

Chapter 16: DeFi will be the New Normal

Bambysheva, N. (2021, March 29). Visa Will Start Settling Transactions With Crypto Partners In USDC On Ethereum. Forbes. https://www.forbes.com/sites/ninabambysheva/2021/03/29/visa-to-start-settling-transactions-with-bitcoin-partners-in-usdc

Bitcoin Headlines. (2021, March 21) Documentation Bitcoin: https://twitter.com/DocumentingBTC/status/1372919635083923460

Buterin, V. (2020, December 28). *Endnotes on 2020: Crypto and Beyond.* https://vitalik.ca/general/2020/12/28/endnotes.html

Cronje, A. (2021, January 12). *Building in defi sucks (part 2)*. Medium. https://andrecronje.medium.com/building-in-defi-sucks-part-2-75df9ee7871b

stani.eth (2021, May 17). Aave Pro for institutions pic.twitter.com/sUWOFDWcxd. Twitter. https://twitter.com/StaniKulechov/status/1394390461968633859.

Thurman, A. (2021, May 12). DeFi lending platform Aave reveals 'permissioned pool' for institutions. Cointelegraph. https://cointelegraph.com/news/defi-lending-platform-aave-reveals-private-pool-for-institutions

GLOSSARY

Index	Term	Description
A	Airdrop	Airdrop refers to the distribution of a reserve of tokens, usually to users who have completed certain actions or fulfill certain criterias.
	Annual Percentage Yield (APY)	It is an annualized return on saving or investment and the interest is compounded based on the period.
	Admin Key Risk	It refers to the risk where the master private key for the protocol could be compromised.
	Algorithmic Stablecoins	Algorithmic stablecoins utilize algorithms to control the stablecoin's market structure and the underlying economics.
	Algorithmic Stableassets	Unlike algorithmic stablecoins, algorithmic stableassets could be seen as another form of collateral rather than units of accounts

Index	Term	Description
	Automated Market Maker (AMM)	Automated Market Maker removes the need for a human to manually quote bids and ask prices in an order book and replaces it with an algorithm.
	Audit	Auditing is a systematic process of examining an organization's records to ensure fair and accurate information the organization claims to represent. Smart contract audit refers to the practice of reviewing the smart contract code to find vulnerabilities so that they can be fixed before it is exploited by hackers.
	An Application Programming Interface (API)	An interface that acts as a bridge that allows two applications to interact with each other. For example, you can use CoinGecko's API to fetch the current market price of cryptocurrencies on your website.
B	Back-running	It is the act of when the attacker sells the tokens right after front-running the victim's trade to make a risk-free arbitrage. See front-running and sandwich attack.
	Buy and Hold	This refers to a TokenSets trading strategy which realigns to its target allocation to prevent overexposure to one coin and spreads risk over multiple tokens.
	Bridge	A protocol that connects two blockchains together, allowing users to transfer assets between them.

Glossary

Index	Term	Description
	Bonding Curve	A bonding curve is a mathematical curve that defines a dynamic relationship between price and token supply. Bonding curves act as an automated market maker where as the number of supply of a token decreases, the price of the token increases. It is useful as it helps buyers and sellers to access an instant market without the need of intermediaries.
C	Cryptocurrency Exchange (Cryptoexchange)	It is a digital exchange that helps users exchange cryptocurrencies. For some exchanges, they also facilitate users to trade fiat currencies to cryptocurrencies.
	Custodian	Custodian refers to the third party to have control over your assets.
	Fiat-collateralized stablecoin	A stablecoin that is backed by fiat-currency. For example, 1 Tether is pegged to $1.
	Crypto-collateralized stablecoin.	A stablecoin that is backed by another cryptocurrency. For example, Dai is backed by Ether at an agreed collateral ratio.
	Centralized Exchange (CEX)	Centralized Exchange (CEX) is an exchange that operates in a centralized manner and requires full custody of users' funds.
	Collateral	Collateral is an asset you will have to lock-in with the lender in order to borrow another asset. It acts as a guarantor that you will repay your loan.

Index	Term	Description
	Collateral Ratio	Collateral ratio refers to the maximum amount of asset that you can borrow after putting collateral into a DeFi decentralized application.
	cTokens	cTokens are proof of certificates that you have supplied tokens to Compound's liquidity pool.
	Cryptoasset	Cryptoasset refers to digital assets on blockchain. Cryptoassets and cryptocurrencies generally refer to the same thing.
	Cover Amount	It refers to the maximum payable money by the insurance company when a claim is made.
	Claim Assessment process	It is the obligation by the insurer to review the claim filed by an insurer. After the process, the insurance company will reimburse the money back to the insured based on the Cover Amount.
	Composability	Composability is a system design principle that enables applications to be created from component parts.
	Cross-chain	Transactions that occur between different blockchains.
D	Decentralized Finance (DeFi)	DeFi is an ecosystem that allows for the utilization of financial services such as borrowing, lending, trading, getting access to insurance, and more without the need to rely on a centralized entity.

Glossary

Index	Term	Description
	Decentralized Applications (Dapps)	Applications that run on decentralized peer-to-peer networks such as Ethereum.
	Decentralized Autonomous Organization (DAO)	Decentralized Autonomous Organizations are rules encoded by smart contracts on the blockchain. The rules and dealings of the DAO are transparent and the DAO is controlled by token holders.
	Decentralized Exchange (DEX)	Decentralized Exchange (DEX) allows for trading and direct swapping of tokens without the need to use a centralized exchange.
	Derivatives	Derivative comes from the word derive because it is a contract that derives its value from an underlying entity/product. Some of the underlying assets can be commodities, currencies, bonds, or cryptocurrencies.
	Dai Saving Rate (DSR)	The Dai Savings Rate (DSR) is an interest earned by holding Dai over time. It also acts as a monetary tool to influence the demand of Dai.
	Dashboard	A dashboard is a simple platform that aggregates all your DeFi activities in one place. It is a useful tool to visualize and track where your assets are across the different DeFi protocols.
	Data Aggregator	Service providers that index and aggregate data so that it be queried by other decentralized applications

Index	Term	Description
E	Ethereum	Ethereum is an open-source, programmable, decentralized platform built on blockchain technology. Compared to Bitcoin, Ethereum allows for scripting languages which has allowed for application development.
	Ether	Ether is the cryptocurrency that powers the Ethereum blockchain. It is the fuel for the apps on the decentralized Ethereum network
	ERC-20	ERC is an abbreviation for Ethereum Request for Comment and 20 is the proposal identifier. It is an official protocol for proposing improvements to the Ethereum network. ERC-20 refers to the commonly adopted standard used to create tokens on Ethereum.
	Exposure	Exposure refers to how much you are 'exposed' to the potential risk of losing your investment. For example, price exposure refers to the potential risk you will face in losing your investment when the price moves.
F	Future Contract	It is a contract which you enter to buy or sell a particular asset at a certain price at a certain date in the future.
	Factory Contract	It is a smart contract that is able to produce other new smart contracts.
	Fixed-Interest Rate Protocol (FIRP)	A new class of protocols that have a fixed interest rate element.

Glossary

Index	Term	Description
	Flash Loans	Borrowers can take up loans with zero collateral if the borrower repays the loan and any additional interest and fees within the same transaction.
	Front-Running	In the cryptocurrency context, frontrunning works in DEX where orders made are broadcasted to the blockchain for all to see, a frontrunner will attempt to listen to the blockchain to pick up suitable orders to frontrun by orders on the market and placing enough fees to have the transaction mined faster than the target's orders.
	Funding Rate	Periodic payments made by traders based on the difference between the perpetual contract prices and spot prices of an asset.
G	Gas	Gas refers to the unit of measure on the amount of computational effort required to execute a smart contract operation on Ethereum.
	Governance	To steer the direction of the DeFi protocol, governance is introduced whereby the project community can decide collectively. To make this possible, governance tokens are pioneered by Compound, allowing token holders to vote on protocol proposals that any community member can submit.

Index	Term	Description
H	Hard Fork	Forced bifurcation of a blockchain, which is usually given when a fairly significant change is implemented in the software code of a network. It results in a permanent divergence of a blockchain into two blockchains. The original blockchain does not recognize the new version.
I	IDO	IDO stands for Initial Decentralized Exchange Offering or Initial DEX offering. This is where tokens are first offered for sale to the public using a DEXs liquidity pool.
	IBCO	IBCO stands for Initial Bonding Curve Offering. Token prices are based on a curve, where subsequent investors will push up the token's price.
	IFO	IFO stands for Initial Farm Offering. Typically, users stake their assets in exchange for the project's tokens. The project then receives the user's staked assets as payment.
	IMAP	IMAP stands for Internet Message Access Protocol. It is an Internet protocol that allows email applications to access email on TCP/IP servers.
	Impermanent Loss	Temporary loss of funds due to volatility leading to divergence in price between token pairs provided by liquidity providers.
	Index	An index measures the performance of a basket of underlying assets. An index moves when the overall performance of the underlying assets in the basket moves.

Glossary

Index	Term	Description
	Insurance	An agreement to provide compensation for losses incurred in exchange for upfront payment.
	Inverse	This Synthetix strategy is meant for those who wish to "short" a benchmark. Traders can purchase this when they think a benchmark is due to decrease.
J		-
K	Know-Your-Customer (KYC)	Know-Your-Customer (KYC) is a compliance process for business entities to verify and assess their clients.
L	Layer-1 Chains	Blockchains where every transaction is settled and verified on the network itself.
	Layer-2 Chains	Layer 2 is a chain that is built on top of the base chain to improve scalability without compromising the security and the decentralization.
	Liquidation Penalty	It is a fee that a borrower has to pay along with their liquidated collateral when the value of their collateral asset falls below the minimum collateral value.
	Liquidation Ratio	The ratio of collateral to debt at which your collateral will be subject to liquidation if it falls below it.
	Liquidity Bootstrapping Pool	Liquidity pools where projects can sell tokens via a configurable AMM. They are mainly used to improve price discovery and reduce volatility.

Index	Term	Description
	Liquidity Pools	Liquidity pools are token reserves that sit on smart contracts and are available for users to exchange tokens. Currently the pools are mainly used for swapping, borrowing, lending, and insurance.
	Liquidity Mining	The reward program of giving out the protocol's native tokens in exchange for capital. It is a novel way to attract the right kind of community participation for DeFi protocols.
	Liquidity Risk	A risk when protocols like Compound could run out of liquidity.
	Liquidity Providers	Liquidity providers are people who loan their assets into the liquidity pool. The liquidity pool will increase as there are more tokens.
	Liquidity Pool Aggregator	It is a system which aggregates liquidity pools from different exchanges and is able to see all available exchange rates in one place. It allows you to compare for the best possible rate.
	Leverage	It is an investment strategy to gain higher potential return of the investment by using borrowed money.
M	MakerDAO	MakerDAO is the creator of Maker Platform and DAO stands for Decentralized Autonomous Organisation. MakerDAO's native token is MKR and it is the protocol behind the stablecoins, SAI and DAI.

Glossary

Index	Term	Description
	Market Maker Mechanisms	A Market Maker Mechanism is an algorithm that uses a bonding curve to quote both a buy and a sell price. In the crypto space, Market Maker Mechanism is mainly used by Uniswap or Kyber to swap tokens.
	Margin Trading	It is a way of investing by borrowing money from a broker to trade. In DeFi, the borrowing requires you to collateralize assets.
	MKR	Maker's governance token. Users can use it to vote for improvement proposal(s) on the Maker Decentralized Autonomous Organization (DAO).
	Mint	It refers to the process of issuing new coins/tokens.
	Multichain	Usually refers to products or tokens that exist on one or more blockchains.
N	Node	Within the blockchain network, the nodes are computers that connect to the network and have an updated copy of the blockchain. Together with the miners they are the guarantors that the network works properly. The nodes in Bitcoin are very important because they help the mission of keeping the network decentralized.
O	Order book	It refers to the list of buying and selling orders for a specific asset at various price levels.

Index	Term	Description
	Over-collateralization	Over-collateralization refers to the value of a collateral asset that must be higher than the value of the borrowed asset.
	Option	Option is a right but not the obligation for someone to buy or sell a particular asset at an agreed price on or before an expiry date.
	Oracle	Service providers which collect and verify off-chain data to be provided to smart contracts on the blockchain.
P	Perpetual Swaps	Enable users to essentially open a leveraged position on a futures contract with no expiration date.
	Prediction Markets	Prediction markets are markets created for participants to bet on the outcomes of future events.
	Price discovery	Price discovery refers to the act of determining the proper price of an asset through several factors such as market demand and supply.
	Protocol	A protocol is a base layer of codes that tells something on how to function. For example, Bitcoin and Ethereum blockchains have different protocols.
	Peer-to-Peer	In blockchain, "peer" refers to a computer system or nodes on a decentralized network. Peer-to-Peer (P2P) is a network where each node has an equal permission to validating data and it allows two individuals to interact directly with each other.

Index	Term	Description
	Perpetuals	It refers to perpetual futures, which is an agreement to purchase or sell an asset in the future without a specified date.
Q		-
R	Range Bound	This TokenSets strategy automates buying and selling within a designated range and is only intended for bearish or neutral markets.
	Rebalance	It is a process of maintaining a desired asset allocation of a portfolio by buying and selling assets in the portfolio.
	Risk Assessor	Someone who stakes value against smart contracts in Nexus Mutual. He/she is incentivized to do so to earn rewards in NXM token, as other users buy insurance on the staked smart contracts.
	Rug-Pull	In the context of crypto and Decentralized Finance (DeFi), having been rug pulled means to have buy support or Decentralized Exchange (DEX) liquidity pool taken away from a market. This results in a sell death spiral as other liquidity providers, holders and traders sell to salvage their holdings. Typically, it is a new form of exit scamming where someone will drain the pool at DEX, leaving the token holders unable to trade.
S	Sandwich Attack	It is a combination attack of front-running and back-running. Thus, the attacker 'sandwiches' the victim's trade to make a risk-free arbitrage.

Index	Term	Description
	Smart Contracts	A smart contract is a programmable contract that allows two counterparties to set conditions of a transaction without needing to trust another third party for the execution.
	Stablecoins	A stablecoin is a cryptocurrency that is pegged to another stableasset such as the US Dollar.
	Staking	Staking can mean various things in crypto space. Generally, staking refers to locking up your cryptoassets in a dApp. Otherwise, it could also refer to participation in a Proof-of-Stake (PoS) system to put your tokens in to serve as a validator to the blockchain and receive rewards.
	Soft Fork	Due to the decentralized nature of the peer-to-peer cryptocurrency network, any updates or changes must be agreed by all participating nodes. Such code changes in the blockchain occur via chain forks, whereby when the network virtually splits in 2, each following different sets of rules. A soft fork event refers to when a fork occurred but old nodes can still participate in the network.
	Spot market	Spot market is the buying and selling of assets with immediate delivery.
	Speculative activity	It is an act of buying and selling, while holding an expectation to gain profit.

Glossary

Index	Term	Description
	Spread Surplus	The net positive difference between swap transactions when the executed price is slightly better than the price quoted
	Stability Fee	It is equivalent to the 'interest rate' which you are required to pay along with the principal debt of the vault.
	Slippage	Slippage is the difference between the expected price and the actual price where an order was filled. It is generally caused by low liquidity.
	Synths	Synths stand for Synthetic Assets. A Synth is an asset or mixture of assets that has/have the same value or effect as another asset.
	Smart Contract Cover	An insurance offer from Nexus Mutual to protect users against hacks in smart contracts that store value.
T	TCP/IP	It stands for Transmission Control Protocol/Internet Protocol. It is a communication protocol to interconnect network devices on the internet.
	Total Value Locked	Total Value Locked refers to the cumulative collateral of all DeFi products.
	Tokens	It is a unit of a digital asset. Token often refers to coins that are issued on existing blockchain.
	Tokenize	It refers to the process of converting things into digital tradable assets

Index	Term	Description
	Technical Risk	It refers to the bugs on smart contracts which can be exploited by hackers and cause unintended consequences.
	Trading Pairs	A trading pair is a base asset that is paired with its target asset in the trading market. For example, for the ETH/DAI trading pair, the base asset is ETH and its target pair is DAI.
	Trend Trading	This strategy uses Technical Analysis indicators to shift from 100% target asset to 100% stableasset based on the implemented strategy.
U	Utilization Ratio	Utilization ratio is a common metric that has been used in legacy finance where you are measuring how much you borrow against your borrowing limit. Similarly, we can calculate decentralized lending application utilization ratio by measuring the borrowing volume against the value locked within the lending dApp.
V	Value Staked	It refers to how much value the insurer will put up against the target risk. If the value that the insurer staked is lower than the target risk, then it is not coverable.

Glossary

Index	Term	Description
	Validators	In contrast to mining on a Proof of Work blockchain network, Proof of Stake blockchain networks are secured by a distributed consensus of dedicated validators who have staked (locked into the network) a significant amount of token as long as the validator nodes are running. Validators are queued for block-signing based on a combination of random selection, amount (weight) staked and length of time staked (age) and others depending on the design of the consensus algorithm.
W	Wallet	A wallet is a user-friendly interface to the blockchain network that can be used as a storage, transaction and interaction bridge between the user and the blockchain.
	Wrapped Asset	Represent assets that exist on other networks besides their native blockchain. For example, WBTC is the ERC-20 version of Bitcoin which exists on the Ethereum blockchain.
X		-
Y	Yield Farming	It refers to the act of staking or lending digital assets in order to generate a return, usually in the form of other tokens.
	Yield Aggregrator	Yield aggregators are born to serve the need of automating users' investment strategies, sparing them the trouble of monitoring the market for the best yield farms.

Index	Term	Description
Z	ZK Rollup	A Layer-2 scaling solution where transfers are bundled together and executed in one transaction on the base chain. Among these solutions are Starkware and Loopring.

Printed in Great Britain
by Amazon